Scientific Advancements in Tribal Farming Knowledge

Ravish Kumar

Copyright © [2023]

Author: Ravish Kumar

Title: Scientific Advancements in Tribal Farming Knowledge

All rights reserved. **Chromium Treatment from Contaminated Soil and Groundwater** No part of this publication may be reproduced, stored in a retrieval system, or transmitted, in any form or by any means, electronic, mechanical, photocopying, recording, or otherwise, without the prior written permission of the publisher or author.

This book was printed and published by in [2023].

ISBN:

CONTENTS

S. No.	Chapters	Page No.
1.	**INTRODUCTION**	**1-22**
	1.1 Concept of Indigenous Technical Knowledge (ITK)	2
	1.2 Tribals – The custodians of ITK	4
	1.3 Role of ITK in sustainable agricultural development	5
	1.4 Knowledge conversion model	8
	1.5 Steps in ITK-based technology development	12
	1.6 Concept of scientisation of ITKs	14
	1.7 Problem Statement	16
	1.8 Researchable questions	18
	1.9 Objectives	19
	1.10 Conceptual framework	19
	1.11 Scope and significance of the study	20
	1.12 Limitations of the study	21
	1.13 Organisation	22
2.	**REVIEW OF LITERATURE**	**23-54**
	2.1 Indigenous Technical Knowledge (ITKs) and its significance	23
	2.2 Documentation of ITKs: Methods and Approaches	26
	2.3 Rationality of ITKs	30
	2.4 Validation of ITKs	33
	2.5 Refinement and Integration of ITKs	37
	2.6 Utilisation of ITKs	41
	2.7 Constraints encountered in utilisation of ITKs	45
	2.8 Framework related to scientisation of ITKs	50

3.	**RESEARCH METHODOLOGY**	55-95
	3.1 Locale of the study	56
	3.2 Research design	56
	3.3 Brief description of the study area	56
	3.4 Sampling plan	62
	3.4.1 Selection of district	62
	3.4.2 Selection of Community development blocks	64
	3.4.3 Selection of Villages	66
	3.4.4 Selection of Respondents	69
	3.5 Variables and their Measurement	70
	3.5.1 Age	72
	3.5.2 Gender	72
	3.5.3 Tribe Type	72
	3.5.4 Education	73
	3.5.5 Land holding	73
	3.5.6 Farming experience (in years)	74
	3.5.7 Social participation	74
	3.5.8 Risk orientation	75
	3.5.9 Innovativeness	75
	3.5.10 Delphi method for Scientisation of Indigenous Technical Knowledge	76
	3.5.11 Scientisation of ITKs	78
	3.5.11.1 Particularisation of ITKs	78
	3.5.11.2 Validation of ITKs	81
	3.5.11.3 Generalisation of ITKs	86
	3.5.12 Constraints encountered in utilisation of Indigenous Technical Knowledge by tribal farmers	86

3.5.13 Framework for systematic documentation and scientisation of Indigenous Technical Knowledge		86
3.6 Methods and tools of data collection		87
3.6.1 Quantitative Research		87
3.6.2 Qualitative Research		88
3.6.3 Documentation tools		89
3.7 Statistical analysis		89
4.	**RESULTS AND DISCUSSION**	**96-192**
	4.1 Demographic profile of tribal farmers	96
	4.1.1 Gender	99
	4.1.2 Age	99
	4.1.3 Tribe type	100
	4.1.4 Education	101
	4.1.5 Land holding	101
	4.1.6 Farming experience	102
	4.1.7 Social participation	103
	4.1.8 Risk orientation	103
	4.1.9 Innovativeness	104
	4.2 Demographic profile of ITK experts	105
	4.3 Identification of the process of systematic documentation and scientisation of Indigenous Technical Knowledge (ITKs)	107
	4.3.4.1 Methods and Activities Related to 'documentation and scientisation of ITKs	114
	4.3.4A Methods and Activities Related to documentation of ITKs	115
	4.3.7B Methods and Activities Related to scientisation of ITKs	116
	4.4 Scientisation of Indigenous Technical Knowledge about pest and disease management among tribal farmers.	128
	4.4.1 Particularisation of ITKs	128

	4.4.1.1	Rationality analysis on a 3-point scale of Dhaliwal and Singh (2010)	128
	4.4.2	Rationality analysis on a 4-point scale of Venkatesan and Sundaramari (2014)	135
	4.4.3	Rationality analysis on a 5-point scale of Hiranand (1979)	140
	4.4.4	Comparative Rationality Analysis of 3 Types of Rating Scales	145
	4.4.5	Validation of ITKs	150
	4.4.5.1	Validation by Quantification of Indigenous Knowledge (QuIK) method	150
	4.4.6	Validation by Mean Perceived Effectiveness Index Methodology (MPEM)	159
	4.4.7	Generalisation of ITKs	163
	4.5	Constraints encountered in utilisation of ITKs by tribal farmers	173
	4.6	Development of a framework for systematic documentation and scientisation of Indigenous Technical Knowledge	180
	4.7 Success story		191
5.	**SUMMARY AND CONCLUSION**		**193-216**
	5.1 Objectives		194
	5.2 Research methodology		194
	5.3 Results and discussion		196
	5.3.1 Demographic profile of tribal farmers		196
	5.3.2 Demographic profile of ITK experts		197
	5.4	Identification of the process of systematic documentation and scientisation of indigenous technical knowledge	197
	5.5	Scientisation of Indigenous Technical Knowledge about pest and disease management among tribal farmers.	203
	5.5.1 Particularisation of ITKs		203
	5.5.1.1	Rationality analysis on a 3-point rating scale of Dhaliwal and Singh (2010)	203

5.5.1.2	Rationality analysis on a 4-point rating scale of Venkatesan and Sundaramarai (2014)	203
5.5.1.3	Rationality analysis on a 5-point rating scale of Hiranand (1979)	204
5.5.1.4	Comparative Rationality Analysis of 3 Types of Rating Scales	204
5.5.2	Validation of ITKs	205
5.5.2.1	Validation by Quantification of Indigenous Knowledge (QuIK) method	205
5.5.2.2	Validation of ITKs by Mean Perceived Effectiveness Methodology (MPEM)	205
5.5.3	Generalisation of ITKs	206
5.6	Constraints encountered in utilisation of ITKs by tribal farmers	207
5.7	Development of a framework for systematic documentation and scientisation of Indigenous Technical Knowledge	208
5.8 Conclusions		209
5.9 Implications of the study		212
5.10 Suggested areas for future research		216

LIST OF TABLES

Table No.	Title	Page No.
3.3.1	Demographic features of population in Jharkhand	61
3.4.1	Ranchi district at a glance	63
3.4.2.1	Agro-ecological features of Angara and Tamar blocks	65
3.4.2.2	Demographic features of Angara and Tamar blocks	65
3.4.4	Distribution of respondents according to different categories	69
3.5	Measurement of variables selected in the study	70
4.1	Distribution of tribal farmers according to their selected demographic profile	97
4.2	Distribution of ITK experts according to their demographic profile in Delphi rounds	106
4.3.1	Distribution of experts' opinion on 'need and relevance of the study' on a 5-point Likert scale	109
4.3.2	Distribution of statements related to need and relevance of the study	110
4.3.3	Distribution of Delphi experts according to their awareness of methods of documentation and scientisation of ITKs	111
4.3.4.(A)	Distribution of Delphi experts according to their opinion 'methods and activities' related to documentation of ITKs	115
4.3.4.(B)	Distribution of Delphi experts according to their opinion on 'methods and activities' related to scientisation of ITKs	117
4.3.4.2	Distribution of Delphi experts according to their opinion on 'competencies required' of personnel involved in ITK-related studies	120
4.3.4.3	Distribution of Delphi experts according to their opinion on 'institutional mechanism' required for ITK-related studies	123
4.3.4.4	Distribution of Delphi experts according to their opinion on 'criteria' for documentation and scientisation of ITKs	125
4.3.4.5	Distribution of Delphi experts according to their opinion on 'barriers' in ITK-related studies	127
4.4.1.1	Rationality scores obtained by selected ITKs on a 3-point continuum	129

4.4.1.2	Distribution of ITKs according to rationality categories of 3-point continuum	135
4.4.2.1	Rationality scores obtained by selected ITKs on a 4-point continuum	136
4.4.2.2	Distribution of ITKs according to rationality categories of 4-point continuum	140
4.4.3.1	Rationality scores obtained by selected ITKs on a 5-point continuum	141
4.4.3.2	Distribution of ITKs according to rationality categories of 5-point continuum	145
4.4.4	Comparative Rationality Analysis of 3 Types of Rating Scales used	146
4.4.5.1	Validation of different alternatives to control Rice hispa	151
4.4.5.2	Validation of different alternatives to control Rice caseworms	153
4.4.5.3	Validation of different alternatives to control Bihar hairy caterpillar	154
4.4.5.4	Validation of different alternatives to control Rice gall fly	156
4.4.5.5	Validation of different alternatives to control Banki disease	157
4.4.6	Mean Perceived Effectiveness scores of ITKs on selected effectiveness parameters	160
4.4.7.1	Distribution of plant protection scientists according to their opinion on generalisation of ITKs	164
4.4.7.2	Distribution of ITKs according to utilisation method suggested by the scientists	167
4.4.7.3	Suggestions on suitable Corresponding Scientific Technology for blending with ITK	168
4.4.7.4	Opinion of tribal farmers on mode of dissemination of ITKs for generalisation	170
4.5	Distribution of tribal farmers according to their opinion on constraints encountered in utilisation of ITKs	174

LIST OF FIGURES

Table No.	Title	Page No.
1.	SECI Model	9
2.	Steps of scientisation of ITKs	15
3.	Conceptual framework	19
4.	Sampling procedure for selection of tribal farmers	70
5.	Flow diagram of Delphi process	78
6.	Distribution of tribal farmers according to their age	99
7.	Distribution of tribal farmers according to their gender	100
8.	Distribution of tribal farmers according to their tribe type	100
9.	Distribution of tribal farmers according to their education	101
10.	Distribution of tribal farmers according to their land holding	102
11.	Distribution of tribal farmers according to their farming experience	102
12.	Distribution of tribal farmers according to their social participation	103
13.	Distribution of tribal farmers according to their risk orientation	104
14.	Distribution of tribal farmers according to their innovativeness	104
15.	Dimensions of framework development	183
16.	Items in the format for documentation of ITKs	185
17.	Particularisation of ITKs involving the three main stakeholders	187
18.	Validation of ITKs involving the three main stakeholders	188
19.	Generalisation of ITKs involving the three main stakeholders	189

LIST OF PLATES

Table No.	Title	Page No.
1.	Map of India showing Jharkhand state	59
2.	Map of Jharkhand state showing Ranchi district	62
3.	Map of Ranchi district showing selected community development blocks	66
4.	ITK Expert of Jharkhand interacting with tribal clan leader	92
5.	Discussion with plant protection scientists	92
6.	Collection of data from tribal farmers	92
7.	Discussion with the oldest tribal farmer	93
8.	Sinduwar leaves	93
9.	Discussion with tribal key informants regarding validation parameters	93
10.	Field of tribal farmers practicing ITKs	94
11.	Focus Group Discussion with farmers practicing ITK for pest and disease management	94
12.	Discussion with tribal farmers practicing ITK in Paddy field.	95
13.	Investigation of ITK material preparation and discussion with tribal farmers.	95

LIST OF ABBREVIATIONS

Abbreviation	Extended form
AI	Artificial Insemination
ANOVA	Analysis of variance
BAIF	Bharatiya Agro Industries Foundation
CBD	Convention on Biological Diversity
CIKARD	Center of indigenous Knowledge for Agriculture and Rural Development
CST	Corresponding Scientific Technology
docs	documents
e-mail	electronic mail
EVM	Ethno-veterinary Medicine
FGD	Focused Group Discussion
ft	Feet
FLD	Frontline Demonstration
FMD	Foot and Mouth disease
GIAN	Grassroots Innovations Augmentation Network
gm	Grams
ICAR	Indian Council of Agricultural Research
ICTs	Information and Communication Technologies
IIHP	Improved Indigenous Horticultural Practices
IIRR	International Institute of Rural Reconstruction
IK	Indigenous Knowledge
IKS	Indigenous Knowledge System
IPM	Integrated Pest Management
IPPP	Indigenous Plant Protection Practices
ITAP	Indigenous Technical Agricultural Practices

ITK	Indigenous Technical Knowledge
IPR	Intellectual Property Rights
KVK	Krishi Vigyan Kendra
Max	Maximum
Min	Minimum
Mid	Middle
mm	Milli meter
M.P	Madhya Pradesh
MPEI	Mean Perceived Effectiveness Index
MPEM	Mean Perceived Effectiveness Methodology
MVD	Modern Veterinary Disease
NATP	National Agricultural Technology Mission
NGO	Non-Government Organisation
NIH	National Institutes of Health
OAM	Office of Alternative Medicine
OFT	On Farm Trial
PEI	Perceived Effectiveness Index
PIC	Prior Informed Consent
PRA	Participatory Rural Appraisal
PST	Parallel Scientific Technology
QuIK	Quantification of Indigenous Knowledge
R&D	Research and Development
RTU	Ready to use
SC	Scheduled Caste
SES	Socio-Economic status
SHG	Self Help Group
ST	Scheduled Tribe

SWOT	Strength Weakness Opportunities Threats
SAU	State Agriculture University
TAP	Technical Agricultural Practices
UNFCCC	United Nations Framework Convention on Climate Change
UOCB	Uttarakhand Organic Commodity Board
USA	United States of America
WORD	Women's Organisation in Rural Development
ZREAC	Zonal Research and Extension Advisory Committee
Fig	Figure

Chapter 1　　　　　　　　　　　　　　　INTRODUCTION

We want to govern with our indigenous ancestors' models: That means a different concept of participation, community and honesty.

Evo Morales

Indian agriculture faces two predominant challenges of increasing income of the farmers by reducing the production cost and enhancing the sustainability of natural resources by using different knowledge systems available in the country. Knowledge is a strategic resource and a powerful tool which facilitates the process of development. Knowledge has been defined as information combined with context, interpretation and experience **(Davenport et al., 1998)**. It becomes imperative in the era of knowledge management to understand and mobilise different forms of knowledge available around the globe.

There are two types of knowledge i.e. explicit and tacit knowledge. Explicit knowledge has been defined as the "knowledge that is documented and public, structured, fixed content, externalized and conscious. The tacit knowledge is personal, undocumented knowledge, context-sensitive, dynamically-created, derived, internalized and experience-based, not codified and often resides in people's mind, behaviour and perception **(Duffy, 2000)**. Explicit knowledge refers to knowledge that can easily be transferred to others and can easily be codified, assessed, and verbalized. An example is information derived from books, papers, documents and databases. This type of knowledge can easily be retrieved, stored, verbalized and transferred to others. Tacit knowledge is the opposite of Explicit Knowledge. It refers to knowledge that is difficult to transfer to others, and that is difficult to codify, assess, and verbalize. It is many times experience based and includes values, skills, and capabilities. Indigenous Knowledge is an integral part of tacit knowledge.

Indigenous knowledge is local knowledge unique to a given culture or society. Indigenous agricultural and environmental knowledge gained global recognition through United Nations Conference on Environment and Development (UNCED) in

1992 and documents such as the World Conservation Strategy (International Union for the Conservation of Nature and Natural Resources (IUCN) 1980), Brundtland Commission's Our Common Future and World Commission on Environment and Development (WCED), 1987. The importance of indigenous knowledge (IK) of the communities in the development process was first highlighted in Global Conference on Knowledge for Development, Nairobi, Kenya (1993). The development process is not possible by keeping the local people's knowledge aside **(Reintjes *et al.*, 1992)**.

In the rapidly globalising world and evolving knowledge systems, the ability of developing countries like India to build and mobilise appropriate and adequate knowledge capital is imperative to attain the goals of sustainable development.

1.1 Concept of Indigenous Technical Knowledge (ITK)

India is one of the recognized mega-diverse countries of the world, harbours nearly 7-8% of the recorded species and representing four of the 34 globally identified biodiversity hotspots *(https://www.cbd.int/)*. India is home to thousands of Indigenous Knowledge (IK), which dates back to the ancient civilization and the localized way of cultivating crops and rearing fish as well as livestock. India's scriptures consisting of four Vedas, 108 Upanishads, two great epics, Bhagavadgita and 'Brahmasutra', 18 'Puranas', 'Kautilyashastra', 'Manusmriti' and other 'Smrities' as well as the teachings of sages, innumerable sayings and proverbs containing profound literature of ideas, folklores, folk songs, mythologies, concepts and practices are designed to address the process of building harmonious relationships among man, animal and nature **(Nene, 2012)**. Indigenous knowledge is dynamic which changes through indigenous creativity and innovativeness as well as through concept of other knowledge systems.

Indigenous Technical Knowledge (ITK) is the product of centuries of trial and error, natural selection and keen observation that can form the knowledge base on which researchers and extension workers can plan their research strategy and experimental procedures. 'Indigenous' implies that, it is generated by local traditional knowledge, external actors, agencies and individual innovations. 'Technical' denotes the fact that this is specific knowledge that some people have as a result of their experience in a particular subject area. Thus, peoples' knowledge is more detailed than that of others, who have not had the same experience or do not have the same skills in observation or analysis **(Sankaran, 2005)**. Traditional knowledge refers to the knowledge, innovations and practices of indigenous and local communities around the world. Indigenous Technical Knowledge (ITK) helps people to overcome uncertainties and prepare for possible adverse or favourable events.

Indigenous technical knowledge is also referred as local or traditional knowledge, people science, ethno science, traditional ecological knowledge etc. ITK is stored in people's memories and activities, and expressed in the form of stories, songs, folklore, dances, myths, cultural values, beliefs, rituals, community laws, local language and taxonomy etc **(Acharya and Shrivastava, 2008)**. ITK is the basis for local level decision-making in agriculture, weather forecasting, soil and water management, post-harvest management, agro-forestry, bio-diversity conservation, livestock management, fish rearing and preservation, food nutrition, climate change and disaster preparedness **(Shenoy, 2012)**. Indigenous technical knowledge is an immensely valuable resource that provides humankind with insights on how communities have interacted with their changing environment It is the cumulative body of knowledge generated and evolved over a long period of time, representing generations of experience, creative thought and actions of societies to earn a livelihood and cope with the changing conditions of the natural, socio-economic and cultural environment **(Morya *et al.* 2016)**.

Indigenous Technical Knowledge (ITK) refers to the unique, traditional and local knowledge existing within and developed around the specific conditions of women and men indigenous to a particular geographic area **(Grenier, 1998)**. **Wang (1988)** defined ITK as "the sum total of knowledge and practices which are based on people's accumulative experiences in dealing with situations and problems in various aspects of life and such practices are special to a particular culture. ITK is the local knowledge that is unique to a given culture or society. This knowledge is the information base for a society; it facilitates communication and decision making **(Warren, 1991)**. ITK is community-based functional knowledge system, developed, preserved and refined by generations of people through continuous interaction, observation and experimentation with their surrounding environment. It is a dynamic system, ever charming, adopting and adjusting to the local situations and has close links with culture, civilization and religious practices of the communities **(Pushpangadan *et al.*, 2002)**.

It is the local knowledge, which has been institutionalized built upon and passed from one generation to the next **(Ajibade, 2008)**. According to **Dey and Sarkar (2011)**, it is built from and based on thousands of years of experience. However, **Ngwasiri (1995)** expresses that the term 'indigenous knowledge has no universality accepted definition rather it has many descriptions such as local knowledge, location specific knowledge, traditional knowledge and localized knowledge systems, which are unique to particular society or ethnic groups. Some of the specific features of ITK are; it is tacit in nature, location-specific, cost-effective, less capital intensive, eco-friendly, efficient by-product, transmitted orally, collectively owned, dynamic, continuously evolving, learned through repetition, regular experimentation, adapted to local culture and environment and minimize risk **(World Bank, 1998)**.

1.2 Tribals – The custodians of ITK

India due to its multitudinous culture and agro-climatic conditions has abundant reservoir of Indigenous Technical Knowledge in every part of the country. The essential characteristics laid down by the **Lokur Committee (1965)** for a community to be identified as Scheduled Tribes are; a) indications of primitive traits b) distinctive culture c) shyness of contact with the community at large d) geographical isolation and e) backwardness. Tribe is a group of people who are historically disadvantaged, non-integrated to the mainstream society, less participative in the opportunity structure of the society **(Panda, 1998)**. *Adivasi* is the collective term for the indigenous people of India. According to **2011 Census**, Scheduled Tribes make up 8.6 per cent of India's population out of which 89.97 per cent live in rural areas and 10.03 per cent in urban areas. Tribal people are rich with their indigenous agricultural practices. They have accumulated their own innovative indigenous technical knowledge and have developed a congenial relationship with the locally available biological resources and diverse agro climatic conditions thus, establishing a perfect harmony with the nature. Indigenous people with their decades of personal experiences combined with that of their ancestors, harbour vast knowledge about the environment and the ecological relationships within them. They rely on cost-effective sustainable indigenous practices due to their poor socio-economic and agro-ecological conditions. The tribal communities in India, deprived of economic, political and social benefits are more dependent on the indigenous knowledge systems for their livelihood.

1.3 Role of ITK in sustainable agricultural development

Introduction and diffusion of standardized technological packages have contributed a lot in the development of agriculture and allied sectors. These packages were based on top-down technology transfer approach which resulted in weakening of the local knowledge possessed by tribal communities, small and marginal farmers, rural artisans, agricultural laborers, and farm women of the country. Knowledge, skill and survival strategies of farmers operating with low external inputs have often ignored to promote modern agriculture **(Ponnusamy et al., 2009)**. ITK possesses practical utility in solving most of the farmers' problems under their own conditions. ITK has evolved through several years of regular experimentation on the day to day life and available resources surrounded by the community **(Majhi, 2008)**. ITK is found to be socially desirable, economically affordable and ecologically sustainable involving minimization of risk **(Bhanotra and Gupta, 2016)**. Although modern agriculture has drastically increased the production and productivity levels but it has harmed the environment and disturbed the ecology too. Hence to develop alternatives to ecologically damaging agricultural practices will lead to sustainability in long term and ITK is one of the viable options. Understanding the strengths and weaknesses of the indigenous practices which have stood the test of time could perhaps give clues in evolving strategies for sustainable agricultural development.

The indigenous knowledge system and scientific knowledge system are two widely acknowledged knowledge systems **(Munyua and Stilwell, 2013)**. ITK is often contrasted with "modern", "scientific", "western" or "international" knowledge – the knowledge developed by universities, research institutions and private agencies using a formal scientific approach. The common differences between Indigenous Technical Knowledge and Scientific Knowledge are that ITK is transmitted orally whereas scientific knowledge is transferred through written words. ITK is developed and acquired through observation and practical experience whereas scientific knowledge is generally developed and learned in a situation which is different from its applied context. ITKs are holistic, intuitive, qualitative and practical whereas scientific knowledge is reductionist, quantitative, analytical and theoretical. The nature and status of ITKs are influenced by socio-cultural factors and held by the community. On the contrary, the nature and status of scientific knowledge are influenced by peer review and held by individual specialists. Explanations behind perceived phenomenon are often spiritual and subjective in the context of ITK whereas explanations behind perceived phenomenon are essentially rational and objective.

ITK converges on western science disciplines like community ecology, emphasizing connectedness and relatedness between human and non-human components of ecological systems and relies on the indigenous concepts of nature, politics and ethics. ITK is inherently inter-disciplinary **(Pierotti and Wildcat, 2000)**. ITK is essentially scientific because it is gathered through methods that are empirical, experimental and systematic, whereas modern science by contrast, may be seen as narrow and naive in the way it considers and define questions **(Klubnikin *et al.*, 2000)**. The importance of wisdom and showing respect as distinctive features of ITK was stressed by **Turner *et al.* (2000) and Long *et al.* (2003)**

According to the viewpoint of organized science, knowledge of other cultures is regarded as 'pre-logical' or 'irrational', and either their validity is dismissed or greatly played down. Many proponents of ITK have argued that it is eminently practical and utilitarian. Despite their importance, ITKs are neglected and often disregarded on the pretext of being unscientific. But, something unexplained is not necessarily unscientific not justifiable. Indigenous practices may have some weaknesses, problems and constraints, but there are evidences that farmers have survived in the past under extreme conditions based only on the local knowledge they possessed

An understanding of similarities and differences between ITK and scientific knowledge and the benefits and challenges of integrating both the knowledge systems was considered and explained by **Berkes *et al.* 2000, Moller *et al.*, 2004 and Davis, 2006**. The rapid change in the way of life of local communities has largely accounted for the loss of IK. Younger generations underestimate the utility of indigenous knowledge systems (IKSs) because of the influence of modern technology and education **(Ulluwishewa, 1993)**. It is evident that if indigenous knowledge is not recorded and preserved, it will be lost and remain inaccessible to other indigenous systems as well as to development workers. Development projects cannot offer sustainable solutions to local problems without integrating local knowledge **(Warren, 1991)**.

Indigenous knowledge must be managed because it plays a crucial role in the sustainable development of society. The fact that indigenous people also hold a wealth of knowledge and experience that represents a significant resource in the sustainable development of society is slowly dawning. It is also difficult for indigenous organizations to motivate people to share knowledge because indigenous knowledge is individualized and used as a source of power, status and income in the communities. It is therefore important to promote integration of indigenous knowledge with other knowledge systems for socio-economic growth and advocating change in institutional structures. Local knowledge is also recognized as scientific **(Guthiga and Newsham, 2011)**. Since Indigenous Technical Knowledge is essential to development, it must be gathered, organized and disseminated in the same systematic way as scientific knowledge **(Agrawal, 1995)**. The main challenges to the management and preservation of indigenous knowledge are issues related to methodology, access, intellectual property rights and the media and formats in which to preserve it. It is no wonder that access to the indigenous information collected so far is very limited, because it is not well organized in terms of being indexed and abstracted **(Warren and McKiernan, 1995)**. This partly explains the underutilization of IK in development projects **(Mathias, 1995)**. Indigenous knowledge systems have never been systematically recorded in written form and therefore are not readily accessible to agricultural researchers, development practitioners and policy makers.

1.4 Knowledge conversion model

The emerging knowledge society makes it mandatory for society to manage both explicit and tacit knowledge **(Drucker, 1995)**. The move towards a knowledge-based society requires a fundamental shift in thinking about the methodology of managing information resources generated by society. Knowledge management, with its emphasis on developing, gathering, utilizing, processing, preserving, and sharing all the existing knowledge. The process of organizing and leveraging knowledge embedded in people's experiences, competencies, talents, ideas, practices, intuitions, skills, wisdom and capabilities, in addition to documented and codified sources, has been characterized as knowledge management **(Todd, 1999)**. The central focus of knowledge management is sharing what people know. The idea is to create a knowledge sharing environment whereby sharing knowledge is power as opposed to the old aged that, simply, knowledge is power.

Encoding indigenous knowledge into valuable information is one of the keys to its successful management and sustainable development **(Ngulube, 2002)**. Organizations and communities have started recognizing the importance of managing tacit indigenous knowledge using various knowledge management models. Within this plethora of knowledge-based theories, concepts, and tools, the SECI model is widely acknowledged as a theoretical landmark and adopted as the framework for most knowledge management conceptualization. The model considers knowledge creation as a dynamic process, in which the continuous dialog between tacit and explicit knowledge generates new knowledge and amplifies it across different ontological levels (individual, organizational, inter-organizational). The model stands out because it not only formalizes a theory of knowledge creation based on the epistemological distinction between tacit and explicit knowledge but also offers practical tool for assessing knowledge creation in organizational contexts.

A SECI model is considered as the most suitable framework to convert tacit knowledge to explicit knowledge so that it can be utilized for the betterment of society **(Nonaka, 1991)**. The SECI Model of Knowledge Dimensions is based on two types of knowledge, explicit knowledge and tacit knowledge. The Knowledge Creation commonly known as Nonaka's theory is based on the possibility of managing tacit knowledge such as indigenous knowledge. Since knowledge is continually obtained and converted by practicing, collaborating, interacting, and learning, the SECI Model of Knowledge Dimensions visualizes a spiral in the model. In this model, knowledge follows a cycle in which implicit knowledge is 'extracted' to become explicit knowledge, and explicit knowledge is "re-internalized' into implicit knowledge. The strength of the theory lies in recognizing, generating, transferring and managing tacit knowledge across time and space dimensions **(Nonaka and Konno, 1994)**.

SECI Model

The SECI model identifies four modes of knowledge conversions in organizations, that is, Socialization–Externalization–Combination–Internalization conversion modes generated by the switching process from one type of knowledge to another **(Nonaka and Takeuchi, 1995)**.

1. Socialization
2. Externalization
3. Combination
4. Internalization

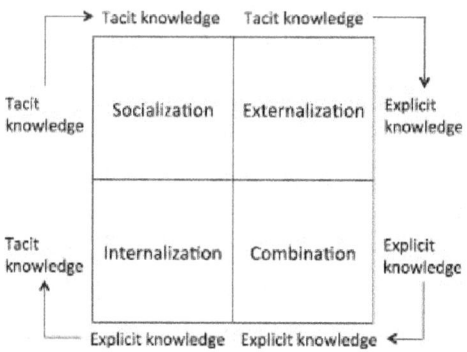

Figure 1: SECI Model

Socialization The spiral starts with the *Socialization* mode. The process that transfers tacit knowledge of one person to tacit knowledge of another person is socialization. Since tacit knowledge is difficult to formalize and often context, space and time specific, it can only be acquired and exchanged by social interaction through sharing experiences. In this regard, experiences, ideas and skills are shared by interaction, observation, and practicing.

Externalization The process of making tacit knowledge explicit is externalization. Tacit knowledge is converted, through the *Externalization* mode, into new explicit knowledge in the form of concepts, images, and written documents. Tacit knowledge is codified and specified in words and put into manuals or other documents so that it can easily be shared among members in the organization. Thus in this process, ideas and narratives are transformed into formats that may be transmitted easily. This is achieved when combining different sets of explicit knowledge such as databases and web-based tools. Other example is the articulation of one's own tacit knowledge i.e. ideas or images in words, metaphors and analogies. A second case is eliciting and translating the tacit knowledge of others like wisdom bearers and experts for example, into a readily understandable form, i.e. explicit knowledge. Dialogue is an important means for both. During such face to face communication people share beliefs and learn how to better articulate their thinking, through instantaneous feedback and the stimulus exchange of ideas.

Combination Once knowledge is explicit, it can be transferred as explicit knowledge through a process, called combination by **Nonaka and Takeuchi (1995)**. Combination is the process of systematizing concepts into a knowledge system. Explicit knowledge is pooled with other intra- or inter-organizational explicit knowledge through the combination mode, being merged, edited, or processed to form more complex and systematic explicit knowledge. This means that existing sources such as books, documents, memos are used and combined to create new knowledge such as a report. This mode of knowledge conversion is many times easily facilitated by online data bases because explicit knowledge is everywhere available online. This is the area where information technology is most helpful, because explicit knowledge can be conveyed in documents, e-mails, data bases, as well as through meetings and briefings. The key steps collecting relevant internal and external knowledge, dissemination, and processing to make it more usable. The creative use of computerized communication networks and large-scale databases can facilitate this mode of knowledge conversion.

Internalization In this process, explicit knowledge is converted into tacit knowledge. Internalization is the process of understanding and absorbing explicit knowledge in to tacit knowledge held by the individuals. Knowledge in the tacit form is actionable by the owner. Internalization is largely experimental, in order to actualize concepts and methods, either through the actual doing or through stimulations. The internalization process transfers organization and group explicit knowledge to be the individual. The SECI spiral concludes with the Internalization mode, where explicit knowledge is absorbed by individuals, enriching their tacit knowledge base: formal knowledge is connected to personal experiences to be subsequently transferred and used in practical situations paving the way to new tacit knowledge generation. The knowledge is next internalized, meaning that that the existing knowledge is being modified. This new internalized knowledge is re-circulated in the spiral of knowledge, initiating further conversion processes. Conversion modes as a whole and in their interaction give rise to the spiral of knowledge generation **(Nonaka, 1991)**.

Managing knowledge in general and indigenous knowledge in particular has become an important and valuable input in the management of sustainable development programmes. However, the growing realization that indigenous knowledge has a role to play in national development as well as the knowledge management environment has led to the growth of interest in preserving and managing it. Although the value of integrating indigenous science with western science has been recognized, we have only begun to scratch the surface of its benefits. Indigenous science is holistic and founded upon interconnectedness, reciprocity and utmost respect for nature. Both western and indigenous science approaches and perspectives have their strengths and can greatly complement one another. The success of humankind is going to largely depend on gathering, analysing, storing, sharing and harnessing what other members of society know as well as drawing upon codified and documented knowledge. Managing and preserving IK will help to 'reduce poverty, enhance equity and reduce environmental degradation' and lead to sustainable development, as well as increased local participation in the development process **(Warren and McKiernan, 1995)**.

1.5 Steps in ITK-based technology development

Indigenous Technical Knowledge and modern scientific knowledge both are equally important for environment conservation. Irrespective of the approach, either modern or indigenous, our aim is to conserve environment and step towards sustainable development. Awareness is growing about the use of indigenous technical knowledge in development initiatives that could bring long term benefits, richly complementing and enhancing the contributions of modern initiatives. Considering ITKs in development projects and locating research, thrust areas are gaining momentum **(Gupta, 1998)**. The followers of traditional knowledge are unaware about the scientific logic behind the practices. Thus there is a need to explore the alternative strategy to provide a scientific basis for the ITKs so that the communities can pursue ITKs utilisation in agricultural development. There are different methodologies for establishing the scientific basis of ITKs so that their utilitarian value can be established. Indigenous knowledge can make a significant contribution to sustainable development and provide a basis for development of highly adoptable and cost effective scientific innovation provided they are documented, verified and refined by blending scientific knowledge. There are mainly four steps for inclusion of ITK in technology generation, reassessment and dissemination i.e. documentation, validation, refinement and integration.

a. Documentation of ITKs: Documentation of ITK is a process in which ITK is identified, collected, organized, registered or recorded as a means to dynamically maintain, manage, use, disseminate or protect according to specific goals. Documentation is essential firstly because economic, social and political factors are gradually uprooting many such untapped resources from their native habitats resulting in loss and erosion of very rich indigenous knowledge Secondly, rapid pace of acculturation or urbanization has tremendous influence on the lives of indigenous communities. Thirdly, modernisation has resulted into loss of their peculiar culture and heritage. Fourthly, the knowledge survives through word of mouth, particularly among the old generation. Thus, it is necessary to document such knowledge, before the old generation passes away. ITKs are the intellectual property of the informant (individual or community). So benefit sharing is required when the data will be used for raising any benefit after the commercialisation of ITKs **(Girach, 2007)**. Some common methods used for documentation are notes, photographs, audio and video recordings **(IIRR, 1996)**.

b. Validation of ITKs: The concept of Validation has been presented under two heads: pre-validation and validation.

i. Pre- validation of ITKs: Rationality of ITK is assessed. Scientific rationality is the degree to which the information on ITK is realistic with a scientific backstopping. Further it refers to the degree to which ITK can be explained or supported with scientific explanations or have been established based on long term experiences **(Husain, and Sundaramari, 2011)**. It is adjudged by the scientists/experts of respective fields and based on review of literature, it can be done by three types of rating scales i.e. 3-point rating scale of **Dhaliwal and Singh (2010)**, 4-point rating scale of **Venkatesan and Sundaramari (2014)** and 5-point rating scale of **Hiranand (1979)**.

ii. Validation of ITKs: Validation of ITK is a logical step to qualify and quantify effectiveness of practices. Validation of ITK can be done by different methods such as QuIK (Quantification of Indigenous Knowledge), Mean Perceived Effectiveness Methodology (MPEM) and experimental validation.

c. Refinement of ITKs: Some ITKs can be used directly after documentation and validation while some ITKs need further modifications for its adoption. Suitable modifications of the local practices, through research and development (R&D) will help to develop appropriate and acceptable technologies that are more suited to our farming situations.

d. Integration of ITKs: ITKs have more adaptability to the local situations and can be used in formal advisory system. A blend of ITK and modern technology may be most appropriate for sustainable development **(Rathakrishnan *et al.*, 2009)**. After documentation of ITKs, those should be integrated with the modern scientific knowledge that will be beneficial to the farmers, scientists and environment and to the national economy.

Utilisation of ITKs: ITKs having high level of rationality and effectiveness scores is to be given priority by extension agents and researchers as they will greatly reduce expenditure of modern practices and benefit farmers when put in use on a regular basis. Research and Development organizations can take up the task of refining the selected ITKs and popularise them among farmers. Scientists and scientific institutions should consider the farmers as active partners in the process of technology generation and dissemination. The indigenous practices are to be promoted and utilised not only for the benefit of the people but also for maintaining agricultural sustainability and ecosystem stability through integration with the modern science.

These steps were widely accepted as standardized steps in appropriate technology development and were modified and renamed in the context of indigenous knowledge management as particularisation, validation and generalisation. This was later termed as the scientisation of ITKs. **(Agrawal 2002, UNESCO Report)**

1.6 Concept of scientisation of ITKs

ITK is often seen as legitimate only when it has been adapted to the specialized narrative of science **(Mauro and Hardison, 2000)**. ITKs which are perceived as directly relevant to specific purpose in a scientific view are most often incorporated into the agricultural technology development process and technology transfer. The step whereby ITKs deemed amenable to technology development and transfer process are separated from other knowledge is the first in the process of ITK documentation, **Agrawal (2002)** describes it as "scientisation." The scientisation process involves distinguishing the descriptive from analytical, the anecdotal from the systematic, and the mythic from the factual **(Raffles, 2002)**. The term scientisation refers to the sequential processes of "particularisation", "validation" and "generalisation" **(Agrawal, 2002)**.

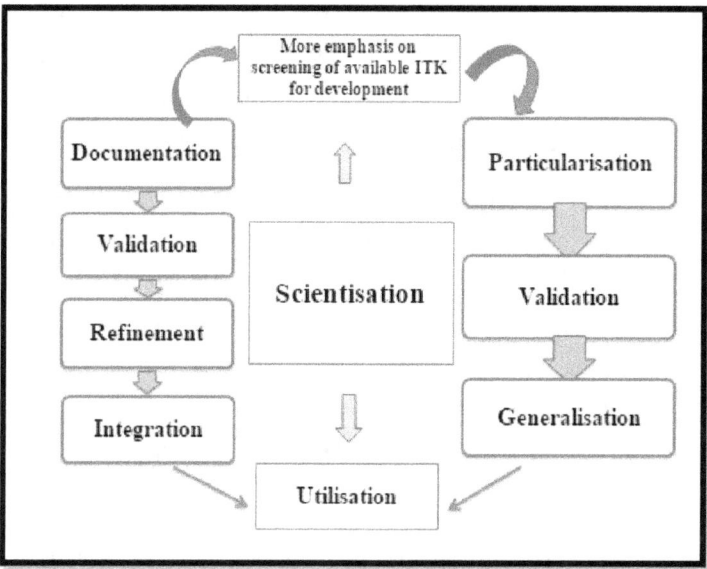

Figure 2: Steps of Scientisation of ITKs

i. Particularisation of ITKs: The process of identification and separation of useful indigenous knowledge is called particularisation. The process of particularisation is the first step in creation of any database of useful knowledge for validation. ITKs which are passed through the process of particularisation are often perceived as confirming to the requirements for using them as a "resource" for agricultural research and technology transfer.

ii. Validation of ITKs: The second step in the process of scientisation of ITK involves testing and validating relevant knowledge using scientific criteria. Various scientific criteria used in validation of ITK are efficacy, replicability, rationality, rigor and universality. It involves generating direct, empirical and quantifiable information to meet various criteria identified. Only the ITKs which satisfy those criteria are most often considered to be valid and useful. The myths, sayings, values, beliefs and other contextual knowledge are discarded **(Pierotti and Wildcat, 1997)**.

iii. Generalisation of ITKs: Once knowledge is particularised and validated, it is considered as truthful, useful and ultimately powerful which needs to be catalogued and archived, and then circulated before it can be used more widely. This is the process of generalisation. Though generalisation helps in cataloging of the useful ITK, it does not end with the inclusion of a validated piece of information in a catalogue. This generalisation process logically leads to further validation.

Hence, scientisation in nutshell, is the basis for establishing the truth content of a particular ITK- based practices. It helps to convert ITK from a myth or tradition to a scientific fact, which will be validated for utilisation. The process of Scientisation entails protection of ITKs through Intellectual Property Rights to prevent illegal use and unwanted commercial exploitation. Past studies on the "scientisation of Indigenous Technical Knowledge" have demonstrated that this process can be effectively applied in climate research also **(Riedlinger and Berkes, 2001)**.

1.7 Problem statement

Advances in agricultural science and technology and their application have revolutionized the agricultural scenario in India. India achieved a distinct status from a food deficit to a food surplus nation. When impact of Green Revolution was studied, it was found that for deriving short term benefits, sustainability was ignored in the long run. Environment has been treated in an unfriendly manner and ecology was disturbed due to intensive farming. So maintaining sustainability of resources is the major concern of the policy makers and development workers **(Bizimana, 1997)**.

While finding viable options to maintain sustainability of resources, the role of ITK has gained momentum. Green Revolution had totally revolutionized the agricultural scenario of the country through intensive package of practices and costly inputs. Even then, the benefits of green revolution could not reach the rainfed areas cultivated by the resource-poor farmers. The suitability of conventional agricultural technology forced them to rely mostly on indigenous technical practices. Indigenous knowledge has elements of natural products which are utilized in solving daily situational and environmental problems faced by the community. Earlier scientists and development practitioners regarded ITKs as ineffective and useless for development projects. Voice of tribal farmers or local communities practicing indigenous practices have often been neglected in the process of in modernizing agriculture.

Thus, there is an immense pressure on research and extension personnel and realisation to collect, preserve and adopt ITKs. This will help in reducing dependence on external inputs, to reduce the cost of production and to propagate eco-friendly agriculture **(Berkes, 1993)**. Several ITKs are at the risk of becoming extinct because of rapidly changing natural environment and fast pacing economic, political and cultural change on global scale. Policy makers and development workers are somewhat skeptical about the benefits of low yielding results of Indigenous Technical Knowledge for competing with the global food demand. The integration of indigenous knowledge system has facilitated improved performance on farming activities in many developing countries **(Ponnusamy et al., 2009)**. Thus there is need for incorporating Indigenous Technical Knowledge with modern scientific technology so that both ITK and the corresponding scientific technology could be used to supplement and complement each other in the development process. Thus technology blending programmes would be an effective step to generate eco-friendly, location-specific, economically-viable and socially acceptable technology **(Gupta, 2008)**.

Proper documentation, validation and refinement of ITKs at different stages will help the mankind to have easy access to ITK-based practices or ITK-based blended technology for agriculture **(Rajesh et al., 2013)**. Although many studies have been conducted so far on this aspect at different locations of the country but all these studies were limited to a narrower domain consisting of either one or two functions involved in ITK integration such as Documentation **(Talukdar et al., 2012)**, Validation **(Ghosh and Sahoo, 2011)**, assessing perceived effectiveness of selected ITK-based practices **(Singh and Chauhan, 2016 and Bhuyan, 2017)**. However, **Das et al.** **(2002)** tried to compile ITK related to agriculture but this is also insufficient to pool this ocean of knowledge. Merely documenting and studying perceived effectiveness of ITK will not bring sustainability unless it is utilised in farming. ITK used by farmers need proper research and validation procedure to provide acceptable scientific evidence to support traditional methods which are presumably eco-friendly and subsequently paving the way to sustainable agriculture. Emphasis should be on reduced dependence on external inputs, cost of cultivation and cost of production and to propagate eco-friendly agriculture. Adequate attention has not been given in upgradation of ITK-based practices and disseminating the documented and validated ITKs to the resource poor farmers belonging to similar environments and commercialising them for the benefit of farming community at large.

The main obstacle in popularisation of ITKs is the unavailability of a standard framework which facilitates systematic documentation, validation and dissemination of ITKs for the socio-economic upliftment of farmers. The function of ITK is confined to only documentation and validation due to unavailability of a systematic framework.

Efforts to collate indigenous technical knowledge and setting up databases were not successful due to inadequate frameworks for capturing and making knowledge available for development. So far the researches carried out on ITKs have not followed systematic and holistic approach. The present study is an attempt to evolve systematic procedure for documentation and scientisation of ITKs. All the efforts to make indigenous knowledge useful for development moves around the gamut of the three processes of particularisation, validation and generalisation which ultimately lead to scientisation **(Agrawal, 2002)**. There are several research issues which demand attention for in-depth analysis of ITKs.

1.8 Researchable questions

- What are the sequential steps to be followed in systematic documentation, validation and generalisation of ITKs?
- How to ascertain the scientific rationale of the documented ITK-based practices?
- How to standardize the scientific procedure of validation of ITKs?
- Is there any framework available for documentation, validation and generalisation of ITKs?
- How would the validated ITKs be utilised in agriculture?
- What would be the appropriate extension mix for disseminating and popularising the locally relevant ITKs?
- How would ready to use ITK-based products be disseminated?

There have been sporadic attempts to study the different dimensions of ITK merely to study the functional aspects. In view of the importance being attached to the role and relevance of ITKs in agriculture and the research questions raised in this regard, the bigger challenge is of scientisation of ITKs. This issue is required to be studied in greater detail. An effort has been made to investigate the research issues involved in documentation and scientisation of ITKs. Thus, a study entitled, "Scientisation of Indigenous Technical Knowledge of Tribal Farmers in Ranchi district of Jharkhand" was undertaken with the following specific objectives:

1.9 Objectives

1. To identify the process of systematic documentation and scientisation of Indigenous Technical Knowledge.

2. To study the process of scientisation of Indigenous Technical Knowledge about pest and disease management among tribal farmers.

3. To delineate the constraints encountered in utilisation of Indigenous Technical Knowledge by tribal farmers.

4. To develop a framework for systematic documentation and scientisation of Indigenous Technical Knowledge.

1.10 Conceptual framework

The study was conducted on the following conceptual framework:

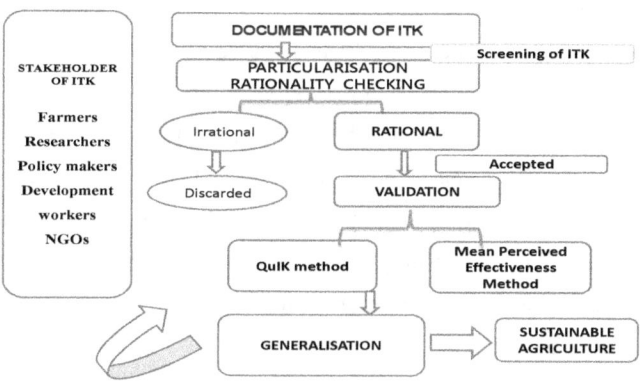

Figure 3: Conceptual framework

In the present investigation, an effort has been made to screen out and popularise relevant ITKs for sustainable agricultural development. This was achieved by following the process of scientisation. Firstly, already documented ITKs were collected from the secondary sources. Although ITKs practiced by tribal farmers were triangulated during primary data collection to know whether those were still prevalent among the communities or not. So after finalising the list of ITKs, first step of scientisation i.e. particularisation was done. Particularisation was done by assessing scientific rationality of ITKs. For this the list of ITK was sent to scientists to assess their rationality. The ITKs which were found rational (scientific backstopping) by the scientists were screened out for validation while rest were discarded. ITKs which were found to be rational were only used for validation. Scientists-farmers interaction is necessary for participatory technology development, therefore community validation as well as scientist validation was used. ITKs which were validated and proved to be efficient were taken up for the next step of scientisation, i.e. Generalisation. The ITKs need to be disseminated and popularised for sustainable agricultural development. Involvement of multiple stakeholders at each step of scientisation would be beneficial for increasing the accessibility of ITKs.

1.11 Scope and significance of the study

Sustainability is the central focus of policy makers and development practitioners. In an effort for seeking alternatives, ITK was identified as a viable option for sustainability. ITK has enormous scope for sustainable agriculture development. The systematic documentation and scientisation of ITK in National Agriculture Research System (NARS) is of utmost importance to achieve sustainability of natural resources. It will help the mankind for easy access of ITK and ITK-based technologies. Scientisation of ITK will lead to location-specific, economically viable and socially acceptable technology to mitigate the environmental problems in different aspects of agriculture and allied fields. This will not only facilitate sustainability but also empower farmers to take active part in participatory technology development.

The scope of the study under reference is very wide as it aims to develop a process framework for systematic documentation and scientisation of Indigenous Technical Knowledge (ITK). This framework will assist in the identification of linkages and relationships between ITK and sustainable agricultural development. The study also focuses on documentation of ITKs followed by their scientisation i.e. particularisation, validation and generalisation. This study includes identification of standard procedures of documentation and assessment of scientific rationality of selected ITKs. It further includes the process of farmer participatory technology development through blending the effective ITKs with their corresponding scientific technologies. Blending will help to enhance their effectiveness and compatibility with existing bio-physical and socio-economic conditions and farming system components as well as household internal resources.

1.12 Limitations of the study

Although every effort was made to make this study as comprehensive as possible but being a social and behavioural science research, it was subjected to the limitations inherent in a single researcher project. Some of the limitations were as indicated below:

1. Due to in-depth nature of the study, it was confined to only one district of the Jharkhand state. Therefore, the findings of the study will also be applicable to the areas similar to the area of study.

2. Establishing rapport with tribal people was a challenge in the beginning which was gradually overcome with the consistent efforts of the researcher in developing a bond of relationship with the villagers.

4. The results of the study are entirely based on the expressed responses of the respondents which might not be completely free from individual bias and prejudices.

5. Farmers were reluctant to disclose the information on ITKs so it was difficult to convince the farmers about the researcher's intentions, genuinity and importance of the investigation.

6. It was a very challenging task to obtain responses of the Delphi questionnaire from the experts as they had a hectic schedule and it was not possible for them to spare time easily for all the three rounds. However regular knock down was made through calls, messages, mails etc.

7. Data collection during the Covid-19 period was a uphill task which had to be discontinued due to the imposed restrictions. It was very difficult to contact tribal farmers due to restrictions imposed due to Covid-19 for detailed investigation.

1.13 Organization

The present investigation has been systematically organized into five chapters in logical sequence. Chapter I attempts to focus on the relevant background information, statement of the problem, objectives and scope of the study along with its limitations i.e. Introduction. Chapter II deals with the Review of Literature related to the research problem. Chapter III elaborates the details of Research Methodology used for conducting research. It covers locale of study area, description of study area, sampling technique, operationalisation and measurement of selected variables, data collection and statistical tools applied to analyse the data. The significant findings of the study along with discussion are presented in Chapter IV i.e. Results and Discussion. Chapter V is on Summary and Conclusions which have emerged from the results of the study. Bibliography, appendices, vita and other relevant information utilized in this study have been presented at the end.

Chapter 2   REVIEW OF LITERATURE

An attempt has been made in this chapter to mention various research studies highlighting relevant literature, research gaps and the areas requiring further studies. The literature reviewed provides readers with a background for understanding current knowledge on a topic and illuminates the significance for the new study. Review of literature establishes a clear tie between the proposed research and the studies which have been already conducted. Review of literature helps the researcher to get acquainted with the subject matter and channelize efforts in desirable direction.

Keeping in view the objectives of the present study, an effort was made to review the available literature having direct or indirect bearing on the present investigation. This chapter has been presented under the following sub-heads:

2.1 Indigenous Technical Knowledge (ITKs) and its significance

2.2 Documentation of ITKs: Methods and Approaches

2.3 Rationality of ITKs

2.4 Validation of ITKs

2.5 Refinement and Integration of ITKs

2.6 Utilisation of ITKs

2.7 Constraints encountered in utilisation of ITKs

2.8 Framework related to scientisation of ITKs

2.1 Indigenous Technical Knowledge (ITKs) and its significance

Chambers *et al.* (1989) observed that some local knowledge systems were responding creatively to challenges through experimentation, innovation, adaptation and transformation under quite diverse conditions.

Warren *et al.* (1991) stated that indigenous knowledge is the systematic body of knowledge acquired by local people through the accumulation of experiences, informal experimentation and intimate understanding of the environment in a given culture. Indigenous knowledge systems are dynamic, changing through indigenous mechanisms of creativity, as well as, through contact with other local and international knowledge systems.

Reijntjes *et al.* (1992) stated that the word 'indigenous' means "native born, originating or produced naturally in a country or in a specified area" and the word 'knowledge' means "assured belief, practical skill, that which is known, learning, enlightenment."

Jena (2007) opined that the community has developed indigenous knowledge systems to conserve and utilize the biological diversity of their surroundings. The recognition of the creativity of the indigenous communities is essential for the conservation of biodiversity as well as conservation of intellectual diversity.

Dilshad *et al.* (2008) concluded that indigenous practices can be used to provide economical solutions to improve productivity of animals and reduction in poverty of the poor farmers.

Gervais (2008) conceptualised that traditional knowledge is an inextricable part of the biocultural heritage of indigenous people and local communities. It is 'traditional' only to the extent that its creation and use are rooted in the cultural norms and practices of a community; it does not necessarily mean ancient or static. Indeed, that which is 'traditional' can be seen as dynamic and evolving.

Gupta (2008) reported that the reasons for protecting traditional knowledge are to improve the livelihoods of ITK holders and communities, to benefit the national economy, to conserve the environment and to prevent the bio-piracy.

Wankhade (2009) reported that developing countries have a valuable but largely untapped reservoir of indigenous agriculture knowledge. Development planners and policy makers are beginning to recognize the need to understand existing knowledge systems and decision making process as they focus their attention on the fact that small scale agriculture can play a better role in achieving national food self sufficiency.

Borthakur and Singh (2012) highlighted that indigenous technical knowledge prevalent in different traditional communities is not properly documented due to which most of them are at the verge of extinction.

Bodapti and Chander (2013) elucidated that farmers prefer more than one measure to solve the problem of dairy animals, i.e. adoption of traditional practices alone or a combination of traditional practices with allopathic medicines was preferred for the treatment of dairy animals.

Devaki and Mathialagan (2015) opined that ITKs are passed from one generation to another by the word of mouth and thought to be the holistic approach for sustainable agricultural development.

Singh *et al.* (2015) stated that indigenous knowledge is characterized as the sum of experiences and knowledge for a given ethnic group, which forms the basis for decision making with regard to familiar and unfamiliar problems and challenges. It can play a key role in designing sustainable farming systems including animal husbandry practices, thereby increasing the livelihoods that rural populations would accept, develop and maintain innovations and interventions.

Singh and Chauhan (2016) opined that due to rapidly changing natural environments and fast pacing economic, political, and cultural changes on a global scale, many indigenous knowledge systems are at risk of becoming extinct. Practices vanish as they become inappropriate for new challenges or because they adapt too slowly. Many practices disappear only because of the intrusion of foreign technologies or development concepts that promise short-term gains or solutions to problems without being capable of sustaining them.

Ponnusamy *et al.* (2017) in a study highlighted some pertinent ITK related issues such as i) Documentation of different ITKs from various regions of the nation ii) The wide variation in formulation of ITK practices for same problem warrants preparation of unique product based on the role of active ingredients in plant parts iii) A ready to use (RTU) product prepared from well validated ITK would enhance the adoption, profitability and sustainability iv) Efforts should be made to validate the use of plants such as pearl millet and sorghum in South India, also as they are widely used in East and West regions v) Need to develop appropriate extension mix for disseminating locally relevant ITK through vernacular language vi) Focus is required on the local innovators to be developed as role models and training centers for out scaling the adoption of ITKs relevant to particular region vii) Many research projects have been carried out in the domain of ITKs but a result framework for monitoring ITKs and its impact on the communities or people need to be developed.

Rai *et al.* (2019) defined ITK as time tested knowledge and experiences of the people in dealing with situations and problems in varying aspects of life and such knowledge and practices are special to a particular culture. Indigenous technical knowledge systems are changing from generation to generation through contact with other localite and cosmopolite knowledge systems as well as through specific process of creativity and innovativeness, finally tuned, adopted both biologically and socially to counter the process of what are often harsh and inimical environment and often represent many years of adaptive evolution.

2.2 Documentation of ITKs: Methods and Approaches

Dana and Kaul (2000) collected data through personal interview schedules and observational techniques. Key informant technique was also used to explore the available indigenous knowledge among the *Ojha*s (village medicine men). Documentation of different plants used by *Santhal* and *Lodha* tribes and also the *Ojhas* for the treatment of different diseases of dairy animals was also done. The respondents being tribals and mostly illiterate, it was decided to use observational technique, diary writing and photography besides the interview schedule.

Dick *et al.* (2004) reported that understanding of the complexities involved in the survey study of ITK can only be achieved by mixing methods such as structured interview schedule, group discussion, key informant interview and observation. This will help the researchers verify and integrate the collected indigenous knowledge into mainstream knowledge development and management.

Rathakrishnan *et al.* (2009) opined that instead of collecting information on indigenous knowledge from individuals, interaction with groups i.e. focused group discussion paved the way for easy documentation and triangulation.

Suresh (2010) identified and documented indigenous agricultural knowledge and practices prevalent among *Mavilan* tribal community of North Kerala by personal interviews and discussions with farmers, aged persons and the community members.

Mishra *et al.* (2011) stated that it is extremely difficult to acquire indigenous knowledge which is regarded as secret or confidential. Since indigenous knowledge is not documented but stored in people's minds, it bears a high risk of losing this valuable knowledge. So, collection of indigenous knowledge is of great significance in conserving and maintaining sustainability of the environment.

Bhanotra (2012) documented ITKs about health care management of dairy animals from Kathua district of Jammu and Kashmir. Prior Informed Consent (PIC) was taken from the *Sarpanch* of the village both orally and in written form to protect intellectual property rights of the wisdom bearers and also for benefit sharing purpose listed in Article 8 (j) of Convention of Biological Diversity (CBD). Focus Group Discussion (FGD), transect walks, observation and key informant interview were used to document and gather information related to ITK on animal healthcare management. Secondary sources were also considered for the triangulation of the results. A list of 25 plant materials (plant species, local name, life form and mode of application) has been recorded to treat 20 ailments of animals.

Singh *et al.* (2012) found that the documentation of indigenous knowledge has gained momentum with the establishment of the Center of Indigenous Knowledge and Rural Development (CIKARD) at IOWA University, USA in 1987 and establishment of Office of Alternative Medicine (OAM) under National Institute of Health (NIH).

Talukdar *et al.* (2012) in a study in Assam explored 57 ITKs under nine selected cultivation practices of Boro rice. The maximum number (33) of ITKs were identified and documented under 'plant protection' and least number (only one) recorded in 'fertility management."

Das *et al.* (2013) stated that in recent era many indigenous technical knowledge systems are at the risk of becoming extinct due to economic, political and cultural changes happening around the globe. As ITK adapt slowly and even get vanished as they become inappropriate to deal with new challenges. Many ITK practices have disappeared due to intrusion of modern technologies so it becomes imperative to document ITK which is believed to carry some substantial scientific logic for sustainability. They also suggested that systematic recording and documentation of ITK in written form will make these practices accessible to researchers, extension workers and development practitioners' for further exploration of scientific possibilities and effective use.

Moreki and Tsopito (2013) used a formal questionnaire which was administered to poultry rearers of Botswana. Data were also collected through direct observation, village walks, interview of passers-by, group interviews, meetings with key informants, traditional leaders, extension agents and chairperson of village development committees and also by reviewing secondary sources of data. The ethno-veterinary practices in 15 villages of Botswana were identified and documented. Nineteen plant species representing 15 families were used by poultry rearers to treat and control poultry diseases and parasites.

Rajesh et al. (2013) documented a suite of 164 traditional practices (indigenous technical knowledge) in different cropping systems of which 39 were pertaining to coconut cultivation at Palakkad district in Kerala. ITK practices were documented by using the key informant method, in-depth informal discussion with the help of semi-structured interview schedule and focus group discussion supplemented with transect walk. Documentation of ITK was done by using both primary and secondary sources of information.

Subrahmanyeswari and Chander (2013) conducted a study with organic farmers of Uttarakhand in which Prior informed consent (PIC) was taken from the registered organic farmers through the network of Uttarakhand Organic Commodity Board (UOCB). Anthropological approaches, interaction with farmers, observation techniques and the secondary data were used to document ITKs of farmers for sustainable organic farming.

Yolmo (2013) conducted a study on "Exploration and Implication of Indigenous Technological Knowledge in Hill ecosystem of West Bengal". Thirty two ITKs were collected and documented based on interaction and discussion with farmers and key informants of the study area. ITK practices were documented in a systematic manner on the basis of the title, general description of indigenous technological knowledge, area of specialization, application of indigenous technological knowledge, cultural compatibility and environmental feasibility, sustainability, scientific rationale, revelation and photographs. The author also emphasized the use of various methods such as interaction with community leaders or elders, rapid rural appraisal, case study, key informant method, history, interview method, participant observation, brain storming, games, group discussion, field observations, surveys and SWOT analysis.

Devi *et al.* (2014) in a study on fish farmers of Assam documented 34 ITKs on different aquaculture practices through interaction, observation and focus group discussion with the use of semi structured interview.

Sahoo *et al.* (2016) adopted four steps for collection and documentation of ITK practices; i) Identification and collection of information: Documentation of oral histories, agro-ecosystem analysis, manual discriminant analysis, use of local resource persons, conducting documentation workshops, continuous interactions during on-farm experiments, local taxonomy, crop histories, in-depth interview of farmers and survey method ii) Documentation: Documenting large variety of practices without scientific validation, documenting prevalent practices and comparing them with traditional ones, documenting the practices of experimentation on a specific aspect and understanding the various linkages and documenting the practices evolved to mitigate specific problems of farming iii) Methods of recording: Identification of indigenous specialists, case studies, field observations, personal observations, interviews, group discussions, historical composition, seasonal pattern chart, taxonomies, cassette documentation, photo/ slide and participatory video iv) Analysis: For analysis of collected and documented ITKs the parameters like IK-based, extent of use, prevent losses, eco-friendly, easy to handle, severity of problem, innovativeness, availability of input, rationality, cost effectiveness were followed and accordingly practices were categorized for further analysis that is validation and standardization.

Singh and Saha (2017) documented indigenous practices regarding farming systems by participant observation, unstructured interaction and recording of oral case histories by tape-recording techniques. The procedures adopted while observing and documenting IK were Observing IK: IK of farmers in their respective farmers Documenting IK: The observed IK was documented by using a camera; Analysing IK: The salient features of IK were recorded in a pocket notebook after carefully observing them, and Titling IK: Later on, an appropriate title for each of the IK recorded was decided through informal discussion either with the participant farmers or with local healers who are encountered on farm holdings.

Venketasan and Sundaramarai (2017) in a study in Kolli Hills of Tamil Nadu aggregated, categorized and reported 23 indigenous agricultural practices practiced in little millet cultivation out of which 19 were related to crop production and 4 were on plant protection.

Devaki *et al.* (2018) reported that indigenous knowledge is not well documented, merely being transmitted verbally from one generation to the next. They emphasized the need for systematic identification, collection and documentation of indigenous knowledge.

Swangla *et al.* (2021) stated that documentation is the conversion of traditional knowledge provided by communities into written documents. The nature and stage of research on indigenous knowledge system guided to qualitative approach supplemented with quantification, wherever required or possible. She documented ITKs of tribal farming systems of Himachal Pradesh by using personal interview method and in-depth informal discussion with the help of semi-structured interview schedule, focus group discussion with respondents supplemented with transect walk.

2.3 Rationality of ITKs

Ponnusamy *et al.* (2009) used a 3-point continuum scale comprising of scientifically valid (5), not considered (3) and not valid (1) to ascertain the scientific rationality of Indigenous Technical Knowledge (ITK) in dairy enterprise in coastal Tamil Nadu. Out of 59 ITK practices, 49 practices i.e. (83.2 %) were found to be scientifically valid indicating their wider usage and applicability in the field of ethno-veterinary practices.

Dhaliwal and Singh (2010) adjudged scientific rationality of traditional food grain storage practices of Punjab by using a 3- point continuum scale i.e. scientifically agreeable, scientifically disagreeable and those need further investigation.

Husain and Sundaramari (2011) in a study in Kerala assessed the rationality of 47 selected Indigenous Plant Protection Practices (IPPPs) on Coconut. It was done by administering the questionnaire to 52 plant protection experts (Agricultural Entomologists and Plant Pathologists) and they were asked to state the rationality/irrationality of each of the IPPPs, by rating them on a four point continuum ranging from 4 to 1. Out of 47 ITK practices, eight were found to be irrational. The rest 39 practices were adjudged by the scientists as rational.

Rajesh *et al.* (2013) evaluated the indigenous technical knowledge (ITK) pertaining to coconut cultivation of Palakkad district of Kerala for their scientific rationality by circulating the list of ITK practices among the extension personnel to assign a score in range of 0-5. Rationality analysis revealed that out of the 39 practices evaluated, 34 were rational and the remaining five were irrational. Such rational and effective ITK practices may directly be recommended by the extension system for their adoption by the farmers.

Devi *et al.* (2014) in a study ascertained the rationality of the documented indigenous practices related to fisheries by listing and sending it to a panel of thirty judges comprising fishery scientists and their response were rated on a 5-point continuum. Rationality analysis revealed that out of 34 ITK practices evaluated, 26 were rational and the remaining eight were found to be irrational as per the perception of the experts. Such rational ITKs suited to the local situation and culture may either be suggested for adoption, or may be recommended to scientists for further examination, or blended with modern technologies, which in turn would promote sustainable farming systems.

Pradhan *et al.* (2017) in a study entitled, 'Indigenous Technological Knowledge regarding Pest control methods in Agriculture' asked 25 scientists to give their rationality scores on a 3-point continuum. Out of seven ITK practices, the rationality score of five practices was found to be above 80. This finding indicated their wider use and compatibility in different agro-climatic zones.

Praveen *et al.* (2018) prepared a list of ITKs on general agriculture of tribal farmers of Telangana region and exposed it to 32 scientists for judging their rationality on a three point scale wherein, 3 is rational, 2 undecided and 1 is irrational. Out of 63 ITKs, 41 ITKs (65.08%) were judged rational by the scientists and 22 ITKs (34.92%) were judged as not rational.

Venketasan and Sundaramarai (2018) assessed the rationality of 41 Indigenous Technical Agricultural Practices (ITAPs) on Insect Pest Management. A set of 41 ITAPs was sent to 50 plant protection scientists in order to assess their rationality of ITAPs on a 4-point continuum i.e. 1) Rationality with scientific evidence, 2) Rational with experience, 3) Rational without experience, 4) Rational without scientific evidence. Rationality analysis showed that 29 ITAPS were found to be rational (70.73 %) and 12 i.e. (29.27%) were found to be irrational.

Rai *et al.* (2019) assessed the scientific rationality of documented indigenous practices related to bovine by sending a specifically constructed questionnaire to 60 experts having expertise in dairy and animal sciences. During the rationality analysis, the experts either declared the ITKs as rational by supplementing them with scientific facts or declared irrational based on their logical thinking and experience. The experts returned the interview schedule after assigning the score from one to four to each ITK based on their assessment of scientific rationality. Out of 110 practices evaluated, 43 were found to be rational (39.09%), while the remaining 67 were rejected as found to be irrational (60.01%).

Sah *et al.* (2019) concluded that 58 per cent of the researchers have favourable perception towards ITKs and perceived to have high scientific base for indigenous practices relating to forecasting of insect-pests in Pulse production of Uttar Pradesh region. Majority of them stressed on the scientific rational of traditional indigenous knowledge resources which need to the confirmed by experimentations.

Biradar (2020) assessed the scientific rationality of 19 indigenous crop management practices of two agro-ecological zones of Karnataka. ITKs were grouped under three categories as highly scientific, moderately scientific and least scientific by using group mean and standard deviation. Out of 19, seven ITKs were categorized as highly rational, eight ITKs were categorized as moderately rational and four ITKs as least rational. Experts expressed multiple opinions about seven ITKs thus indicating difference between sampled experts with that of population.

Khatri *et al.* (2021) tested the rationality of ITKs pertaining to Plant Protection and Post-harvest technology on a 3-point scale viz., a score of 3 for rational, 2 for undecided and 1 for not rationale. The mean score was calculated by summing the overall scores and divided by the number of judges for a given item and if it was more than two, then the item was considered as rational and less than two was considered as irrational. Out of 63 ITKs collected, 41 ITKs (65.08%) were judged rational by the scientists and 22 ITKs (34.92%) were judged as not rational.

2.4 Validation of ITKs

De *et al.* (2004) in a study conducted in West Bengal validated seven ITK practices of Dysentry, Arthritis, Dog bites, Cough and cold, Anoestrum, Wound, Bloat and Diarrhoea through QuIK method. The parameters selected for validation were cost effectiveness, availability, quickness in healing, ease in preparation and side effects. ITK practices were perceived to be comparatively less effective than the Modern Veterinary Drugs (MVD) in number of animals cured and quickness in healing. The indigenous practices were perceived better than MVD in respect of their availability, lesser side effects and lower cost.

Ponnusamy *et al.* (2009) stated that perceived effectiveness implies the degree to which the farm women perceive that a positive outcome is obtainable by using a particular ITK practice in solving the field problems. It is the perception of the respondents about the attributes of the indigenous technology like relative advantage, compatibility, trialability, sustainability and observability. It was measured using the Mean Perceived Effectiveness Index (MPEI) methodology.

Bhanotra (2012) in a study in Kathua region of Jammu and Kashmir validated ITK practices by modified QuIK method. On the basis of literature and consultation with experts, six attributes were selected for rating Modern Veterinary Drug (MVD) and selected Indigenous Technical Knowledge (ITKs). The attributes were: efficacy, side-effects, cost effectiveness, availability, quickness in healing and ease in preparation. The criteria for rating the modern veterinary drug (MVD) and for selected ITKs on the basis of the six selected attributes were done by the scores given by 30 farmers on a five point continuum ranging from least to highly suitable. Scores given by the farmers on several attributes were subjected to one way analysis of variance. Analysis was carried out separately for each group of data under each criterion under a particular disease studied.

Mahto (2012) in a study on Indigenous Technical Knowledge (ITK) in Animal husbandry among Livestock owners of Jharkhand validated 22 ITKs by using QuIK methodology in terms of efficacy, cost effectiveness, quickness in healing, and ease in preparation, side effects and availability against 10 selected commonly occurring diseases viz., diarrhea, fever, fracture, constipation, pneumonia, bloat, gastrointestinal parasites, foot and mouth disease, wound and ecto-parasitic infestation. The scores obtained by all 22 ITKs showed a clear validation by the livestock owners. The investigation showed that all the ITKs were found to be valid and effective as per the observations made by the livestock owners, which need to be validated scientifically and experimentally along with the identification and isolation of active ingredients present in the material used under ITKs.

Sarkar *et al.* (2015) conducted a study on 'Adaptation to Climate Change in the Himalayan and Arid ecosystems'. Community level validation was done through modified Quantification of Indigenous Knowledge (QuIK) method by the key informants of study area. The farmers were asked to rank each ITK based on their degree of use and relevance under changing climatic condition. Validation was done on the parameters like usefulness, cost effectiveness, availability, easiness and side effects on a 5-point scale. Farmers ranked apple paste as the most useful ITK of the area followed by *mind* cultivation, movement of honeybee to forecast rainfall, application of wood ash and eating *siddu* in extreme cold condition. All the ITKs were found to highly useful for the local community to manage climate change induced stresses. So, it was recommended as an immediate need to scientifically validate the technology for their large scale diffusion in the community.

Singh and Chauhan (2016) conducted a study in Bundelkhand region of Uttar Pradesh to identify, document and assess perceived effectiveness of indigenous knowledge possessed by 45 resource persons. ITK practices were enlisted with their Parallel Scientific Technologies (PST). The parameters for perceived effectiveness of ITK and PST among livestock owners for *haemorrhagic septicaemia* disease in livestock were: cost-effectiveness, accessibility, compatibility, sustainability, adaptability, rationality and complexity. ITK was more favourably accepted among the rural communities owing to its cost-effectiveness, local availability in the flora and fauna of the village, less complex in preparation and administration, compatible to social and cultural habitats and sustainable. It is necessary to quantify the perceived effectiveness of such indigenous practices for their further scientific validation in various national and international research organizations.

Bhuyan (2017) assessed the effectiveness of Indigenous Technical Knowledge (ITK) as perceived by 120 farm women of Haryana. The farm women rated each of the six identified ITK practices of mastitis based on seven parameters such as relative advantage, compatibility, trialability, sustainability and observability on a 3-point scale and Mean Perceived Effectiveness Index score for each ITK was then calculated. Farm women were asked to rate each identified ITK practice based on these traits on a 3-point scale i.e. concurred (3), no idea (2) and not concurred (1). The Perceived Effectiveness Index (PEI) score of a particular ITK practice was calculated. Based on those scores, all six ITK practices were categorized into three categories as less, moderate and highly effective. The ITK on mastitis control was perceived to be less effective by farm women.

Ponnusamy *et al.* (2017) defined perceived effectiveness as the degree to which the farm women perceive that a positive outcome is obtainable by using particular ITK practice in solving the field problems. It is the perception of the respondents about the attributes of the indigenous technology like relative advantage, compatibility, trialability, sustainability and observability. It can be measured using the mean perceived effectiveness index (MPEI) methodology.

Swangla (2017) in a study on indigenous technical knowledge (ITKs) in tribal farming systems of Himachal Pradesh validated ITK practices related to tribal farming systems through modified Quantification of Indigenous Knowledge (QuIK) method by the key informants of the study area. They were asked to rank each ITK based on criteria identified by the respondents only such as utility, availability, cost effectiveness, ease in use, time consumption and labour intensiveness on a 5-point scale.

Devaki *et al.* (2018) validated Ethno-veterinary measures (EVMs) through QuIK (Quantification of Indigenous Knowledge) method by some identified persons who were experienced in a particular ITK. The experienced respondents were asked to weigh the EVM(s) in comparison to modern veterinary drugs for its performance on different criteria and effectiveness such as number of animals cured, cost effectiveness, quickness in healing, ease in preparation, side effects and availability.

Vishwatej *et al.* (2018) studied the perceived effectiveness of three ITKs each related to Foot and Mouth Disease (FMD) and Mastitis respectively with the help of 40 farmers and 15 extension agents. The perceived effectiveness of six ITK practices with respect to seven traits i.e. cost effectiveness, adaptability, observability, trialability, complexity, relative advantage, sustainability were analysed using Mean Perceived Effectiveness Index (MPEI). It was found that among three improved ITK practices for treatment of Mastitis, 'topical application of mastilep gel' was perceived as highly effective whereas, 'topical application of dermanol' was perceived as moderately effective and 'topical application of Chenopodium leaf paste' was perceived as less effective. Among three improved ITK for treatment of FMD, practices of 'feeding of roasted Brinjal with ghee and topical application of coconut oil mixed with camphor' and 'feeding lard mixed with banana and sesame oil' were perceived to be moderately effective, while the practice of 'topical application of Babool/ Jamun bark paste' was perceived to be less effective.

Rai et al. (2019) conducted an exploratory study on 'Adoption and Perceived Effectiveness of Indigenous Technical Knowledge among tribal farmers for Bovine Management'. The perceived effectiveness of rational ITKs was measured by using the Mean Perceived Effectiveness Index (MPEI) with slight modifications. The MPEI contained five attributes like efficacy, ease in preparation, availability, cost-effectiveness, side effects. Among 43 ITK practices, 15 practices were found to be highly effective (mean score value >2.5), 24 were found to be effective (mean score value 2 to 2.5) and four practices were found to be less effective (mean score value <2).

2.5 Refinement and integration of ITKs

Rajasekharan (1993) suggested that ITK practices were broad-based, ecologically sound, environmentally safe, socially acceptable and economically resilient. Identification, documentation and incorporation of indigenous knowledge systems into agricultural extension organizations are essential to achieve sustainable agricultural development.

Grenier (1998) reported that studying ITK practices in the context of Intellectual Property Rights (IPR) regime and up scaling ITK practices in agriculture along with modern agricultural practices was the main focus of policymakers and development workers.

World Bank (1998) in a manual stated that the integration of indigenous knowledge in development process is essentially a process of exchange of information and knowledge sharing. The process of exchange of IK within and between developing countries and between developing countries and industrial countries involves recognition, identification, validation, recording and documentation, storage in retrieval repositories, transfer and dissemination.

Gratani et al. (2011) found that there are many evidences available for collating indigenous knowledge but methods for integrating ITK and western knowledge remained debated and still unexplored. More emphasis is required on integrating indigenous knowledge with western scientific knowledge.

Mishra et al. (2011) recommended integration of indigenous knowledge with modern scientific knowledge to generate a wide range of new ideas and practices for the betterment of mankind. The collection of knowledge is of great significance in conserving and maintaining sustainability of the environment.

Mercer et al. (2012) argued that for more effective disaster risk reduction, indigenous knowledge should be integrated with modern technology, moving beyond the dichotomy to bridge the gap between them. This integration of traditional and modern systems demands mutual understanding of the cultural and material basis of each.

Adesiji et al. (2013) stated that despite the fact that efforts have been made towards the fight against climate change from a scientific perspective, research and policies directed towards the incorporation of IK within climate change strategies are desperately needed. The study of local perception is useful in understanding the true implication of a changing climate.

Al-Roubaie (2013) in a study of Arab countries suggested a strategy for narrowing the knowledge gap by building enabling environments driven by digital technologies, investment in human capital, institutional reform, incentive regimes, technological learning and effective knowledge management system. There is a need to identify the best and most effective methods that increase access to knowledge acquisition, promote lifelong learning and strengthen the communication system to share knowledge. Sustaining development requires creation of knowledge at home and also tapping knowledge and skills from abroad.

Rajesh et al. (2013) stated that the importance of indigenous technology and practice to sustainability is being brought through pooling of traditional knowledge, short listing and evaluating them in the context of modern scientific and technological environment and harnessing it for sustainable agriculture growth.

Singh (2013) mentioned that the documentation of utilization pattern of indigenous technical knowledge to pay due respect for people's knowledge and to incorporate this knowledge in rural development planning. It was also revealed that indigenous knowledge can make a significant contribution to sustainable development and provide a basis for development of highly adoptable and cost effective scientific innovation. Thus, there is an urgent need for their systematic documentation, validation, refinement and integration with scientific knowledge.

Yolmo (2013) constructed one neo research and extension paradigm for incorporating the indigenous technological knowledge and scientific knowledge holistically. Furthermore, it was stated that the shrinkage of the bio resources rich areas under indigenous communities and vanishing of indigenous technological knowledge, there is an urgent need for protection, integration and application of indigenous technological knowledge with the scientific knowledge for the sustainable development of local people and local ecological resource management.

Kumar *et al.* (2014) reported blending of ITK with scientific knowledge system is considered vital for sustainable intensification of agriculture. Scientific procedures can identify the active ingredients and could come up with appropriate recommendations in terms of effective application rates. It could be said that ITK provides solutions for low external input but intensive agricultural production. A systematic documentation and blending of available ITK facilitate the process in which researchers and farmers learn from one another. ITKs and blended technologies can be an alternative to modern technologies involving high external inputs.

Sutherland *et al.* (2014) suggested a scientific mechanism to address information from traditional and conventional scientific knowledge can be effectively combined in international assessment. These are the steps for scientific mechanism: i) to recognize that there are different types of knowledge which should be collated and validated; ii) it can be partly combined with available information from conventional scientific knowledge through formal consensus methods like Delphi; iii) institutional structures and capacity required for such knowledge integration and co-production across local and global scales.

Wang (2015) opined that development is widely seen as a modernizing process, the aim of which is to transfer tradition. The path of knowledge development is from traditional to modernized knowledge. Sustainable agricultural knowledge should recognize three different paths to knowledge development: (i) indigenous knowledge to scientific knowledge; (ii) scientific knowledge to indigenous knowledge, and (iii) integration of traditional with modern knowledge. Therefore to better match high level agricultural extension system and on-the ground services with needs of farmers, more in-depth research is needed to elicit the farmers' perspectives of their situation and need for agricultural knowledge. The integration of indigenous with scientific knowledge is the way to form sustainable agricultural knowledge.

Bhanotra and Gupta (2016) in a study suggested that a judicious combination of indigenous and scientific knowledge would help to speed up the adoption of improved practices by the tribal farmers.

Sahoo *et al.* (2016) opined that in spite of advancement in scientific knowledge in agriculture, ITK-based practices still remained in use by the vast majority of the farming community particularly in resource poor farming situations without the knowledge of their scientific rationality. In this context, blending of indigenous knowledge with modern scientific technologies is the need of the day to support sustainable development of agriculture and allied sectors in our country.

Ihenacho *et al.* (2019) documented indigenous knowledge related to climate change adaptation and mitigation in Southeast Nigeria. ITKs were collected, recorded and categorised under crop management, land management, water management and pests/diseases control. Crop diversification, crop rotation, multiple cropping, mulching, soil fertilization, agro forestry, use of planting pits, use of calabashes to store water, use of ashes for pest control and use of cannabis to control new castle diseases were practiced to adapt and mitigate climate change. Since these practices are safe and have proved successful for centuries and so these should be integrated into the modern practices of agriculture.

Rai *et al.* (2019) suggested a scientific blend of both traditional wisdom with modern remedies practiced by the researchers, extension workers, local healers, farmers and the government and non-government organizations would lead to conservation of our rich wisdom for our future generations.

2.6 Utilisation of ITKs

Rajasekharan (1993) stated that it is necessary to understand the scientific rationale underlying each of the ITKs so as to validate and disseminate them through various extension programmes by extension organizations. It is essential to achieve the goal of sustainable agricultural development.

Warren and Rajasekharan (1993) revealed that investigation of scientific logic behind every ITK practice is necessary for better utilisation and management of ITK practices. It was stated that need of the hour is to establish a central apex body for the formulation of policies and programmes for identification of education and training needs to validate and popularise the indigenous knowledge in India as well as establish linkages with other organisations.

Berkes and Folke (1994) lamented that the wisdom possessed by local inhabitants of the tribal region has been emerged as a means to survive under remote, isolated and harsh climatic conditions and considered the ITK practices as the only tool that offers a great potential for their survival. Hence, it is necessary to understand, respect, value and utilise the indigenous knowledge systems.

Benfer *et al.* (1996) stated that it is not essential that IK be validated by scientific criteria. It was added that anthropologists validate models of IK through intensive interviews and through observation of those who held these beliefs.

Jena (2007) opined that the community has developed indigenous knowledge system to conserve and utilise the biological diversity of their surroundings. The recognition of the creativity of the traditional communities is essential for the conservation of biodiversity as well as conservation of intellectual diversity.

Gupta (2008) stated the reasons for protecting traditional knowledge are to improve the livelihoods of ITK holders and communities, to benefit the national economy, to conserve the environment and to prevent the bio-piracy.

Sharma *et al.* (2009) observed that no organisation or institution or individual working in the field respects the legal framework of censorships, co-authorships and ownerships of the products and mechanism of benefit sharing which are some basic ethical issues of documentation.

Review of Literature

Lodhi and Mikulecky (2010) suggested steps for promoting and using indigenous knowledge of local communities in development countries. These are i) Identifying and testing instruments for capture and dissemination of IK; ii) Integration of two knowledge systems i.e. indigenous and modern; iii) Raising awareness of the importance of managing Indigenous Knowledge (IK) among native communities and general public; iv) Protecting the intellectual property rights issue of indigenous knowledge; v) Promoting inter cultural exchange of experiences in education for sustainable development; vi) IK for food preservation, such as drying food fruits and vegetables, should be popularized to ensure food security and reduce dependency on food aid; vii) Developing a framework for incorporating IKS into development programs of government and non-governmental organization (NGOs) and into the curricula at various levels.

Mishra *et al.* (2011) reported that knowledge, skill and survival strategy of farmers operating with low external inputs have often been ignored to promote modern agriculture. Indigenous or traditional knowledge has scientific rationale and great deal of relevance for agricultural productivity and sustainability in the region.

Venkatesan and Sundaramarai (2012) opined that indigenous practices may be promoted not only for the benefit of the people but also for maintaining agricultural sustainability and economic system integrity. Hence the time tested rational and effective indigenous practices suited to the local situations as alternatives or blended with modern crop production technologies which in turn would promote sustainable crop production.

Al-Roubaie (2013) in a study of Arab countries suggested a strategy for narrowing the knowledge gap by building enabling environments driven by digital technologies, investment in human capital, institutional reform, incentive regimes, technological learning and effective knowledge management system. There is a need to identify the best and most effective methods that increase access to knowledge acquisition, promote lifelong learning and strengthen the communication system to share knowledge. Sustaining development requires creation of knowledge at home and also tapping knowledge and skills from abroad.

Rajesh *et al.* (2013) highlighted the importance of indigenous technology and practices for sustainability, which is being brought through pooling of traditional knowledge, short listing and evaluating them in the context of modern scientific and technological environment and harnessing it for sustainable agricultural growth.

Devi *et al.* (2014) suggested ITK practices which have high level of rationality and effectiveness scores should be given priority by extension agents and researchers as they will greatly reduce expenditure on aquacultural practices to benefit farmers. These practices may provide low yields but are sustainable. The author also suggests the scientific testing and refining of this knowledge can help to improve the yield. Hence, research and development organizations should take up the task of refining selected ITK practices and popularise them among the fish farmers.

Suitable modifications of the local practices, through R & D will help to develop appropriate and acceptable methodologies that are more suited to our farming situations. The farmers practicing ITKs may also collaborate with research scientists in refining the knowledge for evolving appropriate technologies. Local ITK practitioners need to be honoured and recognised and publications of local innovation in regional magazines including names and photographs of the innovators can motivate traditional practitioners to disseminate their knowledge. She also suggested that local panchayat has a big role to play in documenting the ITKs in their locality, validating and refining them with the help of researchers and popularising them.

Bhanotra and Gupta (2016) suggested that experimental validation of the ITK practices may be done for identification and isolation of active ingredients which has great bearing on development of herbal drugs. Documentation and validation of ITKs will contribute towards conservation of rich resources which is important for treatment of dairy animals as well as protection of Intellectual Property Rights. The research further studied the determinants, challenges and constraints to enhance the opportunities for ITK so that these are recognized and appropriately used for scaling up and scaling out in the field of agriculture and development.

Singh and Chauhan (2016) stated need of the hour is to establish a central apex body for the formulation of policies and programmes for identification of education and training needs to popularize the indigenous knowledge in India as well as to establish linkages with organizations having experiences in ITK. Experimental trials of ITK practices must also be conducted to identify the cost-effectiveness, accessibility, compatibility and sustainability of ITKs in comparison to modern scientific technologies.

Devaki *et al.* (2018) reported that validated ITK practices can be utilized to formulate the hypotheses for designing and implementing research project on location-specific and farmer's knowledge-based participatory research for efficient natural resource management.

Suganthi and Pirabu (2018) found that indigenous knowledge can play an important role in sustainable agriculture. After validation and standardization of indigenous knowledge by physical and biological scientists, these practices can either be directly disseminated to rural people or these can be blended with scientific technologies. Looking into the future, it cannot be denied that there is a need for institutionalization of traditional knowledge due to its immense utilitarian value in the development process. There is a need to preserve the indigenous knowledge as the documentation of traditional knowledge may create a pressure on policy makers to pay due respect for people's knowledge and to incorporate this knowledge in rural development planning.

Vishwatej *et al.* (2018) concluded that ITK practices can be disseminated among farmers for easy application to reducing cost of production and increase the profitability of livestock farming. The extension officials should be sensitised about these practices and encourages them to disseminate these practices among farmers by conducting extension campaigns or awareness programmes can help the farmers for easy application to reduce their cost of production and increase the profitability of farming practices.

Roy *et al.* (2020) stated that documentation of existing valid ITKs with fisherman's perception and adoption as well as scientific rationale will help in more popularisation, adoption and further improvement to fulfill present need of the people.

Khatri *et al.* (2021) in a study on Indigenous Technological Knowledge on agriculture in Nepal shows that the most important strategies to encourage adoption of ITKs were validation of the ITKs/Assess the ITK for scientific logic, followed by building upon local people's knowledge that is acquired through various processes such as farmer-to-farmer communication, and farmers experimentation, changing poor social perception of farmers, increase awareness among the younger generation and develop appreciation of indigenous system. This shows that the most important strategies to encourage adoption of ITKs were generation and develop appreciation of indigenous system, financial support from Government and other agencies, and focus on future research on adoption of ITK.

2.7 Constraints encountered in utilisation of ITKs

Ranganatha (2002) investigated the adoption of indigenous technical knowledge among tribal farmers and reported various constraints expressed by them. The constraints reported are no land ownership (100%), improper water management practices (98%), less land, more animal menace for crops, lack of proper guidance (92%), lack of extension service (90%), non-availability of extension worker, more of crop failure during blend flowering similarly non- availability of manure (85%), non-availability of labours (74%) and material possession was difficult (68%).

Sahu (2002) identified some common problems related to adoption of ITK in Vizianarangam district which were categorized as inherent disadvantages associated with ITK practices, impact of modernisation, constraints from formal organisations and feelings of farmers. Altogether 66.20 per cent farmers expressed that ITK practices were labor intensive and time-taking. About 50 per cent of farmers faced problems in cultivation because of non-availability of required inputs for cultivation, 40 per cent of farmers said that modern life style has a negative impact on use of ITK practices, 32.50 per cent of the farmers expressed that no support from various government agencies and formal organizations regarding use of ITK practices as the main problem for their adoption, 26.25 per cent of farmers said that because of not having published information the ITK practices were less in practice.

Lakshmana (2003) reported that lack of direct and immediate outcome through use of ITK (57.78%), time taking and labour intensive nature of ITK (47.78%) and bulky nature of indigenous inputs (45.55%) were considered to be major technological constraints by majority of the farmers in adoption of ITK. In addition, a considerable segment of farmers expressed lack of high yielding varieties (23.33%), competition from modern technologies (22.22%) and lack of pest and disease resistant varieties (20.00%) as constraints in adoption of ITK. Very few farmers expressed lack of short duration varieties (17.78%) and lack of information and training pertaining on vermicompost preparation.

Seeralam (2004) reported some major constraints perceived by the farmers regarding use of ITK about animal husbandry in Sivaganga district of Tamil Nadu. No written documents available, inconvenient and time consuming nature of ITKs, no standardization for the proportion and quantity of plants and their products to be given for animals, great pressure through modern techniques and incompatibility of ITK with those modern techniques, no effort has been made for synthesizing modern techniques with ITK, low return, several ITKs become extinct due to non-practice by the younger generation were some of the main constraints reported by the farmers.

Jarial (2006) reported that lack of knowledge about different areas of dairying, non-availability of veterinary staff in the area, poor conception rate through artificial insemination (AI), lack of linkage and coordination among extension agencies were the main factors that promotes the use of ITKs.

Badodiya *et al.* (2011) indicated that lack of input and raw materials, poor financial condition and non-availability of credit facility in time, lack of proper training at grass root level and non availability of appropriate literature were major difficulties faced by the farmers in the study area.

Hosseini *et al.* (2011) in their study observed that lack of access to indigenous knowledge, limited information about indigenous knowledge, lack of training on indigenous knowledge, lack of research on indigenous knowledge, lack of support from government authorities, limited number of experts about indigenous knowledge, weak linkage between government and farmers were the obstacles in adoption of indigenous knowledge in water management.

Hathila (2013) in a study on Utilization Pattern of ITK regarding Paddy Cultivation among the tribal farmers in Hanumana block of Rewa district, (M.P) analysed the constraints encountered while applying indigenous technical knowledge in paddy cultivation.

The major constraints mentioned by the respondents were many ITK practices became extinct due to non-practice by the younger generation (56.67%), incompatibility of ITK with modern techniques (54.17%), local disease and pest resistant varieties were vanishing (48.33%), adoption of chemical pesticides by neighboring farmers compel others to adopt chemical pesticides (46.67%), government officials and educated people gave less recognition to this knowledge, without ascertaining its importance (40.00%), inconvenience and time consuming (35.83%), many herbs are extinct (34.17%) and ITK takes long time to control insect and pest (24.17%).

Devi *et al.* (2014) in a study in Assam reported that the constraints expressed by majority (77.50%) of the farmers were that government officials and educated people used to give less recognition to this knowledge. More than half (52.50%) of the farmers commented that they don't have the knowledge regarding application of ITKs. They also revealed that lack of ability to identify the right medicinal plants/ingredients was the major constraint perceived by majority of the respondents.

Khatri (2014) in an analytical study on management of ITK regarding livestock health practices among the dairy farmers in Hanumana block of Rewa district of M.P documented the constraints faced by them. The major constraints as expressed by the respondents in adoption of indigenous livestock health practices were 'many ITKs became extinct' and 'government officials and educated people used to give less recognition' to this knowledge, without ascertaining its importance (52.50%), extinct due to non-practice by the younger generation (51.66%), preparation of medicine is time consuming (50.84%), lack of required plant materials for treatment and their unavailability, especially in summer (43.33%), allopathic medicines were easily available in the market (42.50%), ITK takes long time to control disease (35.00%) incompatibility of ITK with modern techniques (34.16%), many herbs are extinct (32.50%), lack of ability to identify right plants (24.16.%) and many new diseases have no traditional cure.(15.83%).

Rakesh (2014) studied Indigenous Technical Knowledge of Tribal Farmers of Arunachal Pradesh. The major constraints reported are unavailability of required medicinal plants; preparation of indigenous drugs involves considerable labour and time, waste of time in searching the medicinal plants in surrounding localities and forests, disinterest among the elder farmers in disclosing their valuable knowledge, attitude of government extension personnel, scientists and society, least recognition to indigenous knowledge, young generation farmers may use their knowledge for monetary gains, many new emerging diseases were beyond the control of indigenous drugs, behavior of elderly farmers as old aged farmers did not transfer their knowledge to any other person, except their sons, to maintain the monopoly of their own family. Apathy of young generation towards traditional wisdom and many elders had this superstitious belief that if the names of medicinal plants were told to anybody, their effect would be vanished.

Malhari (2015) revealed factors influencing adoption of indigenous technical knowledge in cereal crops by the farmers, ITKs in descending order were, lack of inputs and raw materials (85.00%), more labour and time required (73.33%), low yielding nature of traditional package of practices (65.00%), lack of training about indigenous knowledge (46.66%), lack of support from govt. authorities (34.16 %) and weak linkage between government and farmers (26.66 %).

Kumar (2016) in an exploratory study in Rajasthan identified ten constraints in adoption of indigenous technical knowledge in indigenous cattle farming practices. The constraints identified were there is no written document about ITK practices available, ITK's nature vitiates through improper application of those techniques and thus, it loses its validity. This was ranked as first and 79.4 per cent of the respondents perceived it as a major constraint. Young farmers were not interested in adoption of ITKs as they mostly rely on modern techniques and their preferences were towards immediate results. About third-fourth (75%) of the respondents perceived it as a major constraint and ranked it as second in order.

Madhukar (2017) in a study on perception of farmers about indigenous technical knowledge in plant protection determined the factors influencing the farmers' behavior. Major factors faced by the farmers of Latur district were; more labour and time required (91.66%) followed by lack of sufficient knowledge about ITK among younger generation (80.00%), lack of training on indigenous knowledge (79.16%), lack of support from government authorities (75.00%), weak linkage between government and farmer (70.00%), low yielding nature of traditional package of practices (68.33%), competition from modern technology as well as no place for indigenous farming practices in scientific recommendation (66.66%), fear of getting labelled as backward (56.66%), bulky nature of indigenous inputs (47.50%), lack of inputs and raw materials (33.33%) and limited number of experts about indigenous knowledge (29.16%).

Arya (2018) in a study on Utilization Pattern of Indigenous Technical Knowledge regarding Rice Cultivation among the tribal farmers in Nagod block of Satna district, (M.P.) indicated that the important constraints experienced by them which were arranged in descending order as, local disease and pest resistant varieties were vanishing (75.83%), followed by lack of ability to identify right plants (70.00%), non-availability of required organic materials as required (65.83), inconvenience and time consuming (64.17%), less recognition by government officials and educated people, without ascertaining its importance (58.33%), take long time to control insect and pest (54.16%), several ITKs become extinct due to non-practice by the younger generation (49.16%), lack of sufficient number of required plants for treatment and their unavailability, especially in summer (45.83%), incompatibility of ITK with modern techniques (40.00%) and adoption of chemical pesticides by neighboring farmers compel others also to adopt chemical pesticides (37.50%).

Kumar *et al.* (2018) found major constraints associated with the adoption of indigenous technical knowledge for management of indigenous cattle as perceived by the respondents were lack of proper ITK documentation, ranked first (79.40%)

followed by young farmers are not interested in adoption of ITKs (75.50%) ranked as second and thirdly, lack of complete knowledge on use of ITKs practices (72.20%).

Khatri *et al.* (2021) reported that the major constraints in adoption of ITKs in agriculture in the study areas were, preference of farmers for sophistication with reliance on readymade inputs, followed by more time required to get the desired results from adoption of ITKs, sociological constraints (social perception of farmers towards use of traditional means), labor-intensive nature of ITKs, lack of expert guidance or extension support for adoption of ITKs, and weak coordination between Research and Development Organizations.

2.8 Framework related to scientisation of ITKs

Rajasekharan (1993) suggested a conceptual framework to incorporate ITK into agricultural research for sustainable development: i) Strengthening of regional research and extension organizations, ii) Working with public extension system, iii) Strengthening of regional research and extension organizations iv) Building upon local people's knowledge, v) Identifying the need for extension scientists/social scientists in an interdisciplinary regional research team, vi) Formation of a sustainable technology development consortium, vii) Generating technological options rather than fixed technical packages, viii) Working with the public extension system, ix) Utilising the academic knowledge gained by Subject Matter Specialists during the process of validating farmer experiments, x) Outlining areas by involving farmers and xi) Considering farmers as partners in technology development.

Roux *et al.* (2006) developed a framework in which he described the relationship between research partners and the recognition given to local opinions and practices. In this framework, he classified participation in terms of levels of involvement of the people and the extent to which their knowledge, opinions and practices are given relevance in research activities, into four (4) categories namely: contractual, consultative, collaborative and collegiate. These categories concern farmers knowledge integration and participation in technology development.

Dekens (2007) reported absence of a framework through which the links between local knowledge and disaster preparedness can be explicitly made. An attempt was made to fill this gap by presenting a general framework for data collection and analysis on local knowledge related to disaster preparedness. The framework can be summarised around the following key areas: i) With respect to understanding of local knowledge: It includes what people know is influenced by what people believe in and what they do and do not do. To understand local knowledge one has to understand and account for people's various ways of knowing (i.e., different knowledge types such as technological and ecological knowledge) as much as people's practices and beliefs, perceptions, and values, ii) With respect to understanding the vulnerability context and contextualising local knowledge/practices and disasters. Local knowledge is influenced by the type, frequency, and intensity of past and present natural hazards as well as by other shocks and global trends for instance increasing the vulnerability of the community instead of exceptional natural event which require emergency operations from outside", iii) With respect to the key dimensions of local knowledge related to disaster preparedness.

Local knowledge on disaster preparedness relates to four major dimensions of people's knowledge: (1) their observations of natural hazards through daily experiences of their local surroundings; (2) their anticipation of natural hazards through identifying and monitoring local indicators such as early warning/environmental signs of eminent hazards, time thresholds, escape routes, safe places for humans and cattle, and key skills and actors; (3) communication strategies on natural hazards among community members and between generations; and (4) adaptation strategies – i.e., how people adjust, experiment, and innovate in the face of natural hazards and learn from it.

Mercer *et al.* (2010) analysed the lacunae of previous framework studies and carried out further research to propose a framework on how to incorporate indigenous knowledge and scientific knowledge to reduce the vulnerability of indigenous communities to environment hazards. The framework is divided into four sections; i) Community engagement ii) Identification of vulnerability factors iii) Identification of indigenous and scientific strategies in addition to potential problems and limitations. iv) Integrated strategy. The implementation of such framework and development of an integrated strategy within a community can only occur through a dialogue based on respect and communication between associated stakeholders.

Mukuna (2013) reported that there is no framework for hybridisation of indigenous and scientific technology in disaster reduction education. IK means of building a culture of safety and resilience. No framework for integrating ITK and ST in DRR education, so as to reduce people's vulnerability and poverty for sustainable development. It is believed that ITK and scientific technology needs to be integrated for sustainable development.

Sannighrahi (2013) recommended a cost-effective networking framework to develop digital databases by exploring ITK of self help group for sustainable agriculture. The data base management system comprises of the following parts i) the stakeholder of ITK being the knowledge bearer, ii) the effective self help groups due to their deep penetration into the society iii) the agricultural experts and policy makers establishing the science behind the use of ITK iv) the information users and the target farmers as the terminal sinks for achieving sustainability in agriculture.

Sutherland (2013) proposed a three step specific mechanism that could help in integrating information from different, parallel knowledge systems into international knowledge assessments. The first step is to recognize that there are fundamentally different types of knowledge, each associated with different needs for different stakeholder groups. It is important to distinguish information (whether drawn from observations or experiment, or from a scientific study or experience, information can be tested in some way) from values (i.e. preferences relating to priorities for action or particular outcomes) and associated mental models (i.e. the cognitive frameworks that people use to interpret and understand the world). The second stage is to collate and validate information from both local and traditional knowledge and conventional scientific knowledge. Finally, information from different sources needs to be combined in a transparent and defensible manner to support joint decision-making.

Hiwasaki *et al.* (2014) presented a process framework for integrating local and indigenous knowledge related to climate change with science. The process involves observation, documentation, validation and categorization of local and indigenous knowledge, which can be then selected for integration with science. This process is unique in that it allows communities identify knowledge which can be integrated with science which could be further disseminated for use by scientists, practitioners and policy makers. It enables communities to increase their resilience against the impacts of climate change.

Karki and Adhikari (2015) suggested a conceptual framework for the research which was drawn from global recognition of indigenous and local practices for adaptation to climate change. It identified a number of practices employing indigenous, traditional and local knowledge and analyses their application for adaptation to climate change and building resilience. The study was designed according to four principles or guidelines: (a) the methods selected were systematic and qualitative in nature; (b) they utilized participatory tools and instruments; (c) research participants, especially key informants and households, were selected purposively; and (d) the study used a process-based framework incorporating mixed methods of social science research. Insights derived from both indigenous and local knowledge and scientific understanding, and incorporating both into a synthesized form, is central to building resilience or reducing vulnerability.

Levac *et al.* (2018) a study in Canada presented an ethical guideline to link different frameworks (taken from disciplines like adult education, rural sociology, education, psychology, ethnographies) related to two ways of knowing i.e. indigenous knowledge and western knowledge with intersectionality. In this they stated seven principles (reciprocity, relationality, reflexivity, respect, reverence, responsivity and responsibility) and methods (inclusion of wisdom keepers, storytelling, sharing circles and talking circles, art based methods, critical ethnography, auto ethnography and collective consensual data analytical procedure) that support intersectionality for holistic development of the society as oppressed and marginalized people as the central focus.

Zulfadrim *et al.* (2019) suggested a process of integrating indigenous and scientific knowledge involves several phases: preparation, data gathering, analysis, validation, integration, and utilization. The first of these (preparation) involves finding out as much as possible about indigenous knowledge in the area of study and categorizing each item of knowledge. In the second phase (data gathering), the researcher observes and records any indigenous knowledge related to disaster risk reduction. In the third phase (analysis and validation), data are interpreted, analyzed and validated in focus groups discussion. In the integration phase, the researcher is not pursuing new knowledge but identifying existing knowledge that can potentially be integrated to enhance the community's capacity to reduce their vulnerability to natural hazards.

Chapter 3 — RESEARCH METHODOLOGY

Research methodology in broad sense refers to the process, principles and procedures by which various stages of research are employed analytically and systematically to solve the research problem in a scientific manner. In social science, "research methodology" is applied to understand how the process of research is carried out. Research methodology is a detailed action plan of investigation which is considered to be a blue-print of the research architect. Every research carried out on scientific lines needs to have a research design to be applied as per the stated problems. Hence, this chapter elaborates the methods and techniques of investigation adopted during the entire course of present investigation to draw rational, logical and meaningful inferences. The research methods and techniques used were based on the requirement of objectives set forth in this study. The methodological details are presented under the following sections:

3.1 Locale of the study

3.2 Research design

3.3 Brief description of the study area

3.4 Sampling plan

    3.4.1 Selection of district

    3.4.2 Selection of community development blocks

    3.4.3 Selection of villages

    3.4.4 Selection of respondents

3.5 Variables and their measurement

3.6 Methods and tools of data collection

3.7 Statistical tools used for analysis of data

3.1 Locale of the study

The study was conducted in purposively selected Ranchi district of Jharkhand, keeping in view the concentration of tribal farmers who are supposed to be the custodians of indigenous and traditional knowledge, which they have been using since ages.

3.2 Research design

Any scientific investigation must begin with some structure or plan. This structure defines the number and the type of variables to be studied and their relationship to one another. Such a structure is termed as design. The term 'research design' refers to drawing a tentative outline, a blue print and a scheme, planning or arranging a strategy of conducting research with thorough knowledge about research methodology. Descriptive research design has been used in conducting the present investigation. Descriptive research is used to "describe" a situation, subject, behavior, or phenomenon. It is used to answer questions of who, what, when, where, and how associated with a particular research question or problem. Descriptive studies are often described as studies that are concerned with finding out "what is". The data collected from descriptive research may be quantitative, qualitative or both.

3.3 Brief description of the study area

State profile

Jharkhand also known as "the land of forests" a state in eastern India, was created on 15 November 2000 by virtue of promulgation of Bihar Reorganization Act. The state was carved out by pooling about 79 lakh hectare (ha) geographical area from the Southern half of undivided Bihar for better planning and execution of developmental activities of an ecologically different zones (Hills & Plateau region compared to Bihar plains). Jharkhand shares its border with the states of Bihar to the north, Uttar Pradesh to the north-west, Chhattisgarh to the west, Odisha to the south and West Bengal to the east. It is the 15th largest state by area, and the 14th largest by population. The city of Ranchi is its capital and Dumka its sub-capital. Jharkhand largely comprises of the tropical dry deciduous forest tracts of Chotanagpur plateau and Santhal Parganas which is thickly wooded and hilly. Jharkhand is adorned with some of the richest deposits of iron ores and coal in the world and accounts for 40%

mineral reserves of India. Jharkhand being the land of Lord Baidyanath and Birsa Munda, freedom fighter known for natural sanctuary of spiritual, cultural and herbal heritage. It is richly endowed with rich flora and fauna. Agro-climatic zone of the state is mostly landscape plateau, undulating, hilly and sloping with mountains, forests and river basins and valleys. It is adorned with distinct cultural traditions.

Jharkhand has 24 districts and 36,620 revenue villages, accounts for 2.4 per cent of the total geographical area of the country. It lies between latitude 22° 00 to 24° 37 N and 83°15 to 87°01E. According to the 2011 Census, Jharkhand has a population of 32.96 million, consisting of 16.93 million males and 16.03 million females. The sex ratio is 947 females to 1000 males. The literacy rate of the state is 67.63% with Ranchi district being most educated at 77.13% compared to rural Pakur district being least at 50.17%.

Climate

Climate of Jharkhand state is sub-humid and average rainfall is 1340 mm. The altitude ranges from 400 to 1000 metre above mean sea level. About 81 per cent of total rain occurs during the monsoon and the remaining 19 per cent during winter and summer.

Cropping pattern

Foodgrains occupy about 75% of the total cultivated area. Rice is the main crop and other important crops are Maize, Ragi, Gundli etc. Wheat is grown in limited extent where there is facility of irrigation is available. Jharkhand has favourable climate for vegetables, and the extensively grown vegetables are: Cabbage, Cauliflower, Tomato, Brinjal, Lady finger, Raddish, Carrot, Onion, Ginger etc are extensively grown here. Apart from coarse grains, pulses like Pigeon pea, Lentil, Kulti, Green gram, Black gram are grown and Linseed and Sarguja as the main oilseed crops.

Livestock and Fisheries

Farmers prefer to keep small animals like goat, pig, sheep and poultry apart from small sized local breeds of cattle. The state is deficient in its milk, meat, egg and fish requirements which imply that the level of production must be increased. The total livestock population of the state is 158.26 lakh which is 3.28% of India's livestock population. The dairy, poultry and fisheries have great scope for expansion and should be strengthened by providing inputs of better breeding stock, disease protection and feed availability.

Agro-ecological features

The state of Jharkhand is characterised by unique land use, agro climatic zones, the cropping pattern and the tribal culture. The agro ecological features have been described below :

Land utilisation pattern

Out of the total geographical area of 79.7 lakh ha of the state, an estimated 38 lakh ha is cultivable. Of this, 18 lakh ha is the net sown area, comprising 22.7 per cent of the total geographical area and 47 per cent of the cultivable area. The state has a total of 23.32 lakh ha of land under forests, comprising 29.26 per cent of the total geographical area, which is much above the national average of about 18 per cent.

Agro-climatic conditions and resources

Based on rainfall, temperature, soil types and physiographic features, the state is divided into three agro-climatic zones namely: Central and North-eastern plateau, Western plateau and South-eastern plateau

Agriculture provides livelihood to about 80% of the state's population. Agriculture is their employment and primary income generating activity. The agricultural economy of Jharkhand is characterized by dependence on nature, low investment, low productivity, mono-cropping with paddy as the dominant crop, inadequate irrigation facilities and small and marginal size of holdings. The cropping pattern of the state is basically rice-based. The dependence of agriculture on the vagaries of the rain-god can be gauged from the fact that as much as 88 per cent of the total cultivated area is rainfed. The cultivable land resources of the state have good potential for higher production of horticulture and forest products. The soil is young and has high capacity of fixation of humus. The forest provides sufficient biomass to feed its soiling. However, soil erosion and failure to recycle the biomass is depleting the soil fertility. Hence, a judicious soil, water and land management is required, only that can improve agricultural productivity. Climate of Jharkhand varies from humid sub-tropical in the north to tropical wet and dry in the south-east.

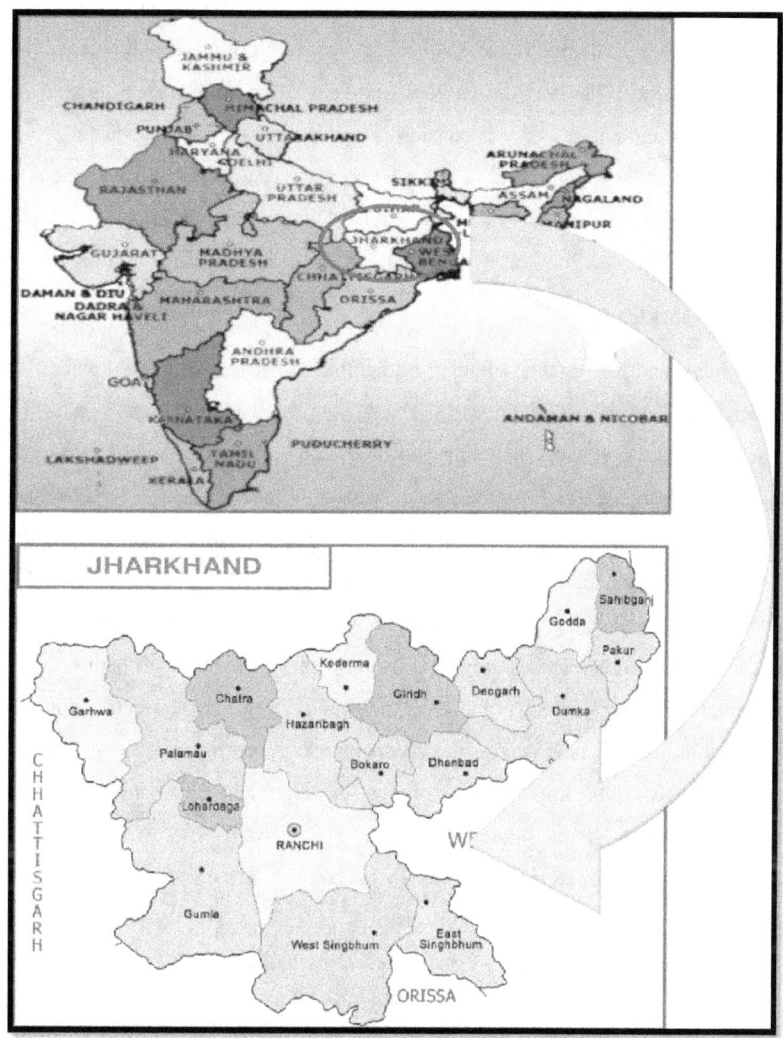

Plate 1: Map of India showing Jharkhand State

Source: www.researchgate.net/Map of India showing Jharkhand state/

The southwest monsoon, from mid-June to October, brings nearly all the state's annual rainfall, which ranges from about 1,000 mm in the West-central part of the state to more than 1,500 mm in the South-west. Nearly half of the annual precipitation falls in July and August. Despite good rainfall in the state, the surface water availability to agriculture is not adequate due to high runoff and inadequate storage facilities etc. As far as the status of ground water is concerned, it is also in the poor state due to little recharging of ground water by natural process in the absence of artificial recharging facilities; as a result, the water table in the plateau is going down.

Tribes of Jharkhand

Jharkhand has remained home to a number of tribal communities since time immemorial. The Scheduled Tribes (ST) population of Jharkhand state as per 2011 census is 8,645,042 (Others including Sarna- 4,012,622, Christian- 1,338,175) of the total of population 32,988,134 of the state. Among all the states and UTs, Jharkhand holds 6th and 10th rank in terms of the ST population and the percentage share of the ST population to the total population of the state respectively. The state has a total of thirty two (32) Scheduled Tribes and all of them have been enumerated at 2011 Census. The Scheduled Tribes are primarily rural as 91.7 per cent of them reside in rural areas including forests and hill tops. Indigenous groups are concentrated mostly in the districts of Ranchi in central Jharkhand, Dumka in the North-east, and East and West Singhbhum in the South-east. District wise distribution of ST population shows that Gumla district has the highest proportion of STs (68.40%). The STs constitute more than half of the total population in Lohardaga and Pashchimi Singhbhum districts whereas Ranchi and Pakur districts have 41.8 – 44.6 per cent tribal population. Koderma district (0.8%) preceded by Chatra (3.8%) has the lowest proportion of the STs population. Out of the total, seven tribes, viz, Santhal, Oraon, Munda, Ho, Kharwar, Bhumij and Lohra are comparatively elevated tribes and make up 83 per cent of the total tribal population. Out of 32 Scheduled Tribes notified for the State, Santhal is the most populous tribe having a population of 2,410,509, constituting 34 per cent of the total ST population of the State. Oraon, Munda and Ho, the 2nd, 3rd and 4th largest tribes respectively in population constitute 19.6, 14.8 and 10.5 per cent respectively of the total ST population of the state. They love to stay in

Research Methodology ....

deep forests and follow their own primitive system. The so called poor *Adivasis* (tribals) are the part of Jharkhand state as well as the economy of the state is mainly based on tapping natural resources like forest produce, mining and agriculture. The tribes, forest dwellers and rural people have a rich oral tradition of native and ethnic knowledge about nature and various farm activities.

Table 3.3.1: Demographic features of population in Jharkhand

Total population (No)	32988134
Male (No)	16930315
Female (No)	16057819
Sex ratio	948
Overall literacy rate (%)	66.41
Male literacy (%)	76.84
Female literacy (%)	55.42
Literate (%)	3.0
Below primary (%)	30.6
Primary (%)	28.6
Middle (%)	17.7
Matric / Intermediate (%)	16.5
Technical & Non-technical (%)	0.1
Graduate and above (%)	3.5
Work participation rate (%)	46.3
Cultivators (%)	52.6
Agricultural labourers (%)	31.0
HHI workers (%)	3.0
Others (%)	13.5

Source-https://www.jharkhand.gov.in/,
https://www.census2011.co.in/census/state/jharkhand.html

3.4 Sampling Plan

A multistage sampling technique was applied to draw the sample for the present investigation. Sampling procedure for the study is given below:

3.4.1 Selection of the district

Jharkhand state in Eastern India consists of 24 districts. Out of these districts, Ranchi district was purposively selected due to substantial tribal population in the research area. Another consideration was the researcher's familiarity with the tribal culture and the rapport with the tribal people of the study area which emanated from the field visits of the researcher prior to carrying out the data collection.

Plate 2: Map of Jharkhand state showing Ranchi district

*Source:*https://store.mapsofindia.com/digital-maps/district-maps/jharkhand-district-map

Study area

Ranchi, the capital of Jharkhand state is also the district headquarter. Ranchi district is divided into two sub-divisions i.e. Ranchi and Bundu and 14 administrative blocks, namely, Angara, Burmu, Bero, Chanho, Kanke, Lapung , Mandar, Namkum, Ormanjhi, Ratu and Silli (Ranchi sub-division). Bundu sub-division comprises of three blocks i.e. Bundu, Sonahatu and Tamar. As of 2011, it is the most populous district of Jharkhand. Ranchi has a humid subtropical climate. Temperature ranges from maximum 42° to 20° C during summer and from 25° to 0° C during winter. The annual rainfall is about 1430 mm. Ranchi has a hilly topography and its combination with dense tropical forests ensures that it enjoys a comparatively moderate climate compared to the rest of the state. According to 2011 Census, Ranchi district had a population of 2,914,253 with population density of 557 inhabitants per square kilometer and sex ratio of 950 females per every 1000 males, and a literacy rate of 77.13%.

Table 3.4.1 Ranchi district at a glance

Latitude	23.23° N
Longitude	85.23° E
Area (in sq km)	5231
Height from sea level	2140 ft
Temperature (°C)	Winter (Min 5.3 Max 22.9) and Summer (Min 20.6 max 37.2)
Annual Rainfall (in mm)	1200
Climate	Humid sub-tropical
Main Tribes	Oraon, Munda
Main minerals	Lime stone, Coal, Asbestos and Ornamental Stones etc
Main crops	Rice, Millets, Pulses and Oil seeds
Language spoken	Hindi, Nagpuri, Oraon, Mundari and Kurmali
Important rivers	Subarnerakha, South Koel and Sankh
Population density (per square km)	557

Source: https://ranchi.nic.in/

3.4.2 Selection of Community development blocks

Ranchi district consists of 14 community development blocks. Out of 14 blocks, two top tribal dominated blocks i.e. Angara and Tamar were selected randomly for the study from among the tribal dominated blocks of the district. The blocks were categorized into tribal dominated and general block according to the tribal population. A block having tribal population more than 50% was considered as tribal dominated block.

a. Angara block

Angara block is situated at a distance of 42 km towards east from Ranchi connected with metalled road. There are 83 villages in Angara block. The total area covered by Angara block is 444.91 sq km. Angara block is characterized by low levels of development such as food insecurity, limited access to basic services and absence of income generating opportunities. Ranchi, the block remained backward with a large portion of the block being inaccessible because of hilly terrain and innumerable fast flowing seasonal rivulets. Farming being the main occupation of farmers of Angara block, farmers grow Paddy as the main crop in the Kharif whereas Potato and Tomato are grown at large scale in Rabi season. Farming is dependent on traditional inputs in Angara. However, use of high yielding varieties and hybrid seeds, chemicals fertilizers and pesticides have gradually increased a lot in the region. It has sub-tropical climate. Summer temperature ranges from 20°C to 42°C and winter temperature 0°C to 25°C. December and January are the coolest months, with temperature dipping to the freezing point in some areas. The annual rainfall is about 1430 mm.

b. Tamar block

Tamar Block has 128 villages. The area is the richest biodiversity centre and a source of ethno-botanical knowledge. The block is having an area of 513.91 km² with forest area of 148.71 Km² (29%) and is situated between 23°3`21``N and 85°39`44``E. Munda and Oraon tribes live in the villages. The Munda tribe is 43 per cent and Oraon tribe is 7 per cent according to 2011 Census. Climate of this block is subtropical. The annual rainfall ranges between 230 mm to 1390 mm and the temperature ranges between 6°-43°C with highest in the month of May and June. November to January are the coldest months. The population of the block is 1,32,702. The livelihood depends mainly on small holding agriculture and livestock production.

Research Methodology ....

Table 3.4.2.1: Agro-ecological features of Angara and Tamar blocks

	Angara	Tamar
Total Geographical area (sq km)	444.91	513.49
Forest (ha)	1383.15	11446.29
Net cultivated area (ha)	12490.01	90.88.89
Cultivated waste land including pasture graze (ha)	4021.92	3457.11
Gross potential for cultivation (ha)	16511.93	12456.00
Not available for cultivation (ha)	6518.81	4400.62

Source: https://www.census2011.co.in/data/district/113-ranchi jharkhand.html

Table 3.4.2.2: Demographic features of Angara and Tamar blocks

	Angara	Tamar
Total population	103155	114115
Rural population	102990	99132
Male	52007	57843
Female	51148	56272
Sex ratio	983	973
Scheduled castes	8116	11911
Scheduled tribes	56521	50345
Total Literacy	42947	47020
Literacy (Male)	28781	32362
Literacy (Female)	14166	14658
No of villages	83	128
No of panchayats	21	23
No of workers	29270	37292
Woman farmers	11293	9570
Cultivators	26073	32969
Agricultural labourers	9745	21113

Source: https://www.census2011.co.in/data/district/113-ranchi-jharkhand.html,
http://www.onefivenine.com/india/villag/Ranchi/Angara,
http://www.onefivenine.com/india/villag/Ranchi/Tamar

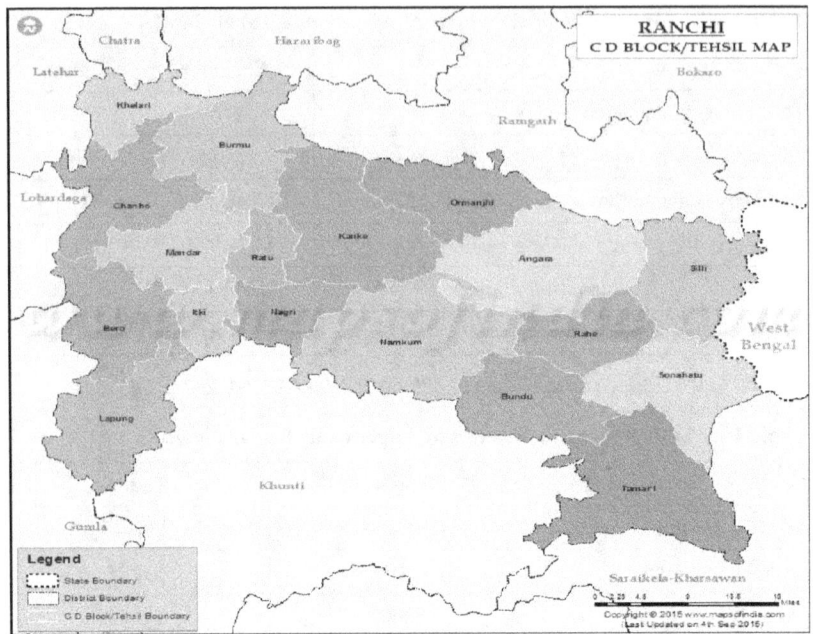

Plate 3: Map of Ranchi district showing selected community development blocks
Source - https://ranchi.nic.in/

3.4.3 Selection of Villages

After selection of the blocks (Tamar and Angara), two tribal dominated villages from each block were selected randomly from the tribal dominated villages for the present investigation. The villages selected were Dhurleta and Jaspur from Angara block and Ulidih and Amhesa from Tamar block. Tribal dominated villages were having more than 50% tribal population.

a. Village Dhurleta

Dhurleta is a small village located in Angara block of Ranchi district, with a total 35 families. Dhurleta village has population of 189 of which 101 were males while 88 were females as per 2011 Census with sex ratio of 871, a bit lower than Jharkhand state of 948. Dhurleta village has lower literacy rate compared to Jharkhand. In 2011, literacy rate of the village was 60.13% compared to 66.41% of

Jharkhand. In Dhurleta male literacy was 73.03% while female literacy rate was 43.48%. As per Constitution of India and Panchayati Raj Act, Dhurleta village was being administrated by Sarpanch (Head of Village) an elected representative of the village. In Dhurleta, majority of the village population was of Scheduled Tribes (STs). STs constituted 89.42% of total population of the village. In Dhurleta, out of total population, 50.79% were engaged in different work activities, of which 69.79% were found to be earning for more than six months, while 30.21% were involved in marginal activities earning livelihood for less than six months. Out of 96 workers engaged in main work, 48 were cultivators (owner or co-owner) while 17 were agricultural labourers and others were involved in different day to day wage activities.

b. Village Jaspur

Jaspur is a village located in Angara block of Ranchi district, inhabited by 135 families. Jaspur village had population of 655 of which 340 were males while 315 were females as per Census 2011 having sex ratio of 926, which is lower than that of Jharkhand state of 948. In 2011, literacy rate of Jaspur village was 70.58% compared to 66.41% of Jharkhand. In Jaspur, male literacy stands at 84.43% while female literacy rate was 55.47%. As per Constitution of India and Panchayati Raj Act, Jaspur village was being administrated by Sarpanch (Head of Village) an elected representative of the village. Jaspur had substantial population of Scheduled Tribes (STs). STs constituted 25.65% while Scheduled Castes (SCs) were 1.53% of total population. In Jaspur village, out of total population, 224 were engaged in various work activities. Altogether 61.61% of workers described their work as the main work (employment or earning for more than 6 months) while 38.39% were involved in marginal activities earning livelihood for less than six months. Of 224 workers engaged in main work, 95 were cultivators (owner or co-owner) while only one was agricultural labourer.

c. Village Amhesa

Amhesa is a village located in Tamar block of Ranchi district, with a total of 375 families. Amhesa village had population of 1629 of which 787 were males and

842 were females as per 2011 Census. Sex ratio in Amhesa village was 1070, higher than Jharkhand state of 948. Amhesa village had higher literacy rate compared to Jharkhand. In 2011, literacy rate of Amhesa village was 71.08% compared to 66.41% of Jharkhand. In Amhesa, male literacy was 89.24% while female literacy was 54.40%. As per Constitution of India and Panchayati Raj Act, Amhesa village was being administered by Sarpanch (Head of Village), an elected representative of the village. In Amhesa, majority of the population was of Scheduled Tribes (STs). STs constituted 56.24% while Scheduled Castes (SCs) were 33.56% of total population in the village. In Amhesa village out of total population, 822 were engaged in various work activities. Altogether 28.71% of workers described their work as main work (employment or earning for more than 6 months), while 71.29% were involved in marginal activities earning livelihood for less than six months. Of 822 workers engaged in main work, 144 were cultivators (owner or co-owner) while 12 were agricultural labourers.

d. Village Ulidih

Ulidih is a village located in Tamar block of Ranchi district, with a total of 373 families. Ulidih village had population of 1515 of which 752 were males while 763 were females as per 2011 Census. Sex ratio of Ulidih village was 1015, higher than Jharkhand of 948. Ulidih village had lower literacy rate compared to Jharkhand. In 2011, literacy rate of Ulidih village was 59.27% compared to 66.41% of Jharkhand. In Ulidih, male literacy was 77.18% while female literacy was 42.64%. As per Constitution of India and Panchayati Raj Act, Ulidih village was being administered by Sarpanch (Head of Village), an elected representative of the village. In Ulidih village, most of the village population was from Scheduled Tribes (STs). STs constituted 86.14% while Scheduled Castes (SCs) were 3.56% of total population in Ulidih village. In Ulidih out of total population, 760 were engaged in various work activities. Altogether 24.47% of workers described their work as main work (employment or earning for more than 6 Months) while 75.53% were involved in marginal activities earning livelihood for less than six months. Of 760 workers engaged in main work, 78 were cultivators (owner or co-owner) while 40 were agricultural labourers.

3.4.4 Selection of Respondents

There were three categories of respondents i.e. i) ITK Experts ii) Tribal Farmers and iii) Scientists with specialization in Plant Protection i.e. Entomologists and Plant Pathologists.

A list of 117 eminent experts of the country having expertise in the field of ITK documentation, validation and utilisation was prepared. Out of those 117, 55 ITK experts were selected randomly for this investigation.

A list of 46 scientists working in different organizations (ICAR, SAUs, KVKs, NGOs and Private sector) in Ranchi having specialization in the field of Entomology and Plant Pathology was prepared. Out of the list 30 scientists were selected through random sampling method for making the sample representative for this study.

Out of four selected villages, tribal farmers from each village were selected from snowball sampling. It was decided beforehand that minimum 10 tribal farmers practicing ITKs should be involved from each village. Hence a total of 45 tribal farmers constituted the sample of farmer respondents in the present investigation. Tribal farmers were utilised here as tribal key informants.

Table 3.4.4: Distribution of respondents according to different categories.

Sl.No	Respondent category	Frequency
1.	ITK Experts	55
2.	Scientists (Entomologist and Plant Pathologsts)	30
3.	Tribal Farmers	45

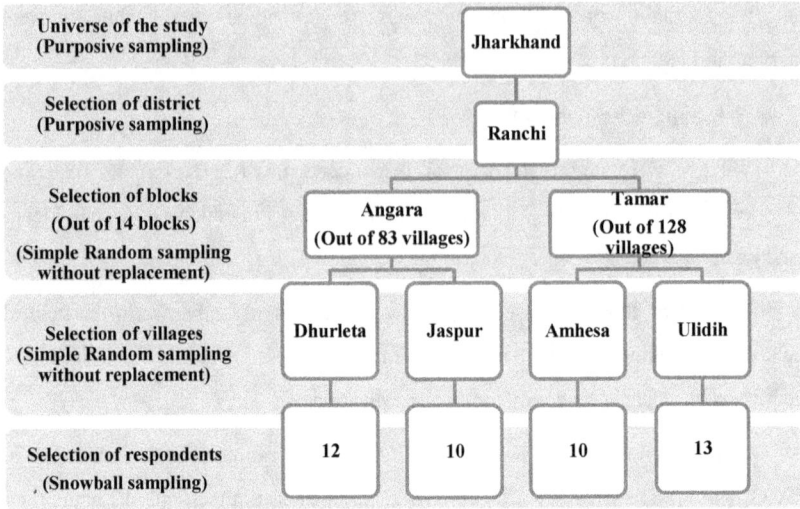

Figure 4: Sampling procedure for selection of tribal farmers

.3.5 Variables and their Measurement

The following variables were selected for the study:

Table 3.5. Measurement of variables selected in the study

S.No	Variable	Measurement
1.	**Profile of tribal farmers**	
i.	Age	Chronological age of respondents on the day of interview
ii.	Gender	Male/Female
iii.	Tribe type	A schedule was developed
iv.	Education	Formal education attained
v.	Land holding	A schedule was developed
vi.	Farming experience	A schedule was developed
vii.	Social participation	Modified scale of Trivedi (1963)
viii.	Risk orientation	Scale developed by Supe (1969)
ix.	Innovativeness	Modified entrepreneurial self assessment scale developed by Technonet Asia (1981)

Research Methodology

2.	**Profile of ITK experts**	
i.	Age	Chronological age of respondents on the day of filling up of questionnaire
ii.	Gender	Male/Female
iii.	Qualification	Educational attainment leading to highest degree
iv.	Designation	As prevalent in SAUs/ICAR and its Institutes
v.	Nature of job	Involvement in teaching/research/extension
vi.	Experience in ITK related works (in years)	Questionnaire was developed
vii.	Level of involvement in ITK-related works	Questionnaire was developed
3.	**Scientisation of ITKs**	
i.	Documentation	A schedule was developed
ii.	Particularisation	
	Rationality	a. A schedule was developed using 3-point Rationality scale of Dhaliwal and Singh (2010)
		b. 4-point Rationality scale developed by Hussain and Sundaramarai (2014)
		c. 5-point Rationality scale developed by Hiranand (1979)
iii	Validation	
		a. Quantification of Indigenous Knowledge (QuIK) developed by De Villiers, A.K. (1996)
		b. Mean Perceived Effectiveness Methodology (MPEM) developed by Sundaramari (2001) with slight modification
iv	Generalisation/Utilisation	A schedule was developed
4.	Constraints encountered in utilisation of ITK	A schedule was developed

The following scoring procedure was followed for the variables selected in the study:

3.5.1 Age

Age of the tribal farmers was measured in terms of chronological age i.e. in actual years on the date of interview. The following scoring procedure was followed for categorization of the tribal farmers:

Category	Scores
Young (Up to 35 years)	1
Middle-aged (36 to 55 years)	2
Old (Above 55 years)	3

3.5.2 Gender

It refers to the difference in man and woman in terms of role and status in society, values, attitude and other socio psychological variables. This was categorized as below:

Male tribal farmer was assigned a score of 1 whereas score of 2 was assigned to a 'female' tribal farmer.

Category	Scores
Male	1
Female	2

3.5.3 Tribe Type

It was operationalised as the clan to which tribal farmers' belonged to. The following scoring procedure was followed for categorization:

Research Methodology

Category	Scores
Kharia	1
Ho	2
Oraon	3
Munda	4

3.5.4 Education

It referred to the level of formal school education of the respondents in terms of years he/she attended the school/college successfully. The following scoring system was followed for categorization:

Category	Scores
Illiterate	0
Can read only	1
Can read and write	2
Primary School	3
Middle School	4
High School	5
Graduate & above	6

3.5.5 Land holding

It was operationalised as the actual size of land holding in hectare possessed by tribal farmers. The following scoring procedure was followed for categorization:

Category	Scores
Marginal (<1 ha)	1
Small (1.0 to 2.0 ha)	2
Medium (2.1 to 4.0 ha)	3
Large (> 4.0 ha)	4

3.5.6 Farming Experience (in years)

It refers to the total number of completed years in which the tribal farmers were involved in farming on the date of interview. The following scoring method was followed for categorization:

Category	Scores
Low (upto 15 years)	1
Medium (16 to 25 years)	2
High (above 25 years)	3

3.5.7 Social participation

Social participation in any of the organization not only indicates a person's social orientation but also provides an opportunity for the individual to have a wider contact and greater influence in the social system, which is very important for securing services and supplies to achieve success in farming. Social participation in this study referred to the degree of involvement or participation of the respondents in formal organizations either as a member or as an office bearer. It was measured with the help of SES scale of **Trivedi (1963)**. Scores of 1, 2 and 3 were assigned to member of only one organization, more than one organization and office bearer respectively and zero was assigned to respondents who were not a member of any organisation.

Categories	Scores
Not a member	0
Member to only one organisation	1
Member of more than on organization	2
Office bearer	3

3.5.8 Risk orientation

It is referred as the degree to which a farmer is oriented towards risk and uncertainty and has courage to face the problems in farming. Risk orientation was measured with the help of a Risk Orientation Scale developed by **Supe (1969)**. This scale included six statements, of which first and fifth statements were negative and four were positive. The items were rated on a 5- point continuum ranging from strongly agree, agree, undecided, disagree and strongly disagree with respective weightage of 5, 4, 3, 2 and 1 for positive statements and 1, 2, 3, 4 and 5 for negative statement, respectively. The maximum and minimum scores obtainable by the respondents were 30 and 6, respectively. The mean risk orientation scores of the respondents were considered for categorizing the respondents into low, medium and high risk orientation.

Category	**Scores**
Low	Upto 7
Medium	8-10
High	11 and above

3.5.9 Innovativeness

Innovativeness was defined as the degree to which a farmer perceived himself/herself to act in a manner so as to introduce new ideas or products and services. The innovativeness of farmers was measured by a scale used by modified **Entrepreneurial Self Assessment Scale - Technonet Asia (1981)**. There were five statements of which one was negative. These statements were rated on a five point continuum ranging from strongly agree, agree, undecided, disagree and strongly disagree with the weightage of 5, 4, 3, 2 and 1 for positive statements and 1, 2, 3, 4 and 5 for the negative statement respectively. Then, the respondents were classified into low, medium and high innovativeness categories according to the scores received.

Categories	Scores
Low	(Up to 11)
Medium	(12 - 15)
High	(16 and above)

3.5.10 Delphi method for Scientisation of Indigenous Technical Knowledge

Delphi method is a technique for arriving at a consensus rapidly for any decision making. It is a judgmental forecasting technique for obtaining, exchanging and developing informed opinion through a consensus about the most probable future through iteration. It is an exercise in group communication among a panel of geographically dispersed experts. In this technique, the pre-selected experts are allowed to systematically deal with a complex problem and reach a consensus straightforward with set rules and principles of its performance. It comprises of series of questionnaires sent to the individual and independent experts. Delphi is generally characterized by anonymity, controlled feedback, and statistical response.

Delphi method in the present study has been operationalised as arriving at a consensus regarding collection, documentation, particularisation, validation and generalisation processes for scientisation of Indigenous Technical Knowledge (ITK) about pest management practices. All the feedback from the selected experts were collected, collated and summarized anonymously by the moderator and most common solutions were selected for sending again to the experts for verification and refinement in the second round. In each round, the solutions were got refined and the least popular ones were dropped by the moderator. Altogether in three rounds the task was completed i.e. the consensus was attained in third round and the data were analysed.

Both quantitative and qualitative i.e. mixed approach was followed for data collection. At the initial stage the prior informed consent was taken as well as broad idea of the research problem was obtained from the experts. For this both closed-ended and open-ended questions were included to have better understanding of the research problem.

The experts were selected based on their expertise in the field of indigenous knowledge, their capacity and willingness in devoting sufficient time devotion to participate in multiple rounds. Altogether 55 experts were selected at the initial stage to seek their willingness and obtain a broad idea of the research problem based on their involvement in the area of research on ITK. Out of 55 experts only 37 turned up by giving their consent for involvement as an expert in Delphi analysis and in the first round their responses were sought through e-mail. Out of 37 experts, responses of only 29 experts were received in the first round. In the second round, questionnaire was mailed to 29 experts, out of which responses were received from 17 experts only. In the third round questionnaire was mailed to 17 experts. In this round all 17 experts sent their responses.

The level of consensus was fixed a priori at 80 per cent. The reliability was greater than 0.80 when Delphi group size exceeded 13 **(Dalkey, 1969)**. The reliability and validity scores of Delphi studies came from combining experts' judgments. It is imperative to note that in the present investigation consensus arrived among the experts was considered when 80% of the experts (i.e. 14 out of 17 experts) agreed or disagreed with a particular statement of the questionnaire administered to them.

Mode of interaction: Initially e-mails and personal calls were made to seek the consent of the experts for being a participant in Delphi technique. Once the consent was obtained then the next steps in the Delphi technique was followed through e-mails only. However, if an expert was busy with his/her own schedule, then a reminder was also given through call and WhatsApp message.

Result analysis: For data interpretation, descriptive statistics was used to analyze the information solicited from Delphi rounds. Data collected using Likert type scale were treated as interval data and reflected as mean and standard deviation for classification and presentation purpose. Nominal data were analysed by using frequencies and percentages.

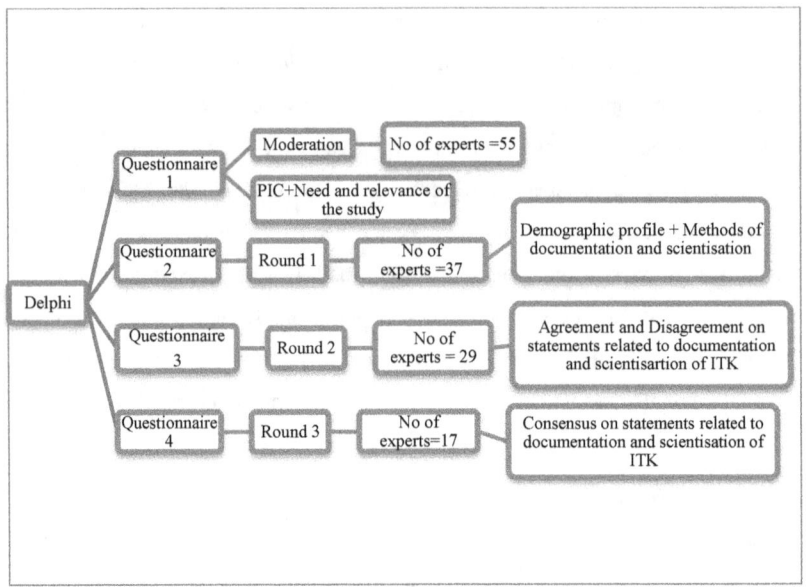

Figure 5: Flow diagram of Delphi process

3.5.11 Scientisation of ITKs

The term scientisation refers to three sequential steps i.e. particularisation, validation and generalisation of ITKs.

3.5.11.1 Particularisation of ITKs

The process of identification and separation of useful indigenous technical knowledge (ITK) from among the collected and documented ITK practices is known as particularisation. The usefulness of ITK is determined by degree of scientific rationality involved therein. Scientific rationality refers to the degree to which the ITK is realistic with a scientific backstopping and explainable facts, based on long term experiences **(Husain and Sundaramarai, 2011)**.

In the present investigation the process of particularisation of ITK has been operationalised as sorting out of the ITKs which can be utilised for solving the production problems and development purposes from among the collected and documented ITKs about pest and disease management in the study area.

Altogether 44 ITKs about pest and disease management were sent to 30 plant protection scientists to adjudge their scientific rationality. The scientists were expected to assess the scientific rationality of ITKs based on their expertise and experience on three types of rating scales which were as follows:

a) 3- point continuum Rating scale of Singh and Dhaliwal (2010)

The experts were asked to indicate their response to each ITK on a 3-point continuum comprising highly rational (score - 3), moderately rational (score - 2) and irrational (score - 1). Thus an ITK can get a maximum score of 90 and a minimum score of 30.

Category	Scores
Highly rational	3
Moderately rational	2
Irrational	1

After calculating the total rationality scores, ITKs which scored equal and above the mean score 60 (Total Rationality Score $\geq$ 60) were considered as rational and those scored below the mean (Total Rationality Score < 60) were deliberated to be irrational.

Category	Scores
Rational	≥ 60
Irrational	< 60

b) 4-point continuum Rating scale of Venkatesan and Sundaramarai (2014)

The experts were asked to indicate the rationality of selected ITKs based on a 4-point continuum i.e. rational based on scientific evidence derived from related studies (4), rational based on logical thinking derived from experiences (3), irrational based on logical thinking derived from experiences (2) and irrational based on scientific evidence derived from related studies (1).

Category	Scores
Rational based on scientific evidence derived from related studies	4
Rational based on logical thinking derived from experiences	3
Irrational based on logical thinking derived from experiences	2
Irrational based on scientific evidence derived from related studies	1

Total and weighted mean score was calculated for each ITK. The ITKs which scored equal or above the mean score were identified as rational and those below the mean score were considered as irrational.

Category	Scores
Rational	≥ 2.5
Irrational	< 2.5

c) 5- point continuum rating scale of Hiranand (1979)

Similarly the experts were asked to indicate their degree of agreement on a 5-point rating scale regarding scientific rationality of selected ITKs as developed by Hiranand (1979). The scoring process followed was: very rational (5), rational (4), undecided (3), irrational (2) and very irrational (1).

Category	Scores
Very rational	5
Rational	4
Undecided	3
Irrational	2
Very irrational	1

After that total and weighted mean score was calculated for each ITK. ITKs which were assigned a weighted mean score above 3.5 were considered to be highly rational, between 2.5 to 3.5 were moderately rational and below 2.5 were rated as irrational. These three categories were further clubbed into two categories i.e. rational (highly rational + moderately rational) and irrational.

Category	Scores
Rational	Highly > 3.5 + Moderately 2.5-3.5
Irrational	< 2.5

3.5.11.2 Validation of ITKs

Validation of ITK is a logical step to qualify and quantify the effectiveness of the indigenous practices. It is also for testing the rationale behind its use and testing the hypothesis based on the claim of the users or the informants. For validation of ITK, generally the following methods are employed:

i. Quantification of Indigenous Knowledge ((QuIK)
ii. Mean Perceived Effectiveness Index Methodology (MPEM)
iii. Experimentation (on-station/ on-farm)
iv. Case study
v. Laboratory experimentation

a) Validation by Quantification of Indigenous Knowledge (QuIK) method

In the present investigation, QuIK methods developed by **De Villiers, A.K. (1996)**, were employed for assessing the performance of selected ITKs as this method being rapid alternative to field trials and relatively lower in cost, owing to suitable for a student researcher. Matrix ranking tool of Participatory Rural Appraisal (PRA) was used in systematic interviews with farmers to generate numerical data on the performance of ITK. Data sets compiled from a number of interviews were subjected to statistical analysis. This enabled hypothesis to be tested and the criteria to be quantified. Criteria for the matrix were defined and derived from interactive farmer-researcher discussion. The factors and their levels were set in such a way that null hypothesis can be tested. The matrix was used as the basis for the interview with a series of independent key informants. Experienced farmers were identified through informal enquiry in the village. The interview process was initiated by drawing skeleton matrix table on the ground or flip chart as per convenience and labeling the columns and rows. The factors were carefully explained to the interviewees to ensure that all respondents refer to same parameters. The factors were defined in terms of farmers' own experience.

The tribal farmers were then asked to score the performance (using a fixed number of stones or other variable counters) against the different factors between the particular ITK and their corresponding scientific technologies. Periodic probing was done to ensure that informants could understand the criteria as intended.

After the matrix was completed by the tribal farmers then they were asked to explain the reasoning behind their decision about the different sources. The farmers were then allowed to modify their initial matrix. The same matrix table was used to interview all the experienced tribal key informants. The parameters in the following order were undertaken:

a) Effective in controlling insect-pests

b) Cost effectiveness

c) Time in problem solving/quickness

d) Ease in preparation

e) Environment friendliness

f) Compatibility with farming system components

Then the data were subjected to the statistical analysis (a standard analysis of variance, ANOVA). Data collected from the respondents on several criteria were subjected to one-way analysis of variance **(Snedecor and Cochran, 1994).** Analysis was carried out separately for each group of data under each criterion under a particular insect- pest disease studied. Duncan's Multiple Range Test as modified by **Kramer (1957)** was used to test the difference of means among alternatives.

b) Validation by Mean Perceived Effectiveness Index Methodology (MPEM)

Parvathi (1995) defined perception as the expressed opinion about a particular object by the individuals in relation to the set criteria. According to **Nagaraju (2001)**, effectiveness perception is the extent of satisfaction derived from various parts of a whole thing. Perceived effectiveness implies the degree to which the farmers perceive that a positive outcome is obtainable by applying a particular ITK in solving the field problems. Perceived effectiveness of the ITK is the degree of relative usefulness of the ITK as perceived by the farmers in resolving the problems in agriculture and allied activities **(Sundaramari and Ranganathan, 2003)**.

In the present investigation, the perceived effectiveness of rational ITKs was measured by using Mean Perceived Effectiveness Index (MPEI) methodology developed and used by **Sundaramari (2001)** with slight modification. The perceived effectiveness of an ITK was operationalised as the extent of ability of that practice, as perceived by tribal key informants, in solving various field problems faced by them in pest and disease management. It is the perception of the respondent about the attributes of the indigenous technology like efficacy, accessibility, cost-effectiveness, observability, adaptability and simplicity. The Mean Perceived Effectiveness Index consisted of six attributes is given with their relevancy weightage:

Weightage of scores of various attributes of ITKs

Attributes	Relevancy weightage
Efficacy	0.86
Accessibility	0.78
Cost-effectiveness	0.79
Observability	0.85
Adaptability	0.68
Simplicity	0.75

The relevancy ratio was defined as the ratio of actual score secured by a trait to maximum possible score that trait could secure. Obviously the ratio was between 0.20 and 1.00. This ratio was taken as the relevancy weightage for each trait. Thus, symbolically if W_1, W_2, W_3, W_4, W_5 and W_6 were the 6 weights on the 5- point continuum and n_1, n_2, ...n_6 were to be the number of judges who gave weights of $W_1, W_2, W_3.....W_6$ etc. Then the relevancy weightage "R" of the trait was calculated by the following formula:

$$= \frac{n_1R_1 + n_2R_2 + n_3R_3 + n_4R_4 + n_5R_5 + n_6W_6}{W\sum nt}$$

Where, W is the maximum of W_1, W_2, W_3, W_4, W_5 and W_6.

W= 6 in the present study

$$\text{i.e. } R = \frac{\sum n_1 W_1 R}{W\sum nt}$$

The finally selected list of six attributes was administered to 45 tribal farmers of the study area. They were asked to rate the effectiveness of each of the selected rational indigenous practices adopted by them against each of the traits on a 3-point continuum, the points being agree, undecided and disagree with scores of 3, 2 and 1 respectively (Agree–3, Undecided–2, Disagree–1). The Perceived Effectiveness Index (PEI) score of a particular ITK pertaining to pest and disease management was calculated using the formula.

$$\text{PEI Score} = \frac{W_1R_1 + W_2R_2 + ... + W_6R_6}{R_1 + R_2 + R_3 + R_4 + R_5 + R_6}$$

where, R_1, R_2, R_3.... R_6 are the relevancy weights of six traits and W_1, W_2 ..... W_6 were the scores obtained for the traits for an ITK from a respondent. To obtain the Mean Perceived Effectiveness Index (MPEI) for a specific ITK, then the mean score of Perceived Effectiveness Index scores obtained to arrive at the acquired from all the respondents for that specific ITK was calculated.

$$\text{MPEI} = \frac{\text{PEI score of Individual tribal key informant for each ITK}}{\text{Total Sample size}}$$

Based on MPEI score, all the ITKs were categorized into three categories: Those ITKs with the MPEI between 2.00 and 2.5 were deliberated as moderately effective ITKs, those having MPEI of above 2.5 were regarded as highly effective and less than 2.0 as less effective.

Category	MPEI Score
Less effective	Less than 2.00
Moderately effective	2.00 – 2.50
Highly effective	More than 2.50

Operational definition of attributes used in validation

i. **Corresponding Scientific Technology (CST)** - CST has been operationalised as the improved practices that have been recommended by the scientists of ICAR Research Institutes or State Agricultural Universities (SAUs), which may be as effective as the ITK.

ii. **Efficacy** is the degree to which an ITK is considered to be effective in the solution of a particular production problem i.e. management of pests and diseases in crop production.

iii. **Accessibility** is the degree to which an ITK related material is easily available in the locality for pest and disease management.

iv. **Cost-effectiveness** is the degree to which an ITK is cheap and affordable for tribal farmers for pest and disease management.

v. **Observability** is the degree to which the results are visible after application of an ITK for pest and disease management.

vi. **Adaptability** is the degree to which an ITK is suitable and compatible to the bio-physical and socio-economic environment of tribal farmers for pest and disease management.

vii. **Simplicity** is the degree to which an ITK is easy and simple in application for pest and disease management.

3.5.11.3 Generalisation of ITKs

Generalisation of ITKs is also called utilisation and popularisation of ITKs. Generalisation of ITKs refers to the degree to which an ITK either in original form or blended or in the form of ready to use (RTU) is of utility for the betterment of the society in the context of sustainable agriculture. In the present investigation, the questionnaire was administered to ITK experts to obtain their opinion on the statements. They were asked to tick the appropriate option given against the listed ITKs to know whether a particular ITK could be used to control the pests and diseases of different crops. If agreed they had to indicate the extent and if disagreed, whether it could be discarded or to use in a completely blended form with corresponding scientific technologies (CSTs). The scientists were asked to suggest the corresponding scientific technology for ITKs which cannot be directly disseminated. Further their opinion on preference on the mode of dissemination was also taken and ranked to prioritize.

3.5.12 Constraints encountered in utilisation of Indigenous Technical Knowledge

Forty five tribal farmers were personally interviewed to know the constraints encountered by them while utilising and popularising ITKs in their fields through a structured schedule. The tribal farmers were asked to give their opinion on different constraints a 3- point continuum i.e. Most important (score - 3), Important (score - 2) and Least important (score - 1).

Category	Scores
Most important	3
Important	2
Least important	1

3.5.13 Framework for systematic documentation and scientisation of Indigenous Technical Knowledge

The output obtained from objectives 1, 2 and 3 was utilised for developing a framework for systematic documentation and scientisation (particularisation, validation and generalisation) of ITKs. The gaps analysed after getting an ideal process of systematic documentation, particularisation, validation and generalisation of ITKs and what is actually practically done for documentation, particularisation, validation and generalisation of ITKs at farmers field keeping in view the various constraints encountered by the tribal farmers, a process framework was suggested to bridge the gap between ITK holders and researchers for better planning, execution and management of development projects. It would be easy to compile data through the use of this framework to have a strong database on ITK about pest and disease management of Jharkhand. The framework developed for the present study can be used by other organisations for systematic documentation, particularisation, validation and generalisation of ITKs in agriculture and allied fields.

3.6 Methods and tools of data collection

A pilot study was conducted in the study area during August 2019 to understand the tribal setting and ITKs prevalent among the tribal farmers of the study area. It helped in identification of villages, tribal groups and selection of ITKs pertaining to pest and disease management. The data collection was started from September 2019 and completed by March 2020. Primary data were collected by survey method with a semi-structured interview schedule. The major techniques used for data collection were personal interviews using interview schedules and focus group discussions. The secondary data were collected from published literature and statistical database.

3.6.1 Quantitative Research

In the present investigation, quantitative approach was used for scientific rationality, validation of ITKs through Mean Perceived Effectiveness Methodology and finding out the constraints in utilisation of ITKs about to pest and disease management. Data were collected with a pre-tested structured questionnaire and interview schedule. Documentation of ITKs was done through secondary sources and also by conducting personal interview with the help of exclusively developed semi-structured interview schedule.

a. Mailed Questionnaire (Google docs): Mailed questionnaire was used to collect data from scientist respondents. These forms were mailed to the respondents who were expected to respond by writing the relevant answers in the spaces provided. Its purpose was to collect information from the respondents located in different parts of the country. Mailed questionnaire technique has an advantage of providing more accurate answer, because respondents can fill up the questionnaire in their spare time.

b. Interview Schedule: A schedule is a structure of a set of questions on a given topic which are asked by the interviewer or investigator personally.

3.6.2 Qualitative Research

Qualitative research provides in-depth understanding of the research problem. Selected tools of Participatory Rural Appraisal (PRA) were used in the initial phase of research. Combinations of PRA methods like direct observation, group discussion with tribal farmers and semi-structured interview schedule were used to document indigenous practices adopted by the farmer respondents in the study villages and to prepare a list of constraints encountered in utilisation of ITKs.

Focus Group Discussion (FGD): FGD was used to supplement and triangulate the data collected from the respondents. A focus group discussion involves gathering people from similar backgrounds or experiences together to discuss a specific topic of interest. It is a form of qualitative research where questions are asked about their perceptions, attitudes, beliefs, opinion or ideas. In focus group discussion participants are free to talk with other group members; unlike other research methods it encourages discussions with other participants. It generally involves group interviewing in a small group of usually 8 to 12 people. It is led by a moderator in a loosely structured discussion of various topics of interest. Additionally, field diary and photographs were also used to document daily account of activities, experiences, people, places and events simultaneously.

In the present investigation, FGDs using semi-structured guidelines were carried out with groups of tribal farmers. The guidelines were prepared for each group. Four groups were formed and five participants from each group for FGDs were selected based on their willingness to participate. Out of the total participants 12 were male and 5 were female household heads and 3 agricultural experts were selected as moderators for focus group discussion.

3.6.3 Documentation tools

a. Field diary

Day to day observations as well as the activities were recorded in the field diary. This technique helped the researcher in documentation of the field activities during the data collection.

b. Photography

Photographs of the tribal community setting, their households and their involvement in various activities were documented. Photographs of the researcher during data collection and conducting focus group discussion were also taken for documentation purpose.

3.7 Statistical analysis

For data interpretation, the data were tabulated and subjected to appropriate statistical tools such as frequency, percentage, arithmetic mean, standard deviation, standard error of mean, weighted mean score, One way analysis of variance and Duncan multiple range test wherever found appropriate and data were analyzed systematically to draw valid inferences.

a. Percentages: Percentages were used in descriptive analysis for making comparisons. For calculating percentages the frequency of a particular cell was multiplied by 100 and divided by the total number of respondents in that particular cell.

$$P = \frac{n}{N} \times 100$$

Where,

P = percentage

n = frequency of particular cell

N = total number of sample respondents

b. **Arithmetic mean:** The mean is the value arrived at by dividing the sum of observations by the total number of observations. x_i

$$\bar{x} = \frac{\sum x_i}{n}$$

c. **Standard deviation:** It is a measure of variability in a set of scores, found by summing up the squared differences from the mean, diving by the number of cases and extracting the square root. It was computed for the [purpose of analysis and further categorisation. The formula was used for calculating standard deviation was as:

$$s = \sqrt{\frac{\sum(x - \bar{x})^2}{n - 1}}$$

Where,

    s = standard deviation

    x = value of individual variable

    $\bar{x}$ = sample mean

    n = sample size

d. **Standard error:** The standard error (SE) of a statistic (usually an estimate of a parameter) is the standard deviation of its sampling distribution or an estimate of that standard deviation.

$$SEM = \frac{s}{\sqrt{n}}$$

Where,

    SEM = standard error of the mean

    σ = sample standard deviation

    n = sample size

e. **Weighted Mean Score:** It is a type of average in which weights are assigned to individual values in order to determine the relative importance of each observation. Weighted mean score was calculated by using the following formula.

$$\overline{X_w} = \frac{\sum W_i X_i}{\sum W_i}$$

Where,

W_i = weight of X_i

X_i = score of X_i

f. ANOVA and Duncan's Multiple Range test: For statistical analysis of validation studies, data collected from the respondents on several criteria were subjected to one way analysis of variance **(Snedecor and Cochran, 1994)**. Analysis was carried out separately for each group of data under each criterion under a particular ITK practiced. To test the difference of means among alternatives, Duncan's Multiple Range Test as modified by **Kramer (1957)** was used.

The linear model chosen for ANOVA was,

$$Y_{ij} = \mu + t_i + e_{ij}$$

Where,

y_{ij} = observation of jth respondent to i^{th} alternative

μ = Overall mean

t_i = Effect of ith alternative

e_{ij} = Residual, distributed normally with mean "0" and variance "1"

Research Methodology

Plate 4: ITK Expert of Jharkhand interacting with tribal clan leader

Plate 5: Discussion with plant protection scientists

Plate 6: Collection of data from tribal farmers

Plate 7: Discussion with the oldest tribal farmer

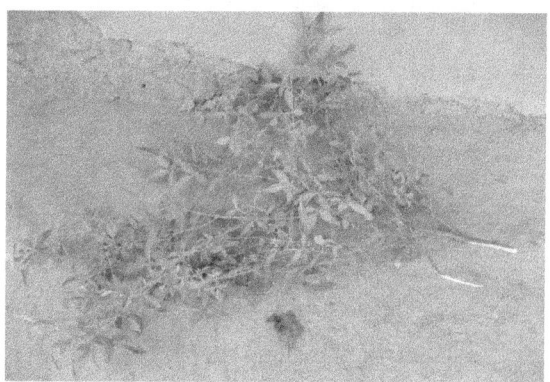

Plate 8: Sinduwar leaves

Plate 9 Discussion with tribal key informants regarding validation parameters

Research Methodology ....

Plate 10: Field of tribal farmers practicing ITKs

Plate 11: Focus Group Discussion with farmers practicing ITK for pest and disease management

Plate 12: Discussion with tribal farmers practicing ITK in Paddy field.

Plate 13: Investigation of ITK material preparation and discussion with tribal farmers.

Chapter 4　　　　RESULTS AND DISCUSSION

The data obtained during the investigation were subjected to statistical analysis according to the objectives. For the convenience of presentation, results obtained are presented and discussed in this chapter under the following sections:

4.1. Demographic profile of tribal farmers

4.2. Demographic profile of ITK experts

4.3. Identification of the process of systematic documentation and scientisation of Indigenous Technical Knowledge

4.4. Scientisation of Indigenous Technical Knowledge about pest and disease management among tribal farmers

4.5. Constraints encountered in utilisation of ITKs by tribal farmers

4.6. Development of a framework for systematic documentation and scientisation of Indigenous Technical Knowledge

4.7 Success story

The main purpose of the present investigation was to develop a systematic framework for documentation and scientisation of ITKs. It was attained by developing a consensus listing of those methods and key activities that help in documentation, particularisation, validation and generalisation of ITKs using an expert panel of scientists, academicians, extension professionals, entrepreneurs working in ICAR, international and national non- profit organizations.

4.1. Demographic profile of tribal farmers

Understanding of socio-personal, economic and demographic profile of the respondents is necessary for understanding the background of the respondents. Profile of the tribal farmers was studied in terms of selected demographic characteristics viz. age, gender, tribe type, education, land holding, farming experience, social participation, risk orientation and innovativeness. Keeping this in view, the demographic profile of the tribal farmers has been presented in Table 4.1.

Table 4.1: Distribution of tribal farmers according to their selected demographic profile (n=45)

S.No	Category	Frequency (f)	Percentage (%)
I	**Gender**		
1.	Male	18	40.00
2.	Female	27	60.00
	Total	45	100.00
II	**Age**		
1.	Young (18 to 35 years)	2	4.45
2.	Middle (36 to 55 years)	11	24.44
3.	Old (56 years and above)	32	71.11
	Total	45	100.00
III	**Tribe type**		
1.	Kharia	6	13.33
2.	Ho	7	15..55
3.	Oraon	21	46.66
4.	Munda	11	24.44
	Total	45	100.00
IV	**Education**		
1.	Illiterate	3	6.66
2.	Can read only	7	15.56
3.	Can read and write	3	6.66
4.	Primary School	14	31.12
5.	Middle School	9	20.00
6.	High School	5	11.12
7.	Graduate & above	4	8.88
	Total	45	100.00

Results and Discussion ....

V	**Land holding**			
1.	Marginal (< 1 ha)		26	57.77
2.	Small (1.0 to 2.0 ha)		9	20.00
3.	Medium (2.1 to 4.0 ha)		6	13.33
4.	Large (> 4.0 ha)		4	8.88
	Total		45	100.00
VI	**Farming experience**			
1.	Low (upto 15 years)		5	11.11
2.	Medium (16 to 25 years)		14	31.11
3.	High (above 25 years)		26	57.78
	Total		45	100.00
VII	**Social participation**			
1.	No membership		19	42.22
2.	Member of one organisation		15	33.34
3.	Member of more than one organisation		4	8.88
4.	Office bearer		7	15.56
	Total		45	100.00
VIII	**Risk orientation**			
1.	Low (scores upto 7)		26	57.77
2.	Medium (8-10)		11	24.45
3.	High (11 and above)		8	17.78
	Total		45	100.00
IX	**Innovativeness**			
1.	Low (scores upto 11)		27	60.00
2.	Medium (12-15)		16	35.55
3.	High (16 and above)		2	4.45
	Total		45	100.00

Results and Discussion ....

4.1.1. Gender

It is evident from Table 4.1 that 60 per cent of the tribal farmers were females and 40 per cent of them were males. The findings highlighted the importance of women's contributions in tribal farming systems. In the study concluded by **Fernandez and Tick (1994)** it was emphasised that an understanding of the role of gender as well as the intrinsic value of the ITK is crucial to the solutions of situation-specific problems.

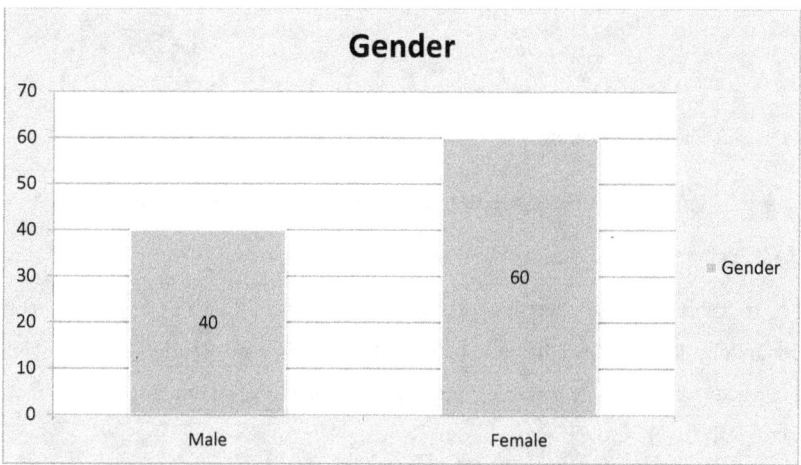

Figure 6: Distribution of tribal farmers according to gender

4.1.2. Age

The data presented in Table 4.1 show that out of total respondents, the highest proportion i.e. 71.11 per cent were found to be in the old age group followed by middle age group (24.44%) and 4.45 per cent were in the category of young age group. This indicated that old age people were the knowledge bearers holding vast knowledge about ITKs which might be lost if they do not share this knowledge with the youngsters. The findings of this study are in line with **Rakesh (2014)** who reported that old people possess more knowledge regarding ITKs than other age groups.

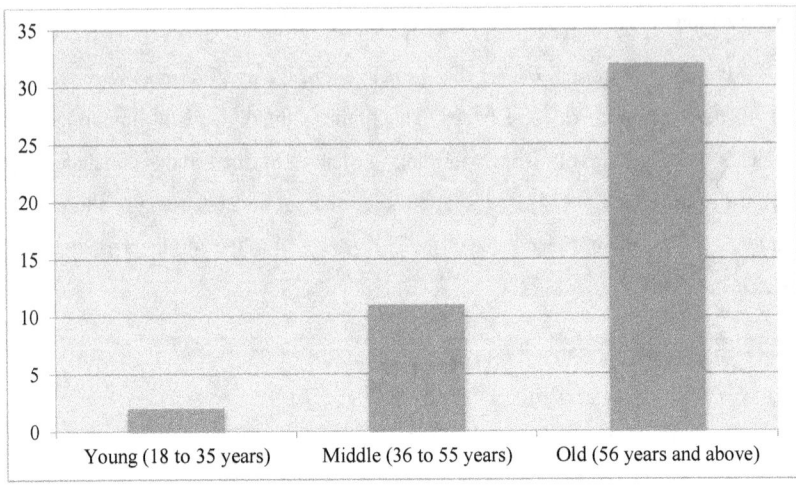

Figure 7: Distribution of tribal farmers according to age

4.1.3. Tribe type

Table 4.1 shows that 46.66 per cent of the tribal farmers belonged to Oraon community followed by Munda (24.46%), Ho (15.55%) and Kharia (13.33%). This indicated that the sample was true representative of the tribal community.

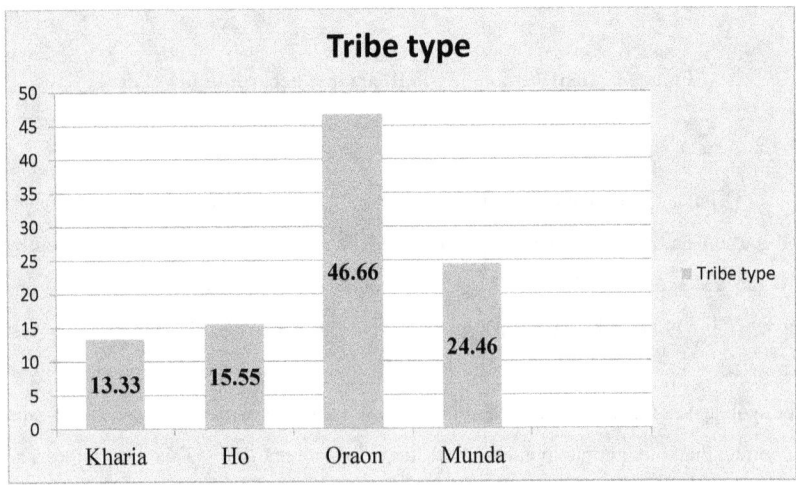

Figure 8: Distribution of tribal farmers according to tribe type

4.1.4. Education

A perusal of the Table 4.1 shows that 31.12 per cent of the tribal farmers had education up to primary level followed by 20 per cent upto middle school and 11.12 percent upto high school. A very less percentage of respondents belonged to the category of graduate and above (8.88%). The remaining respondents were either illiterate (6.66%) or could read and/or write only (28.88%). This indicated that the respondents in the study area had low level of education. **Seeralan (2004), Rai *et al.* (2017), Khan and Nayak (2018)** and **Shakrawar (2018)** also found that respondents practicing ITKs had relatively lower level of education.

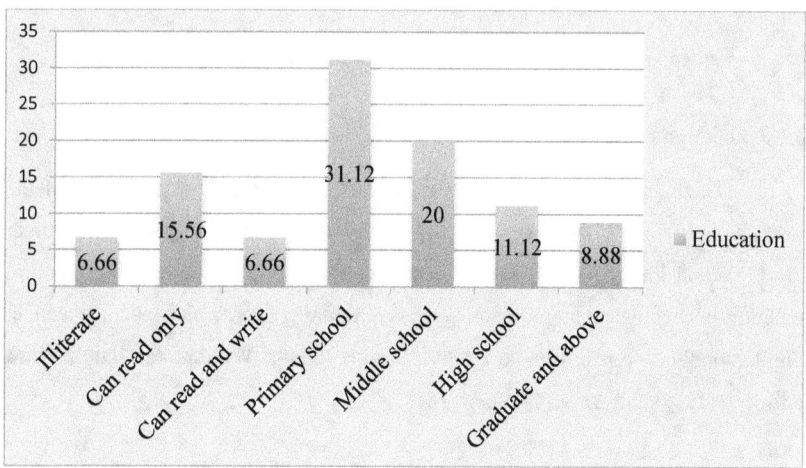

Figure 9: Distribution of tribal farmers according to education

4.1.5. Land holding

It is evident from the Table 4.1 shows that out of total tribal farmers, highest proportion had marginal size of land holdings (57.78%) followed by small (20.00%), medium (13.33%) and large (8.89%). Findings revealed that more than 75 per cent of tribal farmers had small and marginal size holdings and were resource poor utilising the locally available materials in their farming activities rather than relying on input intensive agriculture. The findings are in concurrence with the findings of **Kumari (2008), Singh (2013), Islam *et al.* (2015) and Rakesh (2014).**

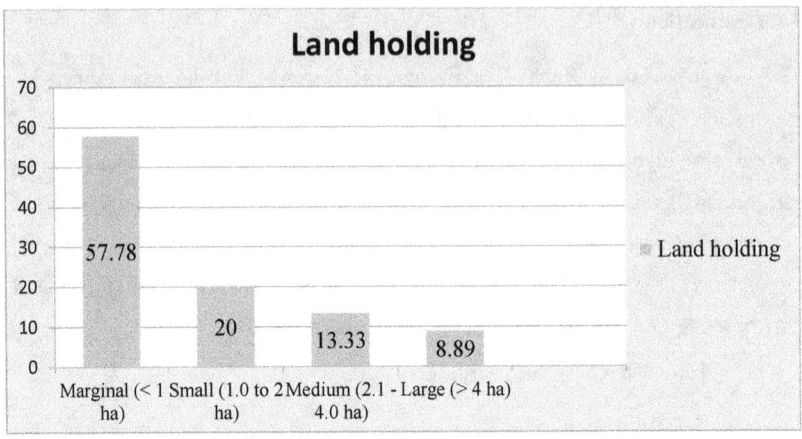

Figure 10: Distribution of tribal farmers according to land holding

4.1.6. Farming experience

The findings presented in Table 4.1 show that the highest proportion of the tribal farmers i.e. 57.78 per cent had high farming experience followed by medium (31.11%) and low (11.11%). This indicated that they had been practicing this oral tradition since long and nurturing as well as contributing to environment conservation. Similar findings were also reported by **Kumari (2008), Wankhade (2009), Tudu and Roy (2015)** and **Arya (2018)**.

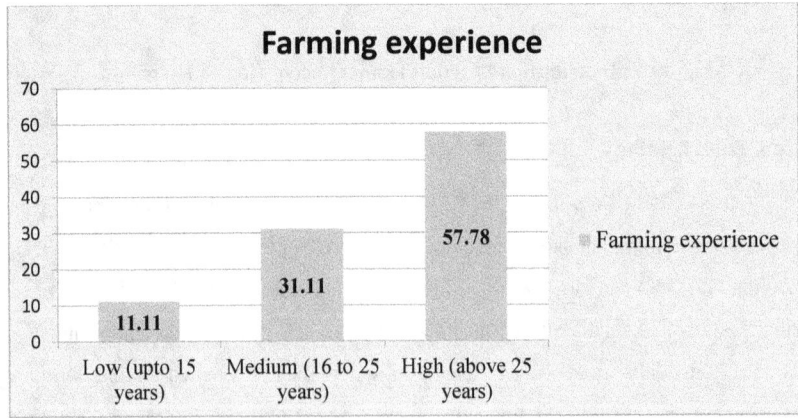

Figure 11: Distribution of tribal farmers according to farming experience

4.1.7 Social participation

The organizations prevalent in the study area were village panchayat, co-operative credit society, milk co-operative society, rural youth club, self help groups (SHGs) etc of which some tribal farmers were either members or office bearers. A cursory look on the table 4.1 shows that 42.22 per cent of the tribal farmers were not associated with any of the formal organizations. 33.34 per cent had membership of only one organization and 8.88 per cent were members of more than one organization and 15.56 per cent tribal farmers were office bearers. The findings are in conformity with the findings of **Singh (2013), Rakesh (2014), Islam *et al.* (2015), Arya (2018) and Shakrawar and Naberia (2018)** which indicated that tribal farming community had low level of participation and like to remain isolated from the mainstream of the society and have rigid social structure and limited social mobility.

Figure 12: Distribution of tribal farmers according to social participation

4.1.8. Risk orientation

It is evident from Table 4.1 that 57.77 per cent of the tribal farmers had low level of risk orientation followed by 24.45 per cent and 17.78 per cent who had medium and high levels of risk orientation respectively. The reason behind this might be that they have low level of education and lower exposure to mainstream society. The findings are in line with those of findings of **Mahto (2012), Patidar (2013) and Rakesh (2014)**.

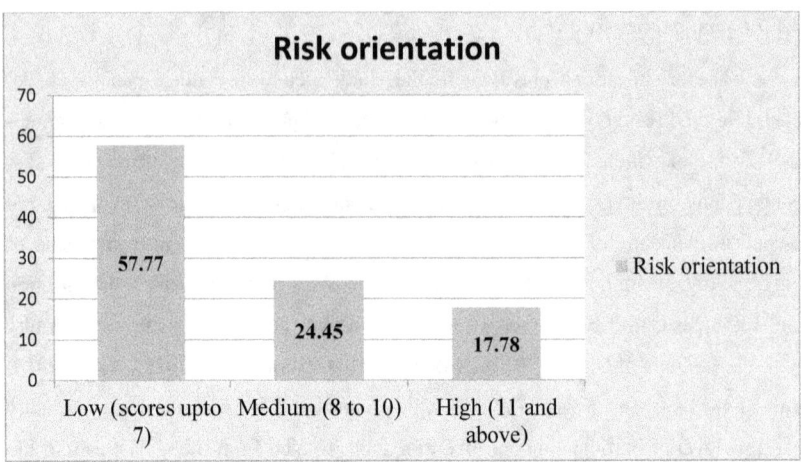

Figure 13: Distribution of tribal farmers according to risk orientation

4.1.9. Innovativeness

Table 4.1 depicts the level of innovativeness of the tribal farmers. It indicates that majority of them (60%) had low level of innovativeness, while 35.55 percent exhibited medium level of innovativeness and remaining 4.45 percent exhibited high level of innovativeness. The results indicated their rigidity and resistance towards any type of change might be the reason for lower level of innovativeness. Similar findings were reported by **Seeralan (2004), Kumari (2008) and Shakrawar (2018)**.

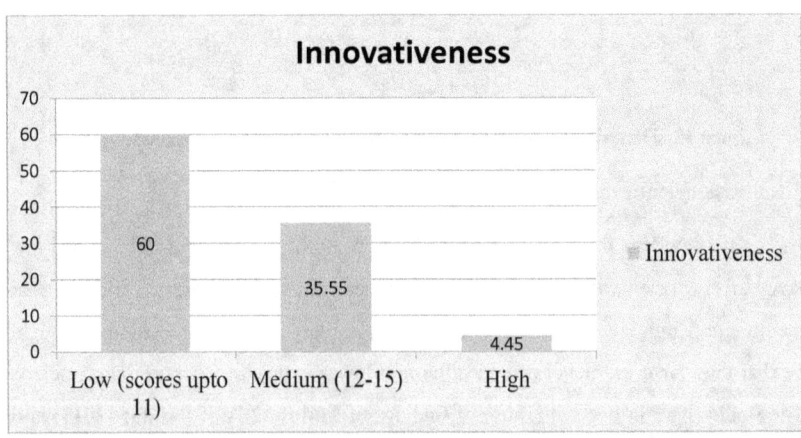

Figure 14: Distribution of tribal farmers according to innovativeness

Results and Discussion

The results and discussion presented in Table 4.1 concluded that majority of the tribal farmers were females (60%) of old age (71.11%) from Oraon community (71.11%) having very low level of literacy. Majority of them were marginal farmers had higher farming experience with very low level of social participation, low risk orientation (57.77%) and innovativeness (60%).

4.2. Demographic profile of ITK experts

It is imperative to study the academic background of the experts involved in the study to gain a better understanding of the ITK related activities and its policy implications. Demographic variables like gender, age, current role, experience in ITK work, nature of work and level of involvement were studied to get a better understanding of the ITK experts and their participation and contribution in ITK-related work. Keeping this in view, the demographic profile of the ITK experts was studied and data have been presented in Table 4.2.

It can be observed in the Table 4.2, that out of 55 experts invited to participate in the Delphi study, 37 experts completed round 1 (response rate – 67.27%) and 29 out of 37 completed round 2 (response rate – 78.37%) and 17 out of 29 completed round 3 (response rate - 58.62%).

Gender-wise distribution shows that majority of the experts were males. In first round, there were two female respondents who were reduced to one and zero in second and third rounds respectively. In each subsequent round, majority of the experts belonged to the age group of 51-65 years (Round 3 - 64.70%). It might be due to the reason that they had acquired the ITK wisdom with passage of time and experience. Majority of the experts were Director/ Dean of SAUs or Director/Assistant Director General of ICAR (Round 3 - 64.70%). In all the three rounds, majority of the experts had the experience of 10-15 years (Round 3 – 88.23%). In the final round, majority of the experts were involved in extension (52.94%) followed by research (35.29%) and teaching (11.77%). The experts who were involved in ITK related work to a greater extent (Round 3 – 82.35%) were found to be quite active in the Delphi process.

Table 4.2. Distribution of ITK experts according to their demographic profile in Delphi rounds

	Round 1 (n=37)	Round 2 (n=29)	Round 3 (n=17)
Gender			
Male	35 (94.59)	28 (96.55)	17 (100)
Female	2 (5.41)	1 (3.45)	0 (0)
Age			
<50 years	3 (8.10)	3 (10.34)	2 (11.76)
51-65 years	26 (70.27)	20 (68.96)	11 (64.70)
>65 years	8 (21.63)	6 (20.68)	4 (23.54)
Current role			
Asst Professor/Scientist	4 (10.8)	2 (6.89)	0 (0)
Associate Professor/ Programme Coordinator/ Senior Scientist	2 (5.40)	1 (3.44)	1 (5.88)
Professor/Principal Scientist	6 (16.21)	6 (20.68)	4 (23.52)
Head of Department	1 (2.70)	0 (0)	0 (0)
Director/Dean/ Assistant Director General	21 (56.75)	18 (62.10)	11 (64.70)
Vice Chancellor	3 (8.10)	2 (6.89)	1 (5.88)
Experience in ITK work			
5-10 years	7 (18.91)	3 (10.34)	3 (17.64)
10-15 years	21 (56.75)	19 (65.51)	15 (88.23)
15-20 years	9 (24.32)	7 (24.13)	2 (11.76)
Nature of job			
Teaching	3 (8.10)	3 (10.34)	2 (11.77)
Research	21 (56.76)	14 (48.28)	6 (35.29)
Extension	13 (35.14)	12 (41.38)	9 (52.94)
Level of involvement			
To some extent	3 (8.10)	0	0
To a moderate extent	6 (16.22)	6 (20.69)	3 (17.65)
To a great extent	28 (75.68)	23 (79.31)	14 (82.35)

Results and Discussion ....

4.3. Identification of the process of systematic documentation and scientisation of indigenous technical knowledge

Prior Informed Consent (PIC) was taken from all the experts as an ethical procedure before involving them in the present investigation as Delphi experts. Anonymity of experts was ensured at all times. Within each round, experts could revise their decision which was supported by a controlled feedback. In all three Delphi rounds were completed in this process. The experts who did not respond in *Round 1* were not invited to the next round. The experts were also requested to provide additional comments.

The statements were collected and collated from extensive review of literature. To meet the objective of the study, the survey was divided into three sections i) PIC and opinion on need and relevance of the study, ii) Open-ended questions with the option of free text and iii) consensus on methods and activities, institutional mechanism, competencies required, criteria and barriers related to documentation and scientisation of ITKs.

The study used a series of four mailed questionnaires uploaded on Google docs. Firstly, PIC form with the questionnaire containing opinion regarding need and relevance of the study was sent to 55 geographically isolated ITK experts. The study demanded this to avoid any ethical issues and to carry out the research in a smooth manner. It also helped to know the excitement and enthusiasm of experts to contribute their valuable opinion in the study. Opinions regarding the need for systematic method of documentation, particularisation, validation and generalisation of ITKs were ascertained on a Likert scale of 5-point continuum. A total of 20 statements were presented to the experts with a free text option available to add any domains that were particularly not listed and needed attention in the study.

Delphi Round 1

PIC was obtained from 37 out of 55 experts who were contacted. In the first round, questionnaires were sent to only 37 experts. The first round included open-ended questions. It enabled identification of domains for the present investigation. An attempt was also made to generate an array of response categories and prepare a list of particulars considered influential in achieving a systematic framework for documentation, particularisation, validation, and generalisation of ITKs and categorize them accordingly. The response of the experts on open-ended questions yielded a list of particulars which were considered during the study. A free text response was made available to the experts within each of the survey domains, provided the opportunity to elaborate the responses. The free text ultimately helped to generate an array of response categories that were used to produce statements for second round of questionnaire. Comments on various aspects of the returned questionnaires indicated that some of the particulars in *Round 1* were too broad and needed revision. After collecting the initial data, the researcher consolidated and grouped the familiar answers through content analysis.

Delphi Round 2

In this round, the experts were sent a revised list containing 120 statements under five domains and they were requested to provide a dichotomous indication of whether they agreed or disagreed.

Delphi Round 3

The third round was sought to arrive at a consensus by reviewing the list of statements to more accurately reflect their opinions. During this round, the experts were presented individual and group results from the second round and were asked to indicate if they agreed or disagreed with each statement.

The results of three delphi rounds enabled in identification of expanded list of total 120 statements from the experts and it was categorized into five main domains namely, methods and activities, competencies required, institutional mechanism, criteria and barriers. The methods and activities section contained larger number of statements. In *Round 1,* participants' demographic profile was collected and documented has been presented in Table 4.2. There was a variation in the proportion of statements that received consensus between domains but the proportion of the consensus increased in each subsequent round across all domains.

The Delphi experts were asked to indicate their agreement or disagreement against the statements given by them based on their experiences about various aspects related to documentation and scientisation (particularisation, validation and generalisation) of ITKs on a 5-point response scale. Need and enthusiasm of the experts in developing a systematic process of documentation and scientisation (particularisation, validation and generalisation) of ITKs was also revealed in the analysis. The mean score of each statement as expressed by the ITK experts is presented in Table 4.3.1.

Table 4.3.1: Distribution of experts' opinion on 'need and relevance of the study' on a 5-point Likert scale

(n=37)

Sl.No	Statement	Mean
1.	There is a need to follow a systematic approach for documentation, particularisation, validation and generalisation of ITKs	4.83
2.	Many ITKs are at brink of extinction and once lost it is impossible to recover	4.89
3.	A systematic approach is essential to generate location-specific solutions for the agricultural problems	4.81
4.	ITKs are time-tested and are the best source for providing solutions to climate-related issues	4.35
5.	The ITKs provide better eco-friendly and sustainable solutions for the agricultural problems than improved technologies	4.54
6.	Scientific validation and utilization of ITKs will lead to value addition to farmers' knowledge	4.83
7.	The current system of documentation of ITKs lacks focus on its validation and utilisation	4.05
8.	Obtaining Prior Informed Consent has to be made mandatory for documenting ITKs	4.29
9.	The research and academic institutions need to develop a sound system for protecting Intellectual Property Rights (IPRs) associated with ITKs	4.21
10.	Validation of ITKs is essential to generate scientific evidence for establishing their efficacy	4.86
11.	The current methods for assessing rationality of ITKs through expert opinion lacks scientific rigor	4.89
12.	There is a need to develop methods and tools for selecting ITKs for validity assessment based on their utility	4.78
13.	There is a need to initiate research works on up scaling of ITKs for developing commercialisable products and services	4.54
14.	There is a need to develop an institutional system for scientific validation of ITKs	4.72
15.	If utilised properly, the ITKs have potential to provide sustainable solutions to problems faced by the society today	4.70
16.	There is a need of developing a policy framework for effective utilisation of ITKs	5.00
17.	There is need to formally recognize the rights of farmers in order to equitably share the benefits	5.00
18.	Involvement of custodian farmers of ITKs in all stages of documentation, particularisation, validation and generalisation is essential	4.97
19.	In the absence of an institutional mechanism for managing ITKs, there is widespread misuse of ITKs documented by various agencies	4.91
20.	Scientific validation of ITKs will generate unique knowledge which can be integrated with modern approaches for developing sound technologies	5.00

It is necessary to know the opinion of the experts whether they feel that there should be a systematic process for documentation and scientisation of ITKs. Once the need and relevance of the study is known then it becomes easy and guiding tool to design the whole process of Delphi. It can be elucidated from Table 4.3.1 that all the 20 statements were found to be relevant and experts felt the need to further explore the topic.

In order to know the degree of their agreement regarding need and relevance of the study the statements were grouped into three categories i.e. low, medium and high having mean scores of <2.5, 2.5-3.5 and >3.5 respectively. The data have been presented in Table 4.3.2.

Table 4.3.2: Distribution of statements related to need and relevance of the study

Category	Score	Number of statements
Low	< 2.5	0
Medium	2.5-3.5	0
High	> 3.5	20

It is evident from Table 4.3.2 that experts opined that there is a strong 'need for developing a policy framework for effective utilisation of ITKs', 'need to formally recognize the rights of farmers in order to equitably share the benefits' and 'scientific validation of ITKs will generate unique knowledge which can be integrated with modern approaches for developing sound technologies'. However all other statements were also rated strongly for their consideration in identification of a systematic process of documentation and scientisation of ITKs.

Apart from the opinions of Delphi experts on various aspects of documentation and scientisation (particularisation, validation and generalisation of ITKs), an attempt was further made to seek their awareness of specific methods of documentation and under headings/sub-headings, different scales for measuring rationality, methods of validation, and preferences for generalisation. The findings are presented in Table 4.3.3.

Results and Discussion ....

Table 4.3.3: Distribution of Delphi experts according to their awareness of methods of documentation and scientisation of ITKs

Sl.No	Methods of Documentation	Frequency (f)	Percentage (%)
1.	Interaction with community leaders including elders	37	67.27
2.	Rapid Rural Appraisal/PRA	37	67.27
3.	Key Informant Method	37	67.27
4.	Historical timeline	37	67.27
5.	Group discussion	37	67.27
6.	Field observations	37	67.27
7.	Surveys	37	67.27
8.	Participant observation	37	67.27
9.	Brain storming	37	67.27
10.	Interview method	35	63.63
11.	Case study	23	41.81
12.	Games	18	32.72
13.	SWOT Analysis	14	25.45
	Heading and sub-headings for documentation		
1.	Name of ITK	37	67.27
2.	Purpose of ITK	37	67.27
3.	Practised by which community	37	67.27
4.	Related material available in the locality	37	67.27
5.	Extent to which the problem is solved by ITK	22	40
6.	Percentage of family using the ITK	6	10.90

Results and Discussion ....

	Particularisation		
	Scales for exploring scientific rationality of the ITKs		
1.	3-point rationality scale of Dhaliwal and Singh (2010)	35	63.63
2.	4- point rationality scale of Hiranand (1979)	31	56.36
3.	5-point rationality scale of Venkatesan and Sundaramarai (2014)	23	41.81
	Validation		
	Methods of validation of ITKs.		
1.	Quantifying Indigenous Knowledge (QuIK) method	34	61.81
2.	Mean Perceived Effectiveness Methodology (MPEM)	29	52.72
3.	Field Experimentation	12	21.81
	Generalisation		
	Generalisation of ITKs.		
1.	Effective at par with corresponding scientific technology		
	Recommendation for large scale dissemination	35	63.63
	Ready to use products	30	54.54
2.	Not Effective but at par with scientific technology		
	Further experimentation for enhancing its effectiveness	36	65.45
	Multi- locational trial should be conducted further	31	56.36

It can be interpreted from Table 4.3.3 that experts felt that a combination of suitable methods should be used for documentation of ITKs as opined by all the ITK experts. The methods most preferred by the experts were interaction with community leaders including elders, rapid rural appraisal, participatory rural appraisal, case study, key informant method, historical timeline, interview method, participant observation, brain storming methods would give better documentation results and would help in proper collection and identification of ITKs from the study area.

Among headings and sub-headings to be covered in documentation of ITKs, 'name of the ITK', 'purpose of ITK', 'community practicing that ITK' and 'availability of ITK material' were most preferred sub-headings to be followed in documentation of ITK followed by extent of adoption of ITK. Percentage of family using ITK was found to be of no relevance for documentation purpose by the experts as only six per cent experts showed their preference to this section.

Results of the scale preferred for scientific rationality showed that experts had awareness of all the three types of rating scales. The most preferred scale to assess the scientific rationality of ITKs was Dhaliwal and Singh (2010) scale which has 3-point scoring procedure followed by 5- point rating scale of Hiranand (1979) and 4-point rating scale of Venkatesan and Sundaramarai (2014).

Validating ITKs to establish their effectiveness is necessary for participatory technology development. Quantifying Indigenous Knowledge (QuIK) method was most preferred method of validation followed by Mean Perceived Effectiveness Methodology (MPEM). It might be due to the fact that QuIK is a community validation method and can be quickly done. It is believed that community practicing ITKs have better understanding of their socio-physical conditions so parameters used by them to assess the effectiveness of ITKs is of great importance. Field experimentation was least preferred as it is time consuming and costly.

After validation of ITKs, generalisation/utilisation needs to be scaled up so it is important to know whether ITK is as effective at par with corresponding scientific technology. After ascertaining this, it should be recommended for large scale dissemination followed by utilising ITKs through ready to use (RTU) products. When ITK is not effective at par with corresponding scientific technology then further experimentation of ITKs for enhancing their effectiveness was most preferred followed by conducting multilocational trials.

After obtaining the results of the PIC format and the opinion on need and relevance of the study, awareness and preference of different methods of documentation and scientisation of ITKs, different statements were framed on different aspects of documentation and scientisation of ITKs to get dichotomous response of the experts in Round 2 and Round 3 to achieve the consensus. The statements were categorised under five domains by the experts and they were: methods and activities to be followed for documentation and scientisation of ITKs, competencies required for personnel involved, institutional mechanism required, criteria and barriers in ITK related studies.

4.3.4.1 Methods and Activities Related to 'documentation and scientisation' of ITKs

Table 4.3.4. (A) and (B) shows that how consensus was arrived on the statements related to documentation, particularisation, validation and generalisation. Methods and activities domain were further categorized into four sub-headings to make a clear cut distinction of the activities to be followed. The four sub-headings were namely documentation, particularisation, validation and generalisation. ITK experts were requested to indicate their agreement or disagreement to 'methods and activities' related to the steps involved in documentation and scientisation of ITKs. The data are presented in the table 4.3.4. (A).

It can be interpreted from Table 4.3.4. (A) that under the domain of documentation, 13 statements were identified which were agreed upon by the experts. Almost all the statements reached at consensus. Out of those 13 statements, experts expressed their cent-per-cent agreement on 9 statements i.e. Statement. No. 1, 3, 4, 5, 10, 11, 12 and 13 followed by 88.23 per cent agreement on 2nd and 8th statement and 76.47 per cent agreement on 7th statement. It might be due to the fact that most of the researches have been conducted on the lines of rapport building through tribal key informants as they are closest to the community members. Elders are being considered as the knowledge bearers of ITK so it becomes very important to contact them for documentation of ITK practices. Elders have gained this knowledge with the years of experimentations, keen observations and trial and error mechanisms with the changing bio-physical environment. Therefore, it becomes imperative to discuss ITKs

Table 4.3.4. (A): Distribution of Delphi experts according to their opinion 'methods and activities' related to documentation of ITKs

Sl.No	Methods and activities	Round 2 (n=29)		Round 3 (n=17)	
		Agree	Disagree	Agree	Disagree
	A. Documentation: Methods and Activities				
1.	Identification of villages practicing ITKs	24 (82.75)	5 (17.24)	17 (100)	0 (0)
2.	Studies on ITKs be conducted on anthropological lines	22 (75.86)	7 (24.13)	15 (88.23)	2 (11.76)
3.	Rapport building through key informants prior to interview	29 (100)	0 (0)	17 (100)	0 (0)
4.	Contacting elders of the village	21 (72.41)	8 (27.58)	17 (100)	0 (0)
5.	Interaction with elderly persons to break the silence	20 (68.96)	9 (31.03)	17 (100)	0 (0)
6.	Transect walk with elders	11 (37.93)	18 (62.06)	8 (47.05)	9 (52.94)
7.	Decide a convenient time and place for focus group discussion with farmers	22 (75.86)	7 (24.13)	13 (76.47)	4 (23.52)
8.	Document the experiences of focus group discussion	24 (82.75)	5 (17.24)	15 (88.23)	2 (11.76)
9.	Visit of fields where ITK is being practiced	24 (82.75)	5 (17.24)	17 (100)	0 (0)
10.	Note down the steps of ITKs	29 (100)	0 (0)	17 (100)	0 (0)
11.	Identify the ITK materials	29 (100)	0 (0)	17 (100)	0 (0)
12.	Videography and photography for better understanding of ITK practices	29 (100)	0 (0)	17 (100)	0 (0)
13.	Properly jot down each aspect related to ITK documentation	29 (100)	0 (0)	17 (100)	0 (0)

Figures in parentheses indicate percentages

with the authentic source of ITKs. Identification of right ITK materials and evidences through photographs for right identification and videography of each step of ITK practice for proper documentation is necessary. These steps were also proved to be standard steps for documenting ITK practices by the research evidences of **Gupta (1990)**, **Pandey *et al.* (2017) and WIPO (2017)**. ITK documentation on anthropological lines was also conducted by **Sarkar *et al.* (2015)** and **Prakash *et al.* (2021)**. Focus group discussions with the community help in identifying ITK practices. Only for the statement at Sl.No. 6, experts showed varied level of opinion i.e. 47.05 per cent agreement and 52.94 per cent disagreement. It might be due to the fact that it is difficult for elders to assist the expert to walk and discuss while walking through the length and breadth of the village due to their old age and health issues. They recommended that it would be a better option to conduct a transect walk with youths of the villages.

B. SCIENTISATION OF ITKs – METHODS AND ACTIVITIES

The process of scientisation was followed after documentation of ITKs. The scientisation process was conceptualized as a three sequential steps of particularisation, validation and generalisation. Table 4.3.4. (B) shows how the consensus was attained on different statements of 'methods and activities' related to particularisation, validation and generalisation i.e. scientisation of ITKs.

In particularisation section of 'methods and activities' domain, there were three statements out of which two i.e. 'identification of needs and problems of farmers' and 'identification of location-specific ITKs available to solve the problem prioritized' reached at cent- per-cent consensus of the experts followed by statement at Sl.No. 2 i.e. 'rank analysis for prioritizing the major problems to be solved' with 94.11 per cent of agreement. It might be due to the reason that first need and problem analysis is necessary to recommend specific ITK to solve the problem in the area. ITKs which have practical utility need to be recommended for solving the problem and particularisation of ITKs would help to screen out relevant ITKs with immediate and high problem solving attribute.

Table 4.3.4. (B): Distribution of Delphi experts according to their opinion on 'methods and activities' related to scientisation of ITKs

Sl. No	Particularisation	Round 2 (n=29)		Round 3 (n=17)	
		Agree	Disagree	Agree	Disagree
1.	Identification of needs and problems of farmers.	29 (100)	0 (0)	17 (100)	0 (0)
2.	Rank analysis for prioritizing the major problems to be solved	24 (82.75)	5 (17.24)	16 (94.11)	1 (5.88)
3.	Identification of location-specific ITKs available to solve the problem prioritized	29 (100)	0 (0)	17 (100)	0 (0)
	Validation				
1.	Framing research trials for solving the problem with ITKs and other options as treatments.	25 (86.20)	4 (13.79)	15 (88.23)	2 (11.76)
2.	Conducting trials at different locations (Multilocational trials)	23 (79.31)	6 (20.68)	14 (82.35)	3 (17.64)
3.	Assessment of technology by KVKs on farmers' field: Context, Circumstances, Situations, ITK materials, Geographic indication of materials used, genuineness, efficiency, pros and cons, sustainability, climatic adaptability, extent of adoption etc.	28 (96.55)	1 (3.44)	17 (100)	0 (0)
4.	Observing the performance	20 (68.96)	9 (31.03)	1 (5.88)	16 (94.11)
5.	If found suitable in On Farm Trials then go for Frontline Demonstrations	22 (75.86)	7 (24.13)	17 (100)	0 (0)
6.	Assess whether ITK is useful in its natural form or it requires some kind of refinement.	24 (82.75)	5 (17.24)	17 (100)	0 (0)
7.	Validation through literature search	28 (96.55)	1 (3.44)	17 (100)	0 (0)
8.	Validation through surveys	6 (20.68)	23 (79.31)	2 (11.76)	15 (88.23)
9.	Validation through Quantification of Indigenous Knowledge (QuIK)	24 (82.75)	5 (17.24)	15 (88.23)	2 (11.76)
10.	Validation through Mean Perceived Effectiveness Methodology (MPEM)	21 (72.41)	8 (27.58)	17 (100)	0 (0)
11.	Validation through field/ laboratory experimentation	18 (62.06)	11 (37.93)	16 (94.11)	1 (5.88)
12.	Refinement through blending with Corresponding Scientific Technologies.	23 (79.31)	6 (20.68)	17 (100)	0 (0)
13.	Mass validation to know the side effects	2 (6.89)	27 (93.10)	1 (5.88)	16 (94.11)

14.	Incorporation in improved package of practices	26 (89.65)	3 (10.34)	17 (100)	0 (0)
	Generalisation				
1.	The validated technologies are to be promoted in the area by training and large scale demonstrations	25 (86.20)	4 (13.79)	17 (100)	0 (0)
2.	Wide publicity to be given through ICTs	3 (10.34)	26 (89.65)	1 (5.88)	16 (94.11)
3.	Very common ITKs may be identified and comments of researchers can be taken	19 (65.51)	10 (34.48)	15 (88.23)	2 (11.76)
4.	Constitution of a National Board / Authority by the Government of India, duly authorized to call for, collect and document ITKs from all sources including the existing work done	24 (82.75)	5 (17.24)	17 (100)	0 (0)
5.	An institutional bottom up approach to be followed	27 (93.10)	2 (6.89)	17 (100)	0 (0)
6.	Successfully assessed technologies to be descended in Zonal Research Extension Advisory Committee	25 (86.20)	4 (13.79)	17 (100)	0 (0)
7.	Promotion and utilisation through various extension approaches	27 (93.10)	2 (6.89)	17 (100)	0 (0)
8.	Provision of regular appointment of experts representing agriculture, health, engineering, resource conservation and innovators	25 (86.20)	4 (13.79)	16 (94.11)	1 (5.88)
9.	Documenting the work already done	29 (100)	0 (0)	17 (100)	0 (0)
10.	Forwarding ITKs to research organizations for their validation and upgradation	28 (96.55)	1 (3.44)	17 (100)	0 (0)
11.	Protection of Intellectual Property Rights	29 (100)	0 (0)	17 (100)	0 (0)
12.	Incorporation of validated ITKs in the package of recommendations relevant to each discipline/ sectors	22 (75.86)	7 (24.13)	15 (88.23)	2 (11.76)
13.	Showcasing the ITKs through demonstrations and field days	24 (82.75)	5 (17.24)	17 (100)	0 (0)
14.	Spread the ITKs through mass media	27 (93.10)	2 (6.89)	17 (100)	0 (0)

Figures in parentheses indicate percentages

In validation section of 'methods and activities' domain, a total number of 14 statements were listed out. Majority of the statements reached at consensus which indicated successful completion of Delphi process. Of the 14 statements, seven statements (Sl.No. 3, 5, 6, 7, 10, 12 and 14) received cent-per-cent agreement of the experts. In respect of statement at Sl.No. 11, 94.11 per cent of agreement was reached followed by statements at Sl.No. 1 and 9 (88.23%) and statement at Sl.No. 2 got 82.35 percent of agreement. This is the only section where maximum number of statements attained consensus with varied level of disagreement. For statements at Sl.No. 4 and 13, the level of disagreement was 94.11 per cent followed by statement at Sl.No 4 with 88.23 per cent of disagreement.

Table 4.3.4 (B) further indicates that altogether 14 statements were listed under generalisation section of methods and activities. Statements at Sl. No. 1, 4, 5, 6, 7, 9, 10, 11, 13 and 14 received cent-per-cent agreement of the experts. However, statement at Sl.No.8 received 94.11 per cent followed by statement at Sl.No 3 and 12, 88.23 per cent of agreement of the experts. There was only one statement i.e. 'wide publicity to be given through ICTs (Sl.No.2) in this section which received consensus on disagreement received 94.11 per cent of disagreement of the experts. It might be due to the reason that tribal farmers are reluctant to adopt any new technologies because of their rigidity and traditional mindset.

b) Competencies Required for Personnel involved in ITK-related studies

The effectiveness of an extension organization is determined by the ability of extension agents to design, deliver, and evaluate effective educational programs, because they are directly serving the needs of the people. To be a successful extension staff today, one must be competent not only in technical matters, but also in areas such as management, programming, communication, human relations and leadership **(Graham, 2009 and Stone and Coppernoll, 2004)**. Keeping this in view, an attempt was made in this section to arrive at the consensus about 'competencies required' for personnel involved in ITK-related studies. The findings are presented in Table 4.3.4.2.

Results and Discussion

Table 4.3.4.2: Distribution of Delphi experts according to their opinion on 'competencies required' of personnel involved in ITK-related studies

Sl. No	Competencies Required	Round 2 (n=29)		Round 3 (n=17)	
		Agree	Disagree	Agree	Disagree
1.	Adequate knowledge about ITKs.	25 (86.20)	2 (6.89)	16 (94.11)	1 (5.88)
2.	Attitude to respect ITKs and farmers' wisdom.	29 (100)	0 (0)	17 (100)	0 (0)
3.	Orientation/training/exposure/capacity building to incorporate ITK in National Agricultural Research System (NARS)	29 (100)	0 (0)	17 (100)	0 (0)
4.	Sensitization of scientists and extension workers regarding myths attached to ITKs.	25 (86.20)	4 (13.79)	17 (100)	0 (0)
5.	Proper utilisation of funds from external agencies to promote ITK work.	10 (34.48)	19 (65.51)	7 (41.17)	8 (47.05)
6.	Designing strategies and linkages to promote ITKs through student researches.	12 (41.37)	17 (58.62)	9 (52.94)	8 (47.05)
7.	Organizing awareness campaigns for multistakeholders to deliver usefulness of ITKs	7 (24.13)	22 (75.86)	2 (11.76)	15 (88.23)
8.	Mechanism formulation for different activities related to ITK studies and their upscaling	23 (79.31)	6 (20.68)	13 (76.47)	4 (23.52)
9.	Establishment of a proper body to conduct academic activities and their monitoring for scaling up use of ITKs	19 (65.51)	10 (34.48)	10 (58.82)	7 (41.17)

Figures in parentheses indicate percentages

Table 4.3.4.2 depicts the Delphi experts' opinion on 'competencies required' of the personnel involved in ITK-related studies. Under the competencies required domain, nine statements were identified by the experts. The table shows that the experts expressed their cent-per-cent agreement with the statement i.e. 'attitude to respect ITK and farmers' wisdom', 'orientation/ training/ exposure/ capacity building to incorporate ITK in National Agricultural Research System' and 'sensitization of scientists and extension workers regarding myths attached to ITKs' followed by 'adequate knowledge about ITKs' (94.11%) and 'mechanism formulation for different activities related to ITK studies and their upscaling' (76.47%).

This might be due to the reason that many extension workers are not aware of the existence of ITKs in related field as those who possessed knowledge, remain isolated from the mainstream society so adequate knowledge is needed through literature and capacity building programmes. Sensitization is required to change the negative attitude towards ITK being illogical, impractical, outdated and unscientific. Technological packages containing ITK recommendations from agricultural extension system is still lacking so formulation of recommendations based on ITK practices should be made and sensitised through awareness campaigns, trainings, demonstrations and farmer field schools.

Table 4.3.4.2 further shows that varied opinions were emerged in this domain as there were no major demarcation between the level of agreement and disagreement for the statements like 'designing strategies and linkages to promote ITKs through student researches' (52.94% for agreement) and (47.05% for disagreement) and 'establishment of a proper body to conduct academic activities and their monitoring for scaling up use of ITKs' achieved 58.82 per cent for agreement and 41.17 per cent for disagreement respectively. It might be due to the fact that the student researches are not well recognised by the promotional agencies and also lack policy support to be incorporated in the NARS. These facts are in line with the suggestions given by **Arya (2008) and Yolmo (2013) and Anbu *et al.* (2018). Hill *et al.* (2020)** who also recommended the requirement for experts that boundary-crossing and bridging knowledge systems are also required.

c) Institutional Mechanism required for ITK-related studies

Under this section, opinion of the Delphi experts' were sought on different statements related to 'institutional mechanism' required for ITK-related studies. The findings are presented in Table 4.3.4.3.

Data presented in the Table 4.3.4.3 show that under 'institutional mechanism' domain of ITK documentation and scientisation (particularisation, validation and generalisation), a total number of 20 statements were identified by the experts. Almost all the statements reached at consensus in the third round. The experts expressed their cent-per-cent agreement on the statements related to 'formation of FPOs/ FIGs/ SHGs/ Forums of ITK wisdom bearers', 'Gram Panchayats should take a lead in popularising ITKs', 'scouts should be utilised', 'a national level institute should be established for coordinating ITK researches', 'village schools should be involved in ITK-related activities', 'package of practices should be formulated taking ITKs into consideration', 'Zonal Research Stations should include ITKs in their experiments', 'a common networking platform should be established', 'linkages of national and international bodies should be initiated and strengthened', 'village clusters should be formed to practice ITKs', 'a national authority should be established', 'computerized and updated database' and 'methodological procedures should be clearly defined' and 'OFT/FLDs should be properly designed'. As it was felt that it would pave the ways for integration of ITKs in development process. It was followed by "farmer-scientist interaction" and "role of KVKs in validation and ATMA in dissemination of ITKs (94.11%) and "ITK cell in every R&D organisations (88.23%)" and "specific portals should be designed (76.47%)". Since the recognition of ITK has just started scratching the surface so recent advancements with mobile apps and websites would take time to come into force, majority of experts expressed their disagreement (88.23%) on designing and developing mobile apps for ITK work. Similarly the experts expressed their disagreement (88.23%) with the statement that farmer radio clubs should be organised as the ITK work has to start first from grassroots' level with full participation of the community.

Table 4.3.4.3: Distribution of Delphi experts according to their opinion on 'institutional mechanism' required for ITK-related studies

Sl. No.	Institutional mechanism	Round 2 (n=29)		Round 3 (n=17)	
		Agree	Disagree	Agree	Disagree
1.	FPOs/FIGs/Clubs/Cooperatives/Forums of ITK wisdom bearers should be formed	26 (89.65)	3 (10.35)	17 (100)	0 (0)
2.	Gram Panchayats should take a lead to popularize ITKs	29 (100)	0 (0)	17 (100)	0 (0)
3.	Farmer-Scientist interaction is required	24 (82.75)	5 (17.25)	16 (94.11)	1 (5.89)
4.	Scouts should be utilised	25 (86.20)	4 (13.8)	17 (100)	0 (0)
5.	Farmer Radio Clubs should be organised	13 (44.82)	16 (55.18)	2 (11.76)	15 (88.24)
6.	Role of KVKs in validation and ATMA in dissemination of ITKs should be ensured	24 (82.75)	5 (17.25)	16 (94.11)	1 (5.89)
7.	Village schools should be involved in ITK-related activities	22 (75.86)	7 (24.15)	17 (100)	0 (0)
8.	A national level institute should be established for coordinating ITK researches	29 (100)	0 (0)	17 (100)	0 (0)
9.	Package of practices should be formulated taking ITKs into consideration	25 (86.26)	4 (13.8)	17 (100)	0 (0)
10.	Zonal Research Stations should include ITKs in their experiments	29 (100)	0 (0)	17 (100)	0 (0)
11.	A common networking platform should be established	27 (93.10)	2 (6.9)	17 (100)	0 (0)
12.	Linkage of national and international bodies should be initiated and strengthened	29 (100)	0 (0)	17 (100)	0 (0)
13.	Village clusters should be formed to practice ITKs	26 (89.65)	3 (10.35)	17 (100)	0 (0)
14.	A national authority should be established	29 (100)	0 (0)	17 (100)	0 (0)
15.	ITK cell in every R&D organisations should be established	22 (75.86)	7 (24.14)	15 (88.26)	2 (11.76)
16.	Computerised & updated database facilities should be created	29 (100)	0 (0)	17 (100)	0 (0)
17.	Methodological procedures should be clearly defined	29 (100)	0 (0)	17 (100)	0 (0)
18.	On-Farm Trials/Frontline Demonstrations should be properly designed	28 (96.55)	1 (3.45)	17 (100)	0 (0)
19.	Specific portals should be designed	20 (68.97)	9 (31.03)	13 (76.47)	4 (23.53)
20.	Mobile Apps should be developed	8 (27.59)	21 (72.41)	2 (11.77)	15 (88.23)

Figures in parentheses indicate percentages

Results and Discussion ....

An informal discussion with the experts revealed that the ITK related activities i.e. documentation, particularisation, validation and their generalisation should be chalked out with the active participation of farmers and scientists. Then efforts should be made to digitalize the ITKs and disseminate them through ICTs. **Bhan *et al.* (2016)** suggested that there is an urgent need to have institutional reforms especially for better coordination, convergence and efficiency in action in recognizing and encouraging the scientific talents behind such grassroot level ITKs across the country. These results are also in concurrence with those of **Talukdar *et al.* (2012)** who highlighted need for an apex body to regulate ITK-related work and **Baliwada *et al.* (2017)** who also recommended appropriate strategies related to policy formulation to improve the accessibility of indigenous knowledge for all the key actors. **Balakrishnan *et al.* (2020)** designed a user friendly database for ITK in agriculture for the multi stakeholders' viz. researchers, extension workers, academicians, policymakers, farmers, NGO etc as a resource base of ITKs.

d) Criteria for Documentation and Scientisation of ITKs

In the process of scientisation, several 'criteria' are used in the methods of documentation and scientisation (i.e. particularisation, validation and generalisation) of ITKs. Thus it was decided to elicit the criteria perceived important by the Delphi experts and further they were asked to indicate their agreement/disagreement with the particulars elicited by them. The findings are presented in the Table 4.3.4.4.

As it appears from Table 4.3.4.4 that altogether 16 statements were considered under the broad domain of 'criteria' to be used for systematic documentation, particularisation, validation and generalisation of ITKs. In the Round 3, there was consensus among the experts with regard to all the statements. The experts showed their cent-per-cent agreement with items at Sl.No. 1 2, 3, 4, 5, 6, 7, 9, 12, 13, 14 and 16. Furthermore 'ability of ITK for large scale demonstrations' (94.11%) followed by 'marketability of ITK' (88.23%), 'problem solving ability of ITK' and suitability of ITK for validation (76.47%) of agreement was expressed by the experts. The results of the criteria domain are in line with the findings of **Pradhan *et al.* (2017) and Ansari *et al.* (2021).**

Table 4.3.4.4: Distribution of Delphi experts according to their opinion on 'criteria' for documentation and scientisation of ITKs

Sl.No.	Criteria	Round 2 (n=29)		Round 3 (n=17)	
		Agree	Disagree	Agree	Disagree
1.	Genuinity of the ITK	26 (89.65)	3 (10.34)	17 (100)	0 (0)
2.	Utility of ITK	29 (100)	0 (0)	17 (100)	0 (0)
3.	Pros and cons of ITK	29 (100)	0 (0)	17 (100)	0 (0)
4.	Extent of adoption of ITK	29 (100)	0 (0)	17 (100)	0 (0)
5.	Sustainability of ITK	29 (100)	0 (0)	17 (100)	0 (0)
6.	Environmental impact of the ITK	24 (82.75)	5 (17.24)	17 (100)	0 (0)
7.	Easy availability of ITK materials	25 (86.20)	4 (13.79)	17 (100)	0 (0)
8.	Ability of ITK for large scale demonstration	26 (89.65)	3 (10.34)	16 (94.11)	1 (5.88)
9.	Compatibility with internal household resources	29 (100)	0 (0)	17 (100)	0 (0)
10.	Marketability of ITK	23 (79.31)	6 (20.68)	15 (88.23)	2 (11.76)
11.	Problem solving ability of ITK	19 (65.51)	10 (34.48)	13 (76.47)	4 (23.53)
12.	Trialability of ITK	23 (79.31)	6 (20.68)	17 (100)	0 (0)
13.	Compatibility with farming system component	29 ((100)	0 (0)	17 (100)	0 (0)
14.	Accessibility of ITK	29 (100)	0 (0)	17 (100)	0 (0)
15.	Suitability for validation	23 (79.31)	6 (20.68)	13 (76.47)	4 (23.53)
16.	Suitability for recording	26 (89.65)	3 (10.35)	17 (100)	0 (0)

Figures in parentheses indicate percentages

e) Barriers in ITK-related studies

Keeping in view several constraints and obstacles in the process of ITK-related studies, an effort was made to identify 'barriers' in the way of ITK-related studies. The findings are presented in Table 4.3.4.5.

Data presented in Table 4.3.4.5 indicate that a total number of 25 statements were identified under the domain of 'barriers' that might obstruct the work of systematic documentation, particularisation, validation and generalisation of ITKs. Out of 25 statements listed in this section, the experts expressed cent-per-cent agreement on 19 statements (Sl.No. 1, 3, 4, 6, 7, 8, 11, 12, 13, 14, 15, 16, 17, 18, 19, 20, 21, 23 and 25). Poor accessibility of ITKs is due to low interest among the users as they are attracted to modern lifestyle and did not want to follow the legacy of traditional farming, ITK wisdom bearers do not want to disclose ITKs to other members (100% agreement) to maintain monopoly in the community. Low profits and returns (100% agreement) are also a major reason behind the restricted use of ITKs. People are not aware of the utility of ITKs (100% agreement) and how sustainable it is. Scientists are advised to recommend and research on modern farming practices, no proper and complete information is available on ITKs and over adoption of modern practices are the prime reasons that hinder the use of ITKs. This implies that the development workers should confirm about the relevance and importance of the research dedicated to ITK work from time to time. Low efficacy in comparison to CSTs, no blending and restricted use due to geographical limitations, IPR issues (94.11%) followed by farmers' reluctance to share and lack of role model (88.23%), negative attitude of stakeholders towards ITK (76.47%) attained agreement. The constraints identified by the experts are similar to that of **Shanjeevika *et al.* (2019) and Sujeetha and Asokhan (2020).**

Table 4.3.4.5: Distribution of Delphi experts according to their opinion on 'barriers' in ITK-related studies

Sl. No.	Barriers	Round 2 (n=29) Agree	Round 2 (n=29) Disagree	Round 3 (n=17) Agree	Round 3 (n=17) Disagree
1.	Lack of knowledge about ITK in terms of environment conservation	27 (93.10)	2 (6.89)	17 (100)	0 (0)
2.	Negative attitude of stakeholders towards ITK	20 (68.96)	9 (31.03)	13 (76.47)	4 (23.52)
3.	Lack of skill to prepare ITK formulations	29 (100)	0 (0)	17 (100)	0 (0)
4.	Inability to identify ITK materials	28 (96.55)	1 (3.44)	17 (100)	0 (0)
5.	Low efficacy in comparison to corresponding scientific technologies	24 (82.75)	3 (10.34)	16 (94.11)	1 (5.88)
6.	Low productivity of ITK	21 (72.41)	8 (27.58)	17 (100)	0 (0)
7.	Lack of awareness about ITK	29 (100)	0 (0)	17 (100)	0 (0)
8.	Lack of value addition opportunities	28 (96.55)	1 (3.44)	17 (100)	0 (0)
9.	No blending with corresponding scientific technology	19 (65.51)	10 (34.48)	16 (94.11)	1 (5.88)
10.	Restricted use of ITK	22 (75.86)	7 (24.13)	16 (94.11)	1 (5.88)
11.	Secretly used by some communities/experts	26 (89.65)	3 (10.34)	17 (100)	0 (0)
12.	Lack of interest of scientific community	20 (68.96)	9 (31.03)	17 (100)	0 (0)
13.	Lack of national institution	21 (72.41)	8 (27.58)	17 (100)	0 (0)
14.	Lack of authorities	24 (82.75)	5 (17.24)	17 (100)	0 (0)
15.	Many works done till date is on library shelfs with no use	29 (100)	0 (0)	17 (100)	0 (0)
16.	No proper description	25 (86.20)	4 (13.79)	17 (100)	0 (0)
17.	No standard procedures for ITK related work	26 (89.65)	3 (10.34)	17 (100)	0 (0)
18.	Location-specificity so difficulty in large scale adoption	28 (96.55)	1 (3.44)	17 (100)	0 (0)
19.	Overdependence on corresponding scientific technologies	29 (100)	0 (0)	17 (100)	0 (0)
20.	Extinction of many ITK plant materials	25 (86.20)	4 (13.79)	17 (100)	0 (0)
21.	Unscientific claims in respecting ITKs	26 (89.65)	3 (10.34)	17 (100)	0 (0)
22.	Intellectual Property Right issues	21 (72.41)	8 (27.58)	16 (94.11)	1 (5.88)
23.	Low profitability	18 (62.06)	11 (37.93)	17 (100)	0 (0)
24.	Lack of role model	20 (68.96)	9 (31.03)	15 (88.23)	2 (11.76)
25.	No cooperation from fellow farmers	26 (89.65)	3 (10.34)	17 (100)	0 (0)

Figures in parentheses indicate percentages

Chatwood *et al.* (2015) for the very first time highlighted the importance of consensus based, mixed method to explore about the significance of indigenous knowledge. Similarly **Sharghi *et al.* (2010)** applied Delphi method to identify the effective factors in achieving sustainable agriculture. They identified a total of 35 factors which were categorized into policy-making, infrastructure, researches, education, extension, economical, social and cooperation. **Diab and Ghany (2014)** conducted a study on work environment and competencies necessary for agricultural extension in Egypt using Delphi technique. In this study also, consensus was attained at round 3. The results are in concurrence with the methods and categorisation adopted by **Buriak ansd Shinn (1993)** in their study on structuring research for agricultural education using national Delphi involving internal experts. The results are also in line with the steps used by **Vogel *et al.* (2019) and Roberts and Dyer (2004)**.

4.4. Scientisation of Indigenous Technical Knowledge about pest and disease management among tribal farmers.

4.4.1. Particularisation of ITKs

Particularisation is a process of identifying and sorting out the ITKs which can be utilised for sustainable agricultural development. Thus it was decided to find out the extent of scientific rationality of selected ITKs and for this all the listed ITKs were mailed to 30 plant protection scientists to adjudge its rationality on three types of selected scales developed by different social scientists. The three scales were: a) three point rating scale developed by **Dhaliwal and Singh (2010)** b) four point rating scale of **Venkatesan and Sundaramarai (2014)** and c) five point rating scale of **Hiranand (1979)**. All the three rating scales were used to see the differences/consistency in the opinion of scientists that may vary on different scales.

4.4.1.1 Rationality analysis on a 3-point scale of Dhaliwal and Singh (2010)

The 3-point rating scale of Dhaliwal and Singh (2010) had 3 continuum i.e. the score of 3 was assigned to highly rational ITK, score 2 to moderately rational ITK and 1 score was given to irrational ITK. The ITKs which scored total rationality score more than 60 was deliberated as rational and which scored less than 60 were deliberated as irrational by the plant protection scientists. The findings of the rationality analysis of all 44 ITKs on 3-point continuum scale developed by Dhaliwal and Singh are presented below in Table 4.4.1.1.

Table 4.4.1.1: Rationality scores obtained by selected ITKs on a 3-point continuum

(n=30)

Sl.No	Pest / disease - wise ITK	HR (3)	MR (2)	IR (1)	Total Rationality scores
	Rice hispa (*Dicladispa armigera*)				
1.	After observing whitening of paddy leaves during vegetative phase, fresh leaves of *Parasi* (*Cleistanthus collinus*) are broadcast in the field to control Rice hispa.	26	4	0	86 (R)
2.	Application of *Baska* i.e. by-product of mahua (*Madhuca indica*) is done to control Rice hispa.	24	6	0	84 (R)
3.	Crushed fruits of *Kendu* trees are applied in paddy field to control Rice hispa.	27	3	0	87 (R)
4.	*Basi mar* is sprayed to control rice hispa.	0	1	29	31 (IR)
5.	Dusting of sand and kerosene oil mixture is done to control Rice hispa.	0	2	28	32 (IR)
	Gundhi bug *(Leptocorisa acuta)*				
6.	Discarded rubber tyres are burnt by holding it in hands to control Gundhi bug *(Leptocorisa acuta)*.	0	3	27	33 (IR)
7.	Neem (*Azadirachta indica*) flowers are tied in small bundles at 5-6 places in the field to control Gundhi bug in paddy.	24	6	0	84 (R)
8.	Branches of *Bhelwa* tree ((*Semecarpus anacardium*) are planted in rice fields to protect it from Lahi and Gundhi bugs.	24	6	0	84 (R)
9.	Dead snake is hanged by the side of the rice field to control Gundhi bug (*Leptocorisa acuta*).	0	0	3	30 (IR)
	Banki disease of rice *(Pyricularia oryzae)*				
10.	Leaves of Neem (*Azadirachta indica*) are spread in the paddy field to control *Banki* disease *(Pyricularia oryzae)*.	29	1	0	89 (R)
11.	*Sandhana* i.e. Bamboo ((*Bambusa vulgaris*) rhizome pieces mixed with water and sprinkled over the affected plants to control *Banki* disease in rice *(Pyricularia oryzae)*.	28	2	0	88 (R)

		Rice caseworm *(Nymphula depunctalis)*			
12.	Kerosene oil soaked chord is used to control rice caseworm *(Nymphula depunctalis)*	0	0	30	30 (IR)
13.	*Sinduwar* leaves are boiled in water and then cooled and the solution is sprayed on Rice to control paddy caseworm *(Nymphula depunctalis)*.	22	8	0	82 (R)
14.	Solution of *Karil* (tender bamboo shoot extract) soaked in water is sprayed in affected paddy field to control rice caseworm (*Nymphula depunctalis*).	24	6	0	84 (R)
15.	Control of rice caseworm by spreading fresh *Parsu (Cleistanthus collinuus)* and *Sali (Boswellia serrata)* leaves in the field.	26	6	0	90 (R)
16.	Branches of Cashewnut are put in the standing paddy crop to control different insects-pests.	23	7	0	83 (R)
17.	*Karanj (Millettia pinnata)*, *Bhelwa (Semacarpus anacardium)* and *Arjun (Terminalia arjuna)* trees are grown along the bunds to control common insects-pests of field crops.	0	2	28	32 (IR)
	Termites *(Coptotermes formosansus)*				
18.	Flooding of paddy field helps in controlling termites (*Coptotermes formosansus*) by disrupting their life cycle.	27	3	0	87 (R)
19.	Horse droppings are mixed with soil during field preparation for Sugarcane cultivation to control termite infestation	29	1	0	89 (R)
20.	To control ants/termites, paddy field is ploughed by desi plough made up of Neem (*Azadirachta indica*) wood.	2	8	22	42 (IR)
	Bihar hairy caterpillar (*Spilosoma oblique*)				
21.	Red colour insects and Bihar hairy caterpillar (*Spilosoma oblique*) is controlled by applying mixture of wood ash and kerosene oil when insects appear on leaves of Cucumber and Bottle gourd crops.	24	6	0	84 (R)
22.	Ash is dusted over Bihar hairy caterpillar (*Spilosoma oblique*) to control it.	16	14	0	76 (R)
23.	Mixture of *Sinduwar* leaves (*Vitex negundo*), sand and kerosene oil is used to control Bihar hairy caterpillar (*Spilosoma oblique*).	27	3	0	87 (R)

Results and Discussion ....

		Potato blight (*Phytophthora infestans*)			
24.	Wood ash is dusted on the leaves at night to control potato blight.	29	1	0	89 (R)
25.	Mixture of wood ash and *Karanj* (*Millettia pinnata*) cake powder is applied on leaves under cloudy conditions to control potato blight.	30	0	0	90 (R)
		Storage			
26.	Dried neem leaves (Azadirachta indica) are mixed with dried wheat seeds to control it from weevil during storage.	28	2	0	88 (R)
27.	Maize (*Zea mays*) cobs are hanged over the chulha (hearth) of the household to get smoke to keep insects-pests away from Maize cobs.	29	1	0	89 (R)
28.	Use of *Bharbhari* (Ocunyn cabyn simo) and *Sinduwar* (*Vitex negundo*) leaves is done for storing grains including pulses	30	0	0	90 (R)
29.	Blackgram is protected from insects by storing it with Fingermillet.	24	6	0	84 (R)
		Leaf eating caterpillar in vegetables			
30.	Extract of Neem leaves (*Azadirachta indica*) is sprayed on vegetable leaves to control leaf-eating caterpillars in cabbage and cauliflower.	22	8	0	82 (R)
31.	Ash of wood or cow dung mixed with kerosene oil is applied on vegetable crops or fruit trees to repel/kill insects-pests.	0	0	30	30 (IR)
		Aphids *(Aphis gossypii)*			
32.	Cooled extract of boiled *Sinduwar* leaves (*Vitex negundo*) and water is sprayed to control aphids in pumpkin, bottlegourd, beans etc.	26	4	0	86 (R)
33.	Cowdung and ash is broadcast on vegetable crops to control insect jugnu.	0	0	30	30 (IR)
		Shoot borer in rice			
34.	Solution of leaves and seeds of Custard apple *(Annona squamosa)* are sprayed to control insects/pests of paddy crop.	19	11	2	79 (R)
35.	Solution of decayed bamboo suckers/young stems with water is applied in field to control pests in paddy.	22	8	0	78 (R)

Results and Discussion ....

		Shoot and fruit borer in vegetables			
36.	Tobacco soaked water with soap/detergent is sprayed on the affected plants for controlling shoot and fruit borers in vegetables.	28	2	0	88 (R)
37.	Mixture of starch, urine and cow dung is sprayed on vegetable plants to control insects/pests.	0	5	25	35 (IR)
38.	Ash of wood is mixed with soil to control insects.	1	6	23	38 (IR)
		Rice gall fly			
39.	Fresh leaves of *Parso/ Persu* (*Creistanthus collinus*) are spread in rice field to control gall fly.	27	3	0	87 (R)
40.	*Sinduwar* (*Vitex negundo*) leaves are broadcast in the paddy field when the plant turn yellow, shoots become dry and pant growth is stunted due to attack of tissue borer, paddy gall fly, rice-root aphid and mealy bugs.	23	7	0	83 (R)
		Soil treatment and nursery raising			
41.	Sterilisation of nursery plots by burning paddy straw after first ploughing to control insects/pests in rice field.	4	9	17	47 (IR)
42.	Powder of Neem (*Azadirachta indica*) and Karanj (*Pongamia pinnata*) cake are mixed with soil while field preparation.	21	8	1	80 (R)
43.	Nursery soil is sterilised by burning of straw and husk of paddy, wheat or fingermillet.	21	9		81 (R)
44.	Plough made up of *Kendu* wood is used to control soil borne insects/pests.	0	0	30	30 (IR)

HR- Highly Rational - 3, MR- Moderately Rational - 2 and Irrational – 1, R- Rational and IR- Irrational

It can be elucidated from Table 4.4.1.1 that in the management of Rice hispa, a total number of five ITKs were documented from the study area. Out of these, three ITKs i.e. ITK 3 (TRS=87) got highest rationality score followed by ITK 1 (TRS=86) and ITK 2 (TRS=84). Two ITKs i.e. ITK 4 (TRS=31) and ITK 5 (RS=32) were found to be irrational. It might be due to the reason that scientists found no logical evidence to support them as having scientific rationality to be used as interventions for sustainable agricultural development. So ITK 3, 1 and 2 having high rationality scores (i.e. TRS ≥ 60) were screened out for further validation and ITK 4 and 5 (i.e. TRS < 60) were discarded by the scientists.

For treating the menace of Gundhi Bug, four ITKs were found to be practiced by the tribal farming community of the study area. Rationality analysis revealed that ITK 7 and 8 (RS=84) got highest rationality score (i.e. TRS ≥ 60) followed by ITK 6 (TRS=33) and ITK 9 (TRS=30). Scientists discarded ITK 6 and 9 (i.e. TRS < 60) for further validation. Rest two i.e. ITK 7 and 8 (i.e. TRS ≥ 60) were screened out for the next step of scientisation i.e. validation.

For the eco-friendly management of Banki disease of Rice, two ITKs were found to practiced by tribal farmers of the study area. Both the ITKs i.e. ITK 10 (TRS=89) and ITK 11 (TRS=88) were found to be highly rational (i.e. TRS ≥ 60). So scientists recommended to accept both the ITKs for validation.

In Rice caseworm management, six ITKs were prevalent among the tribal farming community. Out of those 6, ITK 15 (TRS=87) got highest rationality score followed by ITK 14 (TRS=90), ITK 16 (TRS=83) and ITK 13 (TRS=82). ITK 12 (TRS=30) and ITK 17 (TRS=32) were found to be irrational by the scientists. For scientisation, it was recommended to discard ITK 12 and 17 having low rationality scores (i.e. TRS < 60).

For the treatment of termites, three ITKs were practiced by the tribal farmers. Out of three, ITK 19 (TRS=89) scored highest in rationality analysis followed by ITK 17 (TRS=87) and ITK 20 (TRS=42). So for further validation ITK 18 and 19 were accepted and ITK 20 having lowest rationality score was discarded (i.e. TRS < 60).

Bihar hairy caterpillar was a major pest found in the study area. For its control, tribal farming communities were using three ITKs which were documented. Rationality analysis of these three ITKs affirmed that ITK 23 (TRS=87 ITK) scored highest followed by ITK 21 (TRS=84) and ITK 23 (TRS=76). Scientists suggested to accept all the three ITKs (i.e. TRS ≥ 60) for validation.

For Potato blight infestation, two ITKs were documented from the study area. ITK 25 (TRS=90) was analysed to be highly rational followed by ITK 24 (TRS=89). Both ITK 24 and 25 were accepted for validation by the scientists (i.e. TRS ≥ 60).

To combat storage pest infestation, four ITKs were documented from the tribal farmers of the study area. All of them were found to be highly rational by plant protection scientists. ITK 28 (TRS=90) scored highest among all the ITKs followed by ITK 27 (TRS=89), ITK 26 (TRS=88) and ITK 29 (TRS=84) respectively. Therefore all the four ITKs (i.e. TRS ≥ 60) were taken up for the validation process.

For eradication of leaf eating caterpillar in vegetables, tribal farmers were practicising two ITKs. In rationality analysis, ITK 30 (TRS=82) was found to be highly rational and ITK 31 (TRS=30) was found to be irrational. So ITK 30 was accepted and ITK 31 (i.e. TRS < 60) was discarded for the next stage of scientisation.

To deal with the problem of aphids, ITK 32 (TRS=86) and ITK 33 (TRS=30) were practiced by the tribal farmers. Scientists recommended to accept ITK 32 for validation but discarded ITK 33 for having lowest rationality score (i.e. TRS < 60).

To manage shoot borer infestation in Rice, two ITKs were reported from the study area. Both the ITKs, i.e. ITK 34 (TRS=79) and ITK 35 (TRS=78) were found to be rational (i.e. TRS ≥ 60), so they were further recommended for acceptance for validation process.

Three ITKs were documented from the study area for controlling shoot and fruit borer infestation in vegetables. Out of those three, ITK 36 (TRS=88) was found to be rational whereas ITK 38 (TRS=38) and ITK 37 (TRS=35) were found to be irrational and hence, discarded for validation.

Rice Gall Fly infestation was controlled by tribal farmers by following ITK 39 and ITK 40. Rationality analysis of both the ITKs affirmed that both were found to be rational as ITK 39 (TRS=87) and ITK 40 (TRS=83) scored high. As a result, both the ITKs (i.e. TRS ≥ 60) were accepted for validation.

For soil treatment and nursery raising, four ITKs practiced by the tribal farmers of study area were documented. Rationality analysis results revealed that ITK

43 (TRS=81) scored highest followed by ITK 42 (TRS=80) and both were deemed to be rational by the scientists. ITK 41 (TRS=47) and ITK 44 (TRS=30) were found to be irrational and were discarded by the scientists for the next step.

The results presented in Table 4.4.1.1 have been summarized in Table 4.4.1.2 on the basis of rationality scores.

Table 4.4.1.2: Distribution of ITKs according to rationality categories of 3-point continuum

Category	Rationality scores	No of ITKs	Result
Rational	≥ 60	31 (70.45)	Accepted
Irrational	< 60	13 (29.55)	Discarded

Figures in parentheses indicate percentages

Thus it can be concluded that scientists exhibited varied levels of rationality on different ITKs about pest and disease management. Altogether 31 ITKs (70.45%) scored above 60, which indicated that these were scientifically rational and rest 13 (29.55%) were rated to be irrational and discarded by the scientists. The results are in line with those of **Dhaliwal *et al.* (2004), Ponnusamy *et al.* (2009) and Pradhan *et al.* (2016), Praveen *et al.* (2018)** and **Sah *et al.* (2019),** who also found maximum number of ITKs to be rational on a 3-point continuum. This indicated that majority of the ITKs were having greater degree of scientific rationality.

4.4.2 Rationality analysis on a 4-point scale of Venkatesan and Sundaramari (2014)

An effort was made to obtain the plant protection scientists' response towards scientific rationality of selected ITKs on a 4-point scale developed by Venkatesan and Sundaramari (2014). The ITKs which scored weighted mean scores 2.5 and above were deliberated as rational and those scored less than 2.5 were deliberated as irrational. Perusal of Table 4.4.2.1 shows the rationality scores of selected ITKs about pest and disease management on a 4-point continuum.

Table 4.4.2.1: Rationality scores obtained by selected ITKs on a 4-point continuum

(n=30)

S.No	Pest / disease - wise ITK	4	3	2	1	Total score	WMS
	Rice hispa (*Dicladispa armigera*)						
1.	After observing whitening of paddy leaves during vegetative phase, fresh leaves of *Parasi (Cleistanthus collinus)* are broadcast in the field to control Rice hispa.	30	-	-	-	120	4.00 (R)
2.	Application of *Baska* i.e. by-product of mahua *(Madhuca indica)* is done to control Rice hispa.	27	3	-	-	117	3.90 (R)
3.	Crushed fruits of *Kendu* trees are applied in paddy field to control Rice hispa.	29	1	-	-	119	3.96 (R)
4.	*Basi mar* is sprayed to control Rice hispa.	-	-	3	27	33	1.10 (IR)
5.	Dusting of sand and kerosene oil mixture is done to control Rice hispa.	-	1	27	2	59	1.96 (IR)
	Gundhi bug (*Leptocorisa acuta*)						
6.	Discarded rubber tyres are burnt by holding it in hands to control Gundhi bug *(Leptocorisa acuta)*.	-	-	29	1	60	2.00 (IR)
7.	Neem *(Azadirachta indica)* flowers are tied in small bundles at 5-6 places in the field to control Gundhi bug in paddy.	25	3	1	1	112	3.73 (R)
8.	Branches of *Bhelwa* tree *((Semecarpus anacardium)* are planted in rice fields to protect it from Lahi and Gundhi bugs.	30	-	-	-	120	4.00 (R)
9.	Dead snake is hanged by the side of the rice field to control Gundhi bug *(Leptocorisa acuta)*.	1	1	27	1	61	2.03 (IR)
	Banki disease of rice (*Pyricularia oryzae*)						
10.	Leaves of Neem *(Azadirachta indica)* are spread in the paddy field to control *Banki* disease *(Pyricularia oryzae)*.	15	12	1	2	59	1.96 (IR)
11.	*Sandhana* i.e. Bamboo *((Bambusa vulgaris)* rhizome pieces mixed with water and sprinkled over the affected plants to control *Banki* disease in rice *(Pyricularia oryzae)*.	27	2	1	-	100	3.33 (R)

	Rice caseworm *(Nymphula depunctalis)*					
12.	Kerosene oil soaked chord is used to control rice caseworm *(Nymphula depunctalis)*	-	2	25	3	116	3.86 (R)
13.	*Sinduwar* leaves are boiled in water and then cooled and the solution is sprayed on Rice to control paddy caseworm *(Nymphula depunctalis)*.	26	1	2	1	59	1.96 (IR)
14.	Solution of *Karil* (tender bamboo shoot extract) soaked in water is sprayed in affected paddy field to control rice caseworm *(Nymphula depunctalis)*.	26	2	2	-	112	3.73 (R)
15.	Control of rice caseworm by spreading fresh *Parsu (Cleistanthus collinuus)* and *Sali (Boswellia serrata)* leaves in the field.	19	2	7	2	114	3.80 (R)
16.	Branches of Cashewnut are put in the standing paddy crop to control different insects-pests.	30	-	-	-	120	4.00 (R)
17.	*Karanj (Millettia pinnata)*, *Bhelwa (Semacarpus anacardium)* and *Arjun (Terminalia arjuna)* trees are grown along the bunds to control common insects-pests of field crops.	-	-	-	30	30	1.00 (IR)
	Termites *(Coptotermes formosansus)*						
18.	Flooding of paddy field helps in controlling termites *(Coptotermes formosansus)* by disrupting their life cycle.	21	9	-	-	111	3.70 (R)
19.	Horse droppings are mixed with soil during field preparation for Sugarcane cultivation to control termite infestation	30	-	-	-	120	4.00 (R)
20.	To control ants/termites, paddy field is ploughed by desi plough made up of Neem *(Azadirachta indica)* wood.	-	1	2	27	34	1.13 (IR)
	Bihar hairy caterpillar (*Spilosoma oblique*)						
21.	Red colour insects and Bihar hairy caterpillar *(Spilosoma oblique)* is controlled by applying mixture of wood ash and kerosene oil when insects appear on leaves of Cucumber and Bottle gourd crops.	27	3	-	-	117	3.90 (R)
22.	Ash is dusted over Bihar hairy caterpillar *(Spilosoma oblique)* to control it.	27	3	-	-	117	3.90 (R)
23.	Mixture of *Sinduwar* leaves *(Vitex negundo)*, sand and kerosene oil is used to control Bihar hairy caterpillar *(Spilosoma oblique)*.	26	1	2	1	112	3.73 (R)

Results and Discussion ....

	Potato blight (*Phytophthora infestans*)					
24.	Wood ash is dusted on the leaves at night to control potato blight.	26	4	-	-	116	3.86 (R)
25.	Mixture of wood ash and *Karanj* (*Millettia pinnata*) cake powder is applied on leaves under cloudy conditions to control potato blight.	26	1	2	1	112	3.73 (R)
	Storage					
26.	Dried neem leaves (Azadirachta indica) are mixed with dried wheat seeds to control it from weevil during storage.	29	1	-	-	119	3.96 (R)
27.	Maize (*Zea mays*) cobs are hanged over the chulha (hearth) of the household to get smoke to keep insects-pests away from Maize cobs.	27	3	-	-	117	3.96 (R)
28.	Use of *Bharbhari* (Ocunyn cabyn simo) and *Sinduwar* (*Vitex negundo*) leaves is done for storing grains including pulses	26	1	2	1	112	3.73 (R)
29.	Blackgram is protected from insects by storing it with Fingermillet.	28	2	-	-	118	3.93 (R)
	Leaf eating caterpillar in vegetables					
30.	Extract of Neem leaves (*Azadirachta indica*) is sprayed on vegetable leaves to control leaf-eating caterpillars in cabbage and cauliflower.	30	-	-	-	120	4.00 (R)
31.	Ash of wood or cow dung mixed with kerosene oil is applied on vegetable crops or fruit trees to repel/kill insects-pests.	-	-	-	30	30	1.00 (IR)
	Aphids *(Aphis gossypii)*					
32.	Cooled extract of boiled *Sinduwar* leaves (*Vitex negundo*) and water is sprayed to control aphids in pumpkin, bottlegourd, beans etc.	27	3	-	-	117	3.90 (R)
33.	Cowdung and ash is broadcast on vegetable crops to control insect jugnu.	-	-	4	26	34	1.13 (IR)
	Shoot borer in rice					
34.	Solution of leaves and seeds of Custard apple (*Annona squamosa*) are sprayed to control insects/pests of paddy crop.	30	-	-	-	120	4.00 (R)
35.	Solution of decayed bamboo suckers/young stems with water is applied in field to control pests in paddy.	29	1	-	-	119	3.96 (R)

	Shoot and fruit borer in vegetables						
36.	Tobacco soaked water with soap/detergent is sprayed on the affected plants for controlling shoot and fruit borers in vegetables.	27	3	-	-	117	3.90 (R)
37.	Mixture of starch, urine and cow dung is sprayed on vegetable plants to control insects/pests.	-	3	24	3	60	2.00 (IR)
38.	Ash of wood is mixed with soil to control insects.	-	1	25	4	57	1.90 (IR)
	Rice gall fly						
39.	Fresh leaves of *Parso/ Persu* (*Creistanthus collinus*) are spread in rice field to control gall fly.	27	3	-	-	117	3.90 (R)
40.	*Sinduwar (Vitex negundo)* leaves are broadcast in the paddy field when the plant turn yellow, shoots become dry and pant growth is stunted due to attack of tissue borer, paddy gall fly, rice-root aphid and mealy bugs.	29	1	-	-	119	3.96 (R)
	Soil treatment and nursery raising						
41.	Sterilisation of nursery plots by burning paddy straw after first ploughing to control insects/pests in rice field.	-	3	19	8	55	1.83 (IR)
42.	Powder of Neem *(Azadirachta indica)* and Karanj *(Pongamia pinnata)* cake are mixed with soil while field preparation.	29	1	-	-	119	3.96 (R)
43.	Nursery soil is sterilised by burning of straw and husk of paddy, wheat or fingermillet.	27	3	-	-	117	3.90 (R)
44.	Plough made up of *Kendu* wood is used to control soil borne insects/pests.	-	-	6	24	36	1.20 (IR)

R= Rational and IR=Irrational, 4- Rational based on scientific evidence from related studies, 3- Rational based on logical thinking derived from experiences, 2- Irrational based on logical thinking from experiences, 1- Irrational based on scientific evidence from related studies

Table 4.4.2.1 shows that ITKs listed at Sl.No. 1, 2, 3, 8, 11, 12, 14, 15, 16, 18, 19, 21, 22, 23, 24, 25, 26, 27, 28, 29, 30, 32, 34, 35, 36, 39, 40, 42 and 43 were adjudged rational whereas ITKs at Sl. No. 4, 5, 6, 7, 9, 10, 13, 17, 20, 31, 33, 37, 38, 41 and 44 were deliberated as irrational by the scientists either on the basis of their scientific evidence and their experience of working in the respective fields.

Results and Discussion

The results presented in Table 4.4.2.1 have been summarized in Table 4.4.2.2 on the basis of rationality scores.

Table 4.4.2.2: Distribution of ITKs according to rationality categories of 4-point continuum

Category	Weighted mean scores	No of ITKs	Results
Rational	≥ 2.5	30 (68.18)	Accepted
Irrational	< 2.5	14 (31.82)	Discarded

Figures in parentheses indicate percentages

It can be observed from Table 4.4.2.2 that 30 ITKs (68.18%) were reported to be rational which were accepted for validation and 14 ITKs (31.82%) were reported to be irrational and discarded for the next step. The findings are in concurrence with those of **Kumar *et al.* (2009), Mohapatra *et al.* (2009), Chandola *et al.* (2011), Mehta *et al.* (2012), Majumdar *et al.* (2013), Kumar (2016), Nath *et al.* (2018) and Venkatesan *et al.* (2021)** who also used the same scale for adjudging rationality of different ITK practices of agriculture and allied sectors and found maximum number of ITKs to be rational.

4.4.3 Rationality analysis on a 5-point scale of Hiranand (1979)

The selected ITKs were administered before the plant protection scientists for assessment of their scientific rationality. The findings are presented in Table 4.4.3.1.

A cursory look at Table 4.4.3.1 indicates that a good number of indigenous practices adopted in the area have stood the test of time due to a substantial level of rationality involved in them. It was with this assumption that the identified indigenous practices are still in vogue which was assessed by the scientists on 5-point Hiranand scale (1979). Altogether 32 documented ITKs (ITK at Sl.No. 1, 2, 3, 7, 8, 10, 11, 13, 14, 15, 16, 18, 19, 20, 21, 22, 23, 24, 25, 26, 27, 28, 29, 30, 32, 34, 35, 36, 39, 40, 42 and 43) were adjudged highly rational as they received rationality scores above 3.5 and four practices (Sl.No. 31, 33, 37 and 38) were found to be moderately rational which received rationality scores between 2.5 and 3.5. The remaining eight ITKs (ITKs at Sl.No. 4, 5, 6, 9, 12, 17, 41 and 44) were reported to be irrational which

Table 4.4.3.1: Rationality scores obtained by selected ITKs on a 5-point continuum

S. No.	Pest / disease - wise ITK	HR (5)	R (4)	U (3)	IR (2)	VIR (1)	Total score	WMS
	Rice hispa *(Dicladispa armigera)*							
1.	After observing whitening of paddy leaves during vegetative phase, fresh leaves of *Parasi (Cleistanthus collinus)* are broadcast in the field to control Rice hispa.	23	7	-	-	-	143	4.76 (HR)
2.	Application of *Baska* i.e. by-product of mahua *(Madhuca indica)* is done to control Rice hispa.	26	4	-	-	-	146	4.86 (HR)
3.	Crushed fruits of *Kendu* trees are applied in paddy field to control Rice hispa.	21	9	-	-	-	141	4.70 (HR)
4.	*Basi mar* is sprayed to control Rice hispa.	-	-	17	4	9	68	2.26 (IR)
5.	Dusting of sand and kerosene oil mixture is done to control Rice hispa.	2	3	-	18	7	65	2.16 (IR)
	Gundhi bug *(Leptocorisa acuta)*							
6.	Discarded rubber tyres are burnt by holding it in hands to control Gundhi bug *(Leptocorisa acuta)*.	-	-	-	11	19	41	1.36 (IR)
7.	Neem *(Azadirachta indica)* flowers are tied in small bundles at 5-6 places in the field to control Gundhi bug in paddy.	23	7	-	-	-	143	4.76 (HR)
8.	Branches of *Bhelwa* tree *((Semecarpus anacardium)* are planted in rice fields to protect it from Lahi and Gundhi bugs.	28	2	-	-	-	148	4.93 (HR)
9.	Dead snake is hanged by the side of the rice field to control Gundhi bug *(Leptocorisa acuta)*.	-	-	-	4	26	34	1.13 (IR)
	Banki disease of rice *(Pyricularia oryzae)*							
10.	Leaves of Neem *(Azadirachta indica)* are spread in the paddy field to control *Banki* disease *(Pyricularia oryzae)*.	17	13	-	-	-	137	4.56 (HR)
11.	*Sandhana* i.e. Bamboo *((Bambusa vulgaris)* rhizome pieces mixed with water and sprinkled over the affected plants to control *Banki* disease in rice *(Pyricularia oryzae)*.	28	2	-	-	-	148	4.93 (HR)

	Rice caseworm *(Nymphula depunctalis)*							
12.	Kerosene oil soaked chord is used to control rice caseworm *(Nymphula depunctalis)*	-	2	-	19	9	55	1.83 (IR)
13.	*Sinduwar* leaves are boiled in water and then cooled and the solution is sprayed on Rice to control paddy caseworm *(Nymphula depunctalis)*.	21	9	-	-	-	141	4.70 (HR)
14.	Solution of *Karil* (tender bamboo shoot extract) soaked in water is sprayed in affected paddy field to control rice caseworm (*Nymphula depunctalis*).	26	4	-	-	-	146	4.86 (HR)
15.	Control of rice caseworm by spreading fresh *Parsu (Cleistanthus collinuus)* and *Sali (Boswellia serrata)* leaves in the field.	23	7	-	-	-	143	4.76 (HR)
16.	Branches of Cashewnut are put in the standing paddy crop to control different insects-pests.	14	16	-	-	-	134	4.46 (HR)
17.	*Karanj (Millettia pinnata)*, *Bhelwa (Semacarpus anacardium)* and *Arjun (Terminalia arjuna)* trees are grown along the bunds to control common insects-pests of field crops.	-	2	3	16	9	58	1.93 (IR)
	Termites *(Coptotermes formosansus)*							
18.	Flooding of paddy field helps in controlling termites (*Coptotermes formosansus*) by disrupting their life cycle.	17	13	-	-	-	137	4.56 (HR)
19.	Horse droppings are mixed with soil during field preparation for Sugarcane cultivation to control termite infestation	9	21	-	-	-	129	4.30 (HR)
20.	To control ants/termites, paddy field is ploughed by desi plough made up of Neem (*Azadirachta indica*) wood.	3	19	2	6	-	109	3.63 (HR)
	Bihar hairy caterpillar (*Spilosoma oblique*)							
21.	Red colour insects and Bihar hairy caterpillar (*Spilosoma oblique*) is controlled by applying mixture of wood ash and kerosene oil when insects appear on leaves of Cucumber and Bottle gourd crops.	17	13	-	-	-	137	4.56 (HR)

Results and Discussion ....

22.	Ash is dusted over Bihar hairy caterpillar (Spilosoma oblique) to control it.	15	15	-	-	-	135	4.50 (HR)
23.	Mixture of *Sinduwar* leaves (*Vitex negundo*), sand and kerosene oil is used to control Bihar hairy caterpillar (*Spilosoma oblique*).	24	6	-	-	-	144	4.80 (HR)
	Potato blight (*Phytophthora infestans*)							
24.	Wood ash is dusted on the leaves at night to control potato blight.	19	11	-	-	-	139	4.63 (HR)
25.	Mixture of wood ash and *Karanj* (*Millettia pinnata*) cake powder is applied on leaves under cloudy conditions to control potato blight.	27	3	-	-	-	147	4.90 (HR)
	Storage							
26.	Dried neem leaves (*Azadirachta indica*) are mixed with dried wheat seeds to control it from weevil during storage.	22	8	-	-	-	142	4.73 (HR)
27.	Maize (*Zea mays*) cobs are hanged over the chulha (hearth) of the household to get smoke to keep insects-pests away from Maize cobs.	25	5	-	-	-	145	4.83 (HR)
28.	Use of *Bharbhari* (Ocunyn cabyn simo) and *Sinduwar* (*Vitex negundo*) leaves is done for storing grains including pulses	30	-	-	-	-	150	5.00 (HR)
29.	Blackgram is protected from insects by storing it with Fingermillet.	12	18	-	-	-	132	4.40 (HR)
	Leaf eating caterpillar in vegetables							
30.	Extract of Neem leaves (*Azadirachta indica*) is sprayed on vegetable leaves to control leaf-eating caterpillars in cabbage and cauliflower.	17	13	-	-	-	137	4.56 (HR)
31.	Ash of wood or cow dung mixed with kerosene oil is applied on vegetable crops or fruit trees to repel/kill insects-pests.	4	5	10	6	5	87	2.90 (MR)
	Aphids (*Aphis gossypii*)							
32.	Cooled extract of boiled *Sinduwar* leaves (*Vitex negundo*) and water is sprayed to control aphids in pumpkin, bottlegourd, beans etc.	23	7	-	-	-	143	4.76 (HR)

Results and Discussion ....

33.	Cowdung and ash is broadcast on vegetable crops to control insect jugnu.	3	4	7	9	7	77	2.56 (MR)
	Shoot borer in rice							
34.	Solution of leaves and seeds of Custard apple *(Annona squamosa)* are sprayed to control insects/pests of paddy crop.	18	12	-	-	-	138	4.6 (HR)
35.	Solution of decayed bamboo suckers/young stems with water is applied in field to control pests in paddy.	26	4	-	-	-	146	4.86 (HR)
	Shoot and fruit borer in vegetables							
36.	Tobacco soaked water with soap/detergent is sprayed on the affected plants for controlling shoot and fruit borers in vegetables.	14	16	-	-	-	134	4.46 (HR)
37.	Mixture of starch, urine and cow dung is sprayed on vegetable plants to control insects/pests.	2	9	4	10	5	83	2.76 (MR)
38.	Ash of wood is mixed with soil to control insects.	-	6	7	17	-	79	2.63 (MR)
	Rice gall fly							
39.	Fresh leaves of *Parso/ Persu* (*Creistanthus collinus*) are spread in rice field to control gall fly.	23	7	-	-	-	143	4.76 (HR)
40.	*Sinduwar (Vitex negundo)* leaves are broadcast in the paddy field when the plant turn yellow, shoots become dry and pant growth is stunted due to attack of tissue borer, paddy gall fly, rice-root aphid and mealy bugs.	28	2	-	-	-	148	4.93 (HR)
	Soil treatment and nursery raising							
41.	Sterilisation of nursery plots by burning paddy straw after first ploughing to control insects/pests in rice field.	-	-	-	23	7	53	1.76 (IR)
42.	Powder of Neem (Azadirachta indica) and Karanj (Pongamia pinnata) cake are mixed with soil while field preparation.	17	13	-	-	-	137	4.56 (HR)
43.	Nursery soil is sterilised by burning of straw and husk of paddy, wheat or fingermillet.	11	15	4	-	-	127	4.23 (HR)
44.	Plough made up of *Kendu* wood is used to control soil borne insects/pests.	3	4	2	12	9	70	2.33 (IR)

VR- Very rational, A- Rational, U-Undecided, IR-Irrational and VIR-Very irrational
WMS- Weighted Mean score, HR- Highly Rational >3.5, MR- Moderately Rational - 2.5-3.5 and IR- Irrational - <2.5

received rationality score less than 2.5. Thus altogether 36 ITKs were found to be rational and eight irrational, which were discarded for the next step of scientisation i.e. validation. These findings are in line with those of **Jasuja (2006), Ponnusamy *et al.* (2009), Singh (2013), Rajesh *et al.* (2013) and Devi *et al.* (2014), Naharki and Jaisi (2020) and Rathore *et al.* (2021)** who also reported that majority of ITKs practiced by the tribal farmers were deliberated as rational on a 5-point continuum by the scientists signifying the importance of this time tested knowledge possessed by the farmers.

The results presented in Table 4.4.3.1 have been summarized in Table 4.4.3.2 on the basis of rationality scores.

Table 4.4.3.2: Distribution of ITKs according to rationality categories of 5-point continuum

Category	Weighted mean scores	No of ITKs	Results
Rational	Highly - >3.5 Moderately- 2.5-3.5	36 (81.81)	Accepted
Irrational	<2.5	8 (18.19)	Discarded

Figures in parentheses indicate percentages

It can be seen from the Table 4.4.3.2 that altogether 36 ITKs (81.81%) were found to be rational and eight irrational (18.19%), so discarded for the next step of scientisation i.e. validation.

4.4.4 Comparative Rationality Analysis of 3 Types of Rating Scales

An effort was made to compare three types of scales used for assessing the scientific rationality of selected ITKs by the plant protection scientists. This was done to understand the differences as well as the consistency between the results obtained on three types of rating scales. The results are presented in Table 4.4.4.

Table 4.4.4: Comparative Rationality Analysis of 3 Types of Rating Scales used

Sl. No.	Pest / disease - wise ITK	Dhaliwal and Singh scale	Venkatesan and Sundaramarai scale	Hiranand scale
	Rice hispa (*Dicladispa armigera*)			
1.	After observing whitening of paddy leaves during vegetative phase, fresh leaves of *Parasi (Cleistanthus collinus)* are broadcast in the field to control Rice hispa.	R	R	HR
2.	Application of *Baska* i.e. by-product of mahua *(Madhuca indica)* is done to control Rice hispa.	R	R	HR
3.	Crushed fruits of *Kendu* trees are applied in paddy field to control Rice hispa.	R	R	HR
4.	*Basi mar* is sprayed to control Rice hispa.	IR	IR	IR
5.	Dusting of sand and kerosene oil mixture is done to control Rice hispa.	IR	IR	IR
	Gundhi bug (*Leptocorisa acuta*)			
6.	Discarded rubber tyres are burnt by holding it in hands to control Gundhi bug *(Leptocorisa acuta)*.	IR	IR	IR
7.	Neem *(Azadirachta indica)* flowers are tied in small bundles at 5-6 places in the field to control Gundhi bug in paddy.	R	R	HR
8.	Branches of *Bhelwa* tree *((Semecarpus anacardium)* are planted in rice fields to protect it from Lahi and Gundhi bugs.	R	R	HR
9.	Dead snake is hanged by the side of the rice field to control Gundhi bug *(Leptocorisa acuta)*.	IR	IR	IR
	Banki disease of rice *(Pyricularia oryzae)*			
10.	Leaves of Neem *(Azadirachta indica)* are spread in the paddy field to control *Banki* disease *(Pyricularia oryzae)*.	R	IR	HR
11.	*Sandhana* i.e. Bamboo *((Bambusa vulgaris)* rhizome pieces mixed with water and sprinkled over the affected plants to control *Banki* disease *(Pyricularia oryzae)* in Rice.	R	R	HR
	Rice caseworm *(Nymphula depunctalis)*			
12.	Kerosene oil soaked chord is used to control rice caseworm *(Nymphula depunctalis)*	IR	R	IR
13.	*Sinduwar* leaves are boiled in water and then cooled and the solution is sprayed on Rice to control paddy caseworm *(Nymphula depunctalis)*.	R	IR	HR
14.	Solution of *Karil* (tender bamboo shoot extract) soaked in water is sprayed in affected paddy field to control rice caseworm *(Nymphula depunctalis)*.	R	R	HR

Results and Discussion

15.	Control of rice caseworm by spreading fresh *Parsu* (*Cleistanthus collinuus*) and *Sali* (*Boswellia serrata*) leaves in the field.	R	R	HR
16.	Branches of Cashewnut are put in the standing paddy crop to control different insects-pests.	R	R	HR
17.	*Karanj* (*Millettia pinnata*), *Bhelwa* (*Semacarpus anacardium*) and *Arjun* (*Terminalia arjuna*) trees are grown along the bunds to control common insects-pests of field crops.	IR	IR	IR
	Termites (*Coptotermes formosansus*)			
18.	Flooding of paddy field helps in controlling termites (*Coptotermes formosansus*) by disrupting their life cycle.	R	R	HR
19.	Horse droppings are mixed with soil during field preparation for Sugarcane cultivation to control termite infestation	R	R	HR
20.	To control ants/termites, paddy field is ploughed by desi plough made up of Neem (*Azadirachta indica*) wood.	IR	IR	HR
	Bihar hairy caterpillar (*Spilosoma oblique*)			
21.	Red colour insects and Bihar hairy caterpillar (*Spilosoma oblique*) is controlled by applying mixture of wood ash and kerosene oil when insects appear on leaves of Cucumber and Bottle gourd crops.	R	R	HR
22.	Ash is dusted over Bihar hairy caterpillar (*Spilosoma oblique*) to control it.	R	R	HR
23.	Mixture of *Sinduwar* leaves (*Vitex negundo*), sand and kerosene oil is used to control Bihar hairy caterpillar (*Spilosoma oblique*).	R	R	HR
	Potato blight (*Phytophthora infestans*)			
24.	Wood ash is dusted on the leaves at night to control potato blight.	R	R	HR
25.	Mixture of wood ash and *Karanj* (*Millettia pinnata*) cake powder is applied on leaves under cloudy conditions to control potato blight.	R	R	HR
	Storage			
26.	Dried neem leaves (*Azadirachta indica*) are mixed with dried wheat seeds to control it from weevil during storage.	R	R	HR
27.	Maize (*Zea mays*) cobs are hanged over the chulha (hearth) of the household to get smoke to keep insects-pests away from Maize cobs.	R	R	HR
28.	Use of *Bharbhari* (Ocunyn cabyn simo) and *Sinduwar* (*Vitex negundo*) leaves is done for storing grains including pulses	R	R	HR
29.	Blackgram is protected from insects by storing it with Fingermillet.	R	R	HR

		Leaf eating caterpillar in vegetables			
30.	Extract of Neem leaves (*Azadirachta indica*) is sprayed on vegetable leaves to control leaf-eating caterpillars in cabbage and cauliflower.		R	R	HR
31.	Ash of wood or cow dung mixed with kerosene oil is applied on vegetable crops or fruit trees to repel/kill insects-pests.		IR	IR	MR
		Aphids (*Aphis gossypii*)			
32.	Cooled extract of boiled *Sinduwar* leaves (*Vitex negundo*) and water is sprayed to control aphids in pumpkin, bottlegourd, beans etc.		R	R	HR
33.	Cowdung and ash is broadcast on vegetable crops to control insect jugnu.		IR	IR	MR
		Shoot borer in rice			
34.	Solution of leaves and seeds of Custard apple (*Annona squamosa*) are sprayed to control insects/pests of paddy crop.		R	R	HR
35.	Solution of decayed bamboo suckers/young stems with water is applied in field to control pests in paddy.		R	R	HR
		Shoot and fruit borer in vegetables			
36.	Tobacco soaked water with soap/detergent is sprayed on the affected plants for controlling shoot and fruit borers in vegetables.		R	R	HR
37.	Mixture of starch, urine and cow dung is sprayed on vegetable plants to control insects/pests.		IR	IR	MR
38.	Ash of wood is mixed with soil to control insects.		IR	IR	MR
		Rice gall fly			
39.	Fresh leaves of *Parso/ Persu* (*Creistanthus collinus*) are spread in rice field to control gall fly.		R	R	HR
40.	*Sinduwar (Vitex negundo)* leaves are broadcast in the paddy field when the plant turn yellow, shoots become dry and pant growth is stunted due to attack of tissue borer, paddy gall fly, rice-root aphid and mealy bugs.		R	R	HR
		Soil treatment and nursery raising			
41.	Sterilisation of nursery plots by burning paddy straw after first ploughing to control insects/pests in rice field.		IR	IR	IR
42.	Powder of Neem *(Azadirachta indica)* and *Karanj (Pongamia pinnata)* cake are mixed with soil while field preparation.		R	R	HR
43.	Nursery soil is sterilised by burning of straw and husk of paddy, wheat or fingermillet.		R	R	HR
44.	Plough made up of *Kendu* wood is used to control soil borne insects/pests.		IR	IR	IR

R-Rational, MR- Moderately rational, HR-Highly rational and IR-Irrational,

Results and Discussion ....

It can be seen from Table 4.4.4 that most of the ITKs were found rational in all the three types of rating scales. On the 3-point scale of Dhaliwal and Singh (2010), a total of 31 ITKs were found to be rational, on 4-point scale of Venkatesan and Sundaramarai (2014), 28 ITKs were found to be rational and on 5-point scale of Hiranand (1979) altogether 36 ITKs were rated to be rational. This can be inferred further from Table 4.4.4 that altogether 30 ITKs at Sl.No. 1, 2, 3, 8, 11, 12, 14, 15, 16, 18, 19, 20, 21, 22, 23, 24, 25, 26, 27, 28, 29, 30, 32, 34, 35, 36, 39, 40, 42 and 43 were rated to be rational by the scientists based on their expertise, experience and scientific evidences. As regards consistency of the scales is concerned majority of the ITKs (30) were rated to be rational on all the three types of scales followed by seven ITKs rated to be irrational at Sl.No 4, 5, 6, 9, 17, 41 and 44 and four ITKs at Sl.No 31, 33, 37 and 38 were rated to be irrational on three and 4-point rating scales and rational on 5-point rating scale. It might be due to perceptional differences of the scientists.

As opined by the scientists, Neem, Karanj, Baska, Sinduwar, Bhelwa, Parsu, Keond and Bharbari leaves are of great importance in pest and disease management. In all the three types of rationality analysis, ITKs having these ingredients obtained higher scores, which highlight their importance and relevance in pest and disease management. Due to strong and bitter smell, Parsu leaves acts as a repelling agent to the insects-pests. Baska being toxic and having pungent smell controls the spread of insects-pests. Keond fruits and leaves have a bitter taste and unripe fruits become toxic for insects. Due to insecticidal property of Neem, bugs are repelled. Pungent smell of Bhelwa branches help in repelling insects. Scientists could come up with the ITK based Ready to use (RTU) products to scale up their use among the farming communities to reduce their cost of production and ultimately contributing to attain one of the main objectives of sustainable agriculture i.e. environmental protection through use of botanical (non) chemicals in plant protection and thereby ensuring safety to human and animal health and conservation of natural resources for environment conservation.

Thus such ITKs are to be further tested in order to prove their efficacy. Similarly some illogical and irrational practice of ITKs by the farmers need to be discontinued through capacity building by the extension agents in order to adopt more efficient ITKs with scientific evidences. Slow results, low yield and time consuming nature of these indigenous practices make it imperative to seek an alternative by blending indigenous practices with modern agricultural practices. ITKs which have high levels of rationality scores need to be given due importance by extension agents as they greatly reduce the expenditure of the farmers. Efforts can be made to preserve and popularise various plants, which have high economic importance in terms of their insecticidal properties. If ITKs were used in farming systems along with frontier technologies developed by the agricultural scientists, it would be more practical and not only the farmers would adopt them quickly, but it would also increase the practicability and acceptability of the technology. It also helps in the development of location-specific and sustainable technologies and practices. The importance of the mixture made of Parsu, Sinduwar, Bharbhari and Kendu leaves are of high importance, as reflected from the highest rationality scores obtained. This kind of rationality through experimental approach will help in identifying certain active ingredients responsible for the management of pest and diseases.

4.4.5. Validation of ITKs

The second step of scientisation process is validation. Validation is the process of justifying the effectiveness of selected ITKs. In the present investigation, validation was done both from the scientists and farmers perspective. Validation of selected ITKs about pest and disease management by QuIK method was done on the parameters selected by the tribal farmers. The validation by QuIK method is explained below:

4.4.5.1. Validation by QuIK method

Validation of selected ITKs was done on six parameters namely effectiveness in controlling pests/disease, cost effectiveness, quickness in problem solving, ease in preparation, environment friendliness and farming system compatibility, which were selected by the tribal farmers as they understand their farming situation in a better way than a scientist who is an outsider. However, the QuIK method was done in the presence of one agronomist and one plant protection scientist to facilitate the tribal farmers. A total of 31 ITKs were found to be scientifically rational but it was a difficult task to gather all the 45 tribal farmers at one place and involve them in QuIK method, further time constraints was a limiting factor. Therefore it was decided by the researcher, tribal farmers and the scientists to take up five commonly used ITKs for the QuIK method. The result interpretations of validation of five commonly used selected ITKs are present as below in Table 4.4.5.1

Table 4.4.5.1: Validation of different alternatives to control Rice hispa (n=45) (Mean ± S.E)

Attributes	CST	ITK 1	ITK 2
Effectiveness in controlling pests/disease	8.355 ± 0.235^a	7.11 ± 0.250^b	7.250 ± 0.340^b
Cost effectiveness	4.523 ± 0.292^b	9.713 ± 0.159^a	9.627 ± 0.164^a
Quickness in problem solving	8.712 ± 0.303^a	6.515 ± 0.158^b	6.250 ± 0.135^b
Ease in preparation	9.100 ± 0.148^a	6.615 ± 0.117^b	6.425 ± 0.176^b
Environment friendliness	5.912 ± 6.918^b	9.411 ± 0.173^a	9.520 ± 0.163^a
Farming system compatibility	6.918 ± 0.196^b	9.532 ± 0.105^a	9.200 ± 0.645^a

The multiple comparisons are based on Duncan Multiple Range Test i.e.post hoc test

ab Means bearing different superscripts in a row under each criterion differ significantly (p<0.05)

ITK 1: Fresh Parsu leaves are broadcast

ITK 2: Mahua leaves are applied

It can be elucidated from the Table 4.4.5.1 in case of Rice hispa, DMRT analysis of data revealed that CST varied significantly (p<0.05) over the two ITKs in effectiveness in controlling pests/diseases. However there was no significant difference between the ITKs. CST was found to show better results in controlling the pests/disease effectively so were more preferred by the farmers than ITKs.

Regarding cost effectiveness, CST was found significantly different from the ITKs (p<0.05), whereas, there was no significant difference among the ITKs. CST was least preferred in terms of cost-effectiveness as CSTs are costly than ITKs and

Results and Discussion ....

ITKs are locally and easily available ingredients. Farmers have to pay high amount to purchase a CST.

Considering quickness in problem solving, both the ITKs were found to differ significantly over CST ($p<0.05$). There was no significant difference between the ITKs ($p<0.05$). The high ranking of CST is due to the fact that fast results are observable in case of CST whereas ITKs are slow and time taking in yielding the favourable results.

In case of ease in preparation, CST was significantly different over the ITKs ($p<0.05$), whereas, there was no significant difference among the ITKs. CST was found easier to prepare than ITKs as CST was found in ready to use form, whereas, in case of ITKs, it was a difficult task to identify and collect all the locally available ITK ingredients and then to prepare accordingly.

Regarding environment friendliness, CST was found significantly different from the ITKs ($p<0.05$), whereas, there was no significant difference among the ITKs. CST was perceived to be having side effects to environment in comparison to the ITKs.

In case of farming system compatibility, both the ITKs were significantly different over CST ($P<0.05$). There was no significant difference reported between the ITKs ($p<0.05$). This might be due to the fact that CST was not up to the beliefs of the farmers as they believe in maintaining harmony with the nature. They consider CST as foreign technologies, complex and harmful to their socio-ecological system whereas ingredients of ITKs were locally available and familiar to them. It is clear from Table 4.4.5.1 that ITKs were found to be superior in terms of cost effectiveness, farming system compatibility and environment friendliness, whereas CST was preferred more in terms of effectiveness in controlling pests/disease, quickness in healing and ease in preparation. Experience from discussion with the tribal farmers revealed that ITK 1, ITK 2 could be viable alternatives to control Rice hispa and adaptable to the agro-ecological situation of the tribal farming community.

Results and Discussion ....

Table 4.4.5.2: Validation of different alternatives to control Rice caseworms (n=45) (Mean ± S.E)

Attributes	CST	ITK1	ITK2
Effectiveness in controlling pests/disease	9.261 ± 0.134^a	7.228 ± 0.163^b	7.516 ± 0.124^b
Cost effectiveness	5.918 ± 0.149^b	9.425 ± 0.152^a	9.568 ± 0.234^a
Quickness in problem solving	9.331 ± 0.174^a	6.598 ± 0.185^b	6.740 ± 0.130^b
Ease in preparation	9.424 ± 0.185^a	6.452 ± 0.140^b	5.223 ± 0.164^c
Environment friendliness	5.978 ± 0.189^b	9.113 ± 0.118^a	9.482 ± 0.147^a
Farming system compatibility	6.453 ± 0.187^c	9.521 ± 0.110^a	7.679 ± 0.190^b

The multiple comparisons are based on Duncan Multiple Range Test i.e. post hoc test
ac Means bearing different superscripts in a row under each criterion differ significantly (p<0.05)
*ITK-1: Solution of *Karil* (tender bamboo shoot extract) soaked in water is sprayed in the affected paddy field)
*ITK 2 Spreading fresh *Parsu (Cleistanthus collinuus)* and *Sali (Boswellia serrata)* leaves in the field to control Rice caseworm *(Nymphula depunctalis)*

The validation of ITK was done by QuIK method on six parameters selected by the tribal farmers. From the matrix ranking, it can be revealed that CST was significantly different over the ITKs (p<0.05) regarding effectiveness in controlling pests/diseases. CST ranked first followed by ITK-2 and ITK-1. There was no significant difference among ITKs (P<0.05) in this regard. In case of cost effectiveness, there was significant difference between the CST and ITKs (p<0.05), whereas, there was no significant difference between the ITKs. ITKs were cheaper than CST. This might to due to fact that materials of the ITKs were easily available in the locality and tribal farmers did not have to buy those from the market.

Regarding quickness in problem solving, the DMRT data revealed that CST was highly effective as compared to the selected ITKs and differ significantly over the ITKs. There was no significant difference among the ITKs (p<0.05) in this regard.

In case of ease in preparation, CST was significantly different over the ITKs (p<0.05) whereas there was significant difference also reported among the ITKs. CST was found highly easier to prepare than ITKs. This might be due to the fact that CST was found in packaged form, whereas, in case of ITKs, it was a difficult task to identify and collect all the related ITK materials and then to prepare the solution accordingly. Regarding environment friendliness, CST was found significantly different from the ITKs (p<0.05), whereas, there was no significant difference among the ITKs. CST was perceived to be less safe than the ITKs for the environment as it might have hazardous effects in the long term. In case of farming system compatibility, ITKs were significantly different over CST (p<0.05). There was significant difference also found among the selected ITKs (p<0.05). CST was least preferred in terms of farming system compatibility than the ITKs. This might be due to the fact that CST was introduced into the social system by the outsiders so did not match with their socio-economic and agro-ecological conditions, whereas, ingredients of ITKs were locally available and they were well aware with its usage and suitable to their values and beliefs.

It is clear from Table 4.4.5.2 that ITKs were preferred in terms of cost effectiveness, environment friendliness and farming system compatibility whereas CST was found to be superior regarding effectiveness in controlling pests/diseases, quickness in problem solving and ease in preparation.

Table 4.4.5.3 Validation of different alternatives to control Bihar hairy caterpillar (n=45) (Mean ± S.E)

Attributes	CST	ITK1	ITK2
Effectiveness in controlling pests/disease	8.528 ± 0.173^a	7.113 ± 0.252^b	7.317 ± 0.268^b
Cost effectiveness	4.562 ± 0.256^b	9.713 ± 0.155^a	9.014 ± 0.119^a
Quickness in problem solving	8.614 ± 0.144^a	6.519 ± 0.165^b	6.315 ± 0.243^b
Ease in preparation	9.113 ± 0.147^a	6.725 ± 0.112^b	6.235 ± 0.124^b
Environment friendliness	7.529 ± 0.237^a	9.417 ± 0.171^b	9.514 ± 0.168^b
Farming system compatibility	6.820 ± 0.195^b	9.528 ± 0.107^a	9.512 ± 0.121^a

The multiple comparisons are based on Duncan Multiple Range Test i.e. post hoc test

ab Means bearing different superscripts in a row under each criterion differ significantly (p<0.05)

ITK 1: Mixture of Ash and Kerosene oil

ITK 2: Sinduwar leaves + Sand + Kerosene oil to control Bihar hairy caterpillar

A cursory look at Table 4.4.5.3 shows in the context of effectiveness in controlling pests/disease, there was significance difference found between CST, ITK 1 and ITK 2 but CST was found to be more effective in controlling pests/diseases in comparison with the selected ITKs. However among the ITKs, no significance difference was found. CST ranked higher in terms of effectiveness in controlling pests/diseases.

CST was perceived to be more costly than the ITK 1 and ITK 2. Both the ITKs were found to be relatively cheaper than CST. This might be due to the fact that CST was not easily accessible, whereas, ingredients of ITKs were locally and easily available so use of both the ITKs was highly cost effective over CST. There were no significant difference found between the ITKs but both the ITKs vary significantly over the CST.

In case of quickness in problem solving, DMRT analysis of the data revealed that CST was highly effective as compared to the selected ITKs, whereas, there was no significant difference between ITK 1, and ITK 2. CST was preferred more than ITKs in quickness in problem solving.

About ease in preparation, CST was found in packaged form, whereas, in case of ITKs, the farmers had to collect the ingredients first, then to process and apply it. For this reason, CST might be easier to prepare than ITKs due to its easily accessibility. There was significant difference found between the CST and the ITKs but there was no significant difference found between both the ITKs.

CST was perceived to be having more side effects than the ITK 1 and ITK 2. ITK 1 and ITK 2 were considered environmental friendly and in harmony with the ecosystem so preferred more than CST. CST vary significantly over the ITKs. No significant difference was reported between the ITKs.

In terms of farming system compatibility, both the ITKs were rated better than CST. This might be due to the fact that CST was introduced into the social system by the outsiders i.e. scientists whereas ITKs are the results of curiosity, keen observation, trials and error and experimentation of tribal farmers in their natural setting. Although CST recorded higher ranking in criteria like effectiveness, quickness in healing and ease in preparation, the critical perusal of the data revealed that the farmers, keeping all the six criteria in view favourably accepted the ITK 1 and ITK 2. The viable alternative on the basis of available criteria seemed to be the indigenous technical knowledge from the farmer s perspective which would reduce agricultural expenditure.

Table 4.4.5.4: Validation of different alternatives to control Rice gall fly (n=45) (Mean ± S.E)

Attributes	CST	ITK1	ITK2
Effectiveness in controlling pests/disease	8.814 ± 0.153^a	7.424 ± 0.236^b	7.292 ± 0.241^b
Cost effectiveness	4.652 ± 0.329^b	9.274 ± 0.216^a	9.145 ± 0.216^a
Quickness in problem solving	8.567 ± 0.223^a	6.438 ± 0.217^b	6.397 ± 0.250^b
Ease in preparation	9.164 ± 0.217^a	6.219 ± 0.248^b	6.417 ± 0.126^b
Environment friendliness	7.363 ± 0.212^b	9.642 ± 0.143^a	9.723 ± 0.143^a
Farming system compatibility	6.245 ± 0.256^b	9.423 ± 0.154^a	9.312 ± 0.148^a

The multiple comparisons are based on Duncan Multiple Range Test i.e. post hoc test
ab Means bearing different superscripts in a row under each criterion differ significantly ($p<0.05$)
ITK 1: Fresh leaves of Parso/ Persu (*Creistanthus collinus*) are spread in rice field to control Gall fly.
ITK 2: Sinduwar (*Vitex negundo*) leaves are broadcast in the paddy field when the plant turn yellow, shoots become dry and plant growth is stunted due to attack of tissue borer, paddy gall fly, Rice-root aphid and mealy bugs.

In effectiveness in controlling pests/diseases, the results revealed that CST was significantly different as compared to ITK 1 and ITK 2 ($p<0.05$). CST was found more effectiveness than ITK 1 and ITK 2, whereas, there was no significant difference between ITK 1 and ITK 2 ($p<0.05$) in this regard.

In case of cost effectiveness, there was significant difference between the CST and ITKs ($p<0.05$), whereas, there was no significant difference between the ITKs. ITKs were cheaper than CST. This might to due to the fact that materials of the ITKs were easily available in the study area and tribal key informants did not require to purchase those from shops. Regarding quickness in problem solving, the ANOVA of the data revealed that CST was highly effective as compared to the selected ITKs, whereas, there was no significant difference between ITK 1, and ITK 2. In case of ease in preparation, CST was significantly different (p<0.05) than the ITK 1 and ITK 2, whereas, there was no significant difference between the ITKs. CST was found highly easier to prepare than ITKs. This might be due to the facts that CST was found in readymade form, whereas, in case of ITKs, it was a difficult task to identify, collect all the materials and then to prepare accordingly. Regarding environment friendliness, CST was found significantly different from the ITKs (p<0.05), whereas, there was no significant difference between the ITKs. MST was perceived to be having more side effects than the ITKs. In case of farming system compatibility, both the ITKs were significantly different over CST (P<0.05). There was no significant difference between the ITKs (p<0.05). This might be due to the facts that CST was not easily available in the study area whereas, ingredients of ITKs were locally available. It is clear from Table 4.4.5.4 that ITK 1 and ITK 2 were superior in terms of cost effectiveness, environment friendliness and farming system compatibility whereas, CST was superior regarding effectiveness in controlling pests/diseases, quickness in problem solving and ease in preparation.

Table 4.4.5.5: Validation of different alternatives to control Banki disease (n=45) (Mean ± S.E)

Attributes	CST	ITK1	ITK2
Effectiveness in controlling pests/disease	8.813 ± 0.187^b	7.408 ± 0.113^c	9.424 ± 0.276^a
Cost effectiveness	5.324 ± 0.246^b	9.327 ± 0.340^a	9.196 ± 0.113^a
Quickness in problem solving	8.653 ± 0.162^a	6.432 ± 0.213^b	6.342 ± 0.145^b
Ease in preparation	9.448 ± 0.217^a	6.323 ± 0.125^b	6.528 ± 0.191^b
Environment friendliness	7.312 ± 0.182^b	9.439 ± 0.126^a	9.536 ± 1.118^a
Farming system compatibility	6.761 ± 0.273^b	9.231 ± 0.123^a	9.565 ± 0.187^a

The multiple comparisons are based on Duncan Multiple Range Test i.e. post hoc test
ac Means bearing different superscripts in a row under each criterion differ significantly (p<0.05)
ITK 1: Sandhana i.e. Bamboo *(Bambusa vulgaris)* rhizome pieces mixed with water
ITK 2: Leaves of Neem *(Azadirachta indica)* are spread in the paddy field to control Banki disease *(Pyricularia oryzae)*

A cursory look at the Table 4.4.5.5 indicates that in case of effectiveness in controlling pests-diseases there were significant difference found between all the three CST, ITK 1 and ITK 2 ($p<0.05$). However ITK 2 was found to be more effective than CST and ITK 1. In comparison to ITK 1 and CST, CST was perceived to be more effective. There was significant difference found between CST and both ITKs in terms of cost effectiveness. It might be due to the fact that ITKs are composed of ingredients available locally and in natural setting and CST has to be purchased from outside i.e. shops and it is relatively costly than ITKs. However no significant difference was reported between both ITKs. CST was perceived more effective in quickness in problem solving because fast results are obtained after applying CST to a particular problem whereas ITKs take time to show the desirable results. Regarding ease in preparation, CST was significantly different ($p<0.05$) than the ITK 1 and ITK 2, whereas, there was no significant difference between the ITKs. CST was found quite easier to prepare than respective ITKs. This might be due to the fact that CST was found in ready to use form, whereas, in case of ITKs, it was a very difficult task to identify and collect all the related materials from the proximity and then to prepare them accordingly.

Regarding environment friendliness, CST was found significantly different from the ITKs ($p<0.05$), whereas, there was no significant difference between the ITKs. CST was perceived to be less environment friendly than the ITKs as it has harmful effects on both the soil health and human health and ultimately the environment. In case of farming system compatibility, both the ITKs were significantly different over CST ($p<0.05$). There was no significant difference between the ITKs ($p<0.05$). This might be due to the fact that use of ITKs are in synchronization with the values and beliefs of the tribal farming community as they believe in environment conservation through sustainable agricultural practices whereas CST was something out of their understanding and context. They were reluctant to use it as it might harm their soil and crops health and create imbalance in the environment.

It is clear from Table 4.4.5.5 that ITK 1 and ITK 2 were superior in terms of cost effectiveness, environment friendliness and farming system compatibility

Results and Discussion ....

whereas CST was superior in terms of effectiveness in controlling pests-diseases, quickness in problem solving and ease in preparation. Discussions with the tribal farmers revealed that ITK 1, and ITK 2 could come up as a viable alternatives to Banki disease of Rice as they are suitable to the agro-ecological condition of the tribal farmers.

Similarly, QuIK method was also used by **Saha (2014)** in validating ITKs in animal husbandry, **Singh and Chauhan (2010)** in validating ITK of Hemorrhagic Septicemia disease in animals of Bundelkhand region, **Maiti et al. (2013)** in Yak treatment and **Bhanotra and Gupta (2016)** in ITKs used in treating pneumonia in dairy animals and **Devaki et al. (2019)** in anoestrum treatment. In all these studies ITKs were the preference of the tribal farmers for its effectiveness, cost-effectiveness and easy availability in the area.

4.4.6 Validation by Mean Perceived Effectiveness Methodology

Out of 44 identified and documented ITKs about pest and disease management, 31 ITKs were found to be rational by the experts and accepted for further validation in the particularisation step. Six parameters namely, efficacy, accessibility, cost-effectiveness, observability, adaptability and simplicity were identified to assess the mean perceived effectiveness of the particularised ITKs. The scientists identified and assessed each ITK on the basis of these parameters by indicating their preference on a 3-point continuum, i.e. score 3 for concur, score 2 for no idea and score 1 for not concur. The expressed response of 30 plant protection scientists on the selected parameters are presented in the Table 4.4.6.

Table 4.4.6 shows that out of 31 ITKs listed, 29 were found to be highly effective, whereas ITK 4 and ITK 15 were marked as moderately effective. Not a single ITK was reported under less effective category. It can be concluded that ITKs have great potential to be incorporated in National Agricultural Research System so that farming community can utilise it to the maximum for better results and it should reduce the cost of cultivation and suitable to their agro-ecological system. It will be very easy for tribal farmers to adopt ITK-based package of practices as they are well known to them and less complex to their understanding and use.

Table 4.4.6: Mean Perceived Effectiveness scores of ITKs on selected effectiveness parameters

Sl.No	ITK	MPEM	Effectiveness Results
	Rice hispa *(Dicladispa armigera)*		
1.	After observing whitening of paddy leaves during vegetative phase, fresh leaves of *Parasi (Cleistanthus collinus)* are broadcast in the field to control rice hispa.	2.89	HE
2.	Crushed fruits of *Kendu* trees are applied in paddy field to control rice hispa.	2.90	HE
	Gundhi bug *(Leptocorisa acuta)*		
3.	Neem *(Azadirachta indica)* flowers are tied in small bundles at 5-6 places in the field to control Gundhi bug in paddy.	2.83	HE
4.	Branches of *Bhelwa* tree (*(Semecarpus anacardium)* are planted in rice fields to protect it from Lahi and Gandhi bugs.	2.38	ME
	Banki disease of rice *(Pyricularia oryzae)*		
5.	Leaves of Neem *(Azadirachta indica)* are spread in the paddy field to control *Banki* disease *(Pyricularia oryzae)*.	2.75	HE
6.	*Sandhana* i.e. Bamboo *((Bambusa vulgaris)* rhizome pieces mixed with water and sprinkled over the affected planst to control *Banki* disease in rice *(Pyricularia oryzae)*.	2.67	HE
	Rice caseworm *(Nymphula depunctalis)*		
7.	*Sinduwar* leaves are boiled in water and then cooled and the solution is sprayed on Rice to control paddy caseworm *(Nymphula depunctalis)*.	2.89	HE
8.	Solution of *Karil* (tender bamboo shoot extract) soaked in water is sprayed in affected paddy field to control rice caseworm *(Nymphula depunctalis)*.	2.97	HE
9.	Control of rice caseworm by spreading fresh *Parsu (Cleistanthus collinuus)* and *Sali (Boswellia serrata)* leaves in the field.	2.75	HE
10.	Branches of Cashewnut are put in the standing paddy crop to control different insects-pests.	2.66	HE
11.	*Karanj (Millettia pinnata), Bhelwa (Semacarpus anacardium)* and *Arjun (Terminalia arjuna)* trees are grown along the bunds to control common insects-pests of field crops.	2.90	HE

Results and Discussion ....

	Termites *(Coptotermes formosansus)*		
12.	Flooding of paddy field helps in controlling termites *(Coptotermes formosansus)* by disrupting their life cycle.	2.52	HE
13.	To control ants/termites, paddy field is ploughed by desi plough made up of Neem *(Azadirachta indica)* wood.	2.58	HE
	Bihar hairy caterpillar *(Spilosoma oblique)*		
14.	Red colour insects and Bihar hairy caterpillar *(Spilosoma oblique)* is controlled by applying mixture of wood ash and kerosene oil when insects appear on leaves of Cucumber and Bottle gourd crops.	2.83	HE
15.	Mixture of *Sinduwar* leaves *(Vitex negundo)*, sand and kerosene oil is used to control Bihar hairy caterpillar *(Spilosoma oblique)*.	2.48	ME
	Potato blight *(Phytophthora infestans)*		
16.	Wood ash is dusted on the leaves at night to control potato blight.	2.59	HE
17.	Mixture of wood ash and *Karanj (Millettia pinnata)* cake powder is applied on leaves under cloudy conditions to control potato blight.	2.75	HE
	Storage		
18.	Dried neem leaves (Azadirachta indica) are mixed with dried wheat seeds to control it from weevil during storage.	2.76	HE
19.	Maize *(Zea mays)* cobs are hanged over the chulha (hearth) of the household to get smoke to keep insects-pests away from Maize cobs.	2.57	HE
20.	Use of *Bharbhari* (Ocunyn cabyn simo) and *Sinduwar (Vitex negundo)* leaves is done for storing grains including pulses	2.63	HE
21.	Blackgram is protected from insects by storing it with Fingermillet.	2.55	HE
	Leaf eating caterpillar in vegetables		
22.	Extract of Neem leaves *(Azadirachta indica)* is sprayed on vegetable leaves to control leaf-eating caterpillars in cabbage and cauliflower.	2.64	HE
23.	Ash of wood or cow dung mixed with kerosene oil is applied on vegetable crops or fruit trees to repel/kill insects-pests.	2.85	HE

Results and Discussion

	Aphids *(Aphis gossypii)*		
24.	Cooled extract of boiled *Sinduwar* leaves (*Vitex negundo*) and water is sprayed to control aphids in pumpkin, bottlegourd, beans etc.	2.52	HE
	Shoot borer in rice		
25.	Solution of decayed bamboo suckers/young stems with water is applied in field to control pests in paddy.	2.64	HE
	Shoot and fruit borer in vegetables		
26.	Tobacco soaked water with soap/detergent is sprayed on the affected plants for controlling shoot and fruit borers in vegetables.	2.59	HE
27.	Mixture of starch, urine and cow dung is sprayed on vegetable plants to control insects/pests.	2.58	HE
28.	Ash of wood is mixed with soil to control insects.		
	Rice gall fly		
29.	Fresh leaves of *Parso/ Persu* (*Creistanthus collinus*) are spread in rice field to control gall fly.	2.83	HE
30.	*Sinduwar (Vitex negundo)* leaves are broadcast in the paddy field when the plant turn yellow, shoots become dry and pant growth is stunted due to attack of tissue borer, paddy gall fly, rice-root aphid and mealy bugs.	2.81	HE
	Soil treatment and nursery raising		
31.	Powder of Neem *(Azadirachta indica)* and *Karanj (Pongamia pinnata)* cake are mixed with soil while field preparation.	2.76	HE

HE = Highly Effective, ME = Moderately Effective and MPES = Mean Perceived Effectiveness score

Similar effectiveness criteria in Mean Perceived Effectiveness Methodology of validation were used by **Debnath (2010), Singh and Chauhan (2010), Bhuyan (2017),** and **Rai** *et al.* **(2017)** in their studies. Most of the ITKs were deliberated under highly effective category followed by moderately and less effective ITKs. This shows that ITK can be a viable alternative option for the stakeholders' to utilise in the eco-friendly farming. Scientific community can ponder over integrating ITK-based practices in the recommended package of practices. Furthermore less effective ITKs can be further improved through researches in the research centers.

The findings are in concurrence with that of study of **Singh and Swami (2020)**, **Talukdar** *et al.* **(2012), Singh and Sharma (2013), Saha** *et al.* **(2015), Singh and Chauhan (2016), Halder** *et al.* **(2018), Kumar** *et al.* **(2018), Nath** *et al.* **(2018), Husain and Sundaramari (2019), Rai** *et al.* **(2019), Roy** *et al.* **(2020) and Sindhu and Malik (2020)** where ITKs were preferred over MVDs in terms of cost effectiveness, sustainability, simplicity, adaptability etc. In all the above mentioned studies, Mean Perceived Effectiveness Methodology (MPEM) was used to assess the validity of rational ITKs for future use.

4.4.7. Generalisation of ITKs

The last step of scientisation process is Generalisation. Generalisation is a process through which ITKs are disseminated and popularised for its wider application and preservation it in relevant form for its sustainable use. It is commonly known as utilisation of ITKs in the technology dissemination studies. Many studies have been conducted so far on developing utilisation index and utilisation of ITKs but there is still a wide gap between the practical application of ITKs and research findings suggesting its wider usage. So to scale up the usages of ITKs in agriculture in general and pest and disease management in particular, it is necessary that ITKs need to be studied from the perspective of both scientists and farmers. Thus an effort was made to obtain the opinion of plant protection scientists regarding the mode through which ITKs can be widely disseminated and adopted in farming practices. It is needed to develop appropriate technologies and also to reduce the expenditure cost of farming. The findings are presented in the Table 4.4.7.1.

Table 4.4.7.1: Distribution of plant protection scientists according to their opinion on generalisation of ITKs (n=30)

Sl.No	Pest/disease-wise ITK practices	ADD	ACM
	Rice hispa		
1.	After observing whitening of paddy leaves during vegetative phase, fresh leaves of Parsu are broadcasted in the paddy field to control Rice hispa.	30 (100)	-
2.	Application of baska (by product of mahua) is done to control rice hispa in paddy.	26 (86.66)	4 (13.34)
3.	Crushed fruits of kendu trees are applied in paddy field to control rice hispa.	29 (96.66)	1 (3.34)
	Gundhi Bug		
4.	Neem flowers are tied in small bundles at 5-6 places in the field to control Gandhi bug in paddy.	19 (63.34)	11 (36.66)
5.	Branches of Bhelwa tree are planted in rice fields to protect it from Lahi and Gandhi bugs.	21 (70)	9 (30)
	Banki disease of rice		
6.	Leaves of Neem are spread in the paddy field to control Banki disease.	13 (43.34)	17 (56.66)
7.	Sandhana leaves are mixed with water and sprinkled over the affected plant to control banki disease in rice.	26 (86.66)	4 (13.34)
	Rice caseworm		
8.	Sinduwar leaves are boiled in water and then cooled and this solution is used sprayed to control paddy caseworm *(Nymphula depunctalis)*.	13 (43.34)	17 (56.66)
9.	Solution of Karil (tender bamboo shoot extract) soaked in water is sprayed in affected paddy field to control rice caseworm *(Nymphula depunctalis)*.	16 (53.34)	14 (46.66)
10.	Control of rice caseworm by sparying fresh pasu *(Cleistanthus collinuus)* and sali *(Boswellia serrata)* leaves.	18 (60)	12 (40)
11.	Branches of Cashewnut are put in the standing paddy crop to control different pests.	17 (56.66)	13 (43.34)

Results and Discussion ....

	Termites		
12.	Flooding of paddy field helps in controlling termites by disrupting their life cycle.	19 (63.34)	11 (36.66)
13.	Horse droppings are mixed with soil of sugarcane field to control termite infestation	20 (66.66)	10 (33.34)
	Bihar hairy caterpillar		
14.	Red colour insects and Bihar hairy caterpillar is controlled by applying mixture of wooden ash and kerosene oil when insects appear on leaves of cucumber and bottle gourd crops.	13 (43.34)	17 (56.66)
15.	Ash is dusted over Bihar hairy caterpillar to control it.	9 (30)	21 (70)
16.	Mixture of Sinduwar leaves, sand kerosene oil is used to control Bihar hairy caterpillar.	13 (43.34)	17 (56.66)
	Potato Blight		
17.	Wooden ash is dusted on the leaves at night to control potato blight.	6 (20)	24 (80)
18.	Mixture of wooden ash and karanj cake powder is applied on leaves under cloudy conditions to control potato blight.	16 (53.33)	14 (46.66)
	Storage		
19.	Dried neem leaves are mixed with dried wheat seeds to control it from weevil during storage.	7 (23.33)	23 (76.66)
20.	Maize cobs are hanged over the chulha of the household to get smoke to keep insects/pests away from maize grains	15 (50)	15 (50)
21.	Use of bharbhari *(Ocunyn cabyn simo)* and sinduwar (*Vitex negundo*) leaves for storing grains and pulses	18 (60)	12 (40)
22.	Blackgram is protected from insects by storing it with fingermillet.	12 (40)	18 (60)
	Leaf eating caterpillar in vegetables		
23.	Extract of neem leaves are sprayed on vegetable leaves to control leaf-eating insects in cabbage and cauliflower.	16 (53.33)	14 (46.66)

Results and Discussion ....

		ADD	ACM
	Aphids		
24.	Cooled extract of boiled sinduwar leaves sand water is sprayed to control aphids in pumpkin, bottlegourd, beans etc.	18 (60)	12 (40)
	Fruit & Shoot borer		
25.	Leaves and seeds of custard apple *(Annona squamosa)* are broadcasted to control insects/pests of paddy crop.	7 (23.34)	23 (76.66)
26.	Solution of decayed bamboo suckers/young stems and water is applied in paddy field to control pests in paddy.	27 (90)	3 (10)
	Shoot and fruit borer in vegetables		
27.	Tobacco soaked water and soap/detergent is sprayed on the affected plants for controlling shoot and fruit borers.	24 (80)	6 (20)
	Gall fly		
28.	Fresh leaves of parso/ persu *(Creistanthus collinus)* are spread to control gall fly in rice.	23 (76.67)	7 (23.33)
29.	Sinduwar *(Vitex negundo)* leaves are broadcasted in the paddy field when the plant turn yellow, shoots become dry and pant growth is stunted due to the attack of tissue borer, paddy gall fly, rice-root aphid and mealy bugs.	26 (86.66)	4 (13.34)
	Soil treatment and Nursery raising		
30.	Powder of Neem *(Azadirachta indica)* and karanj *(Pongamia pinnata)* cake are mixed with soil while field is prepared for sowing.	22 (73.33)	8 (26.67)
31.	Nursery soil is sterilised by burning of straw and husk of paddy, wheat and fingermillet.	24 (80)	6 (20)

Figures in parentheses represent percentage

ADD- Agreed for direct dissemination among farmers by the extension agencies

ACM- Agreed with certain modifications such as blending with Corresponding Scientific Technology

Table 4.4.7.1 indicates that plant protection scientists had varied opinions on generalisation of the selected ITKs. They were asked to judge whether an ITK can be directly recommended for its dissemination to the farmers for its use as it was found to be effective and suitable to the agro-ecological conditions or need to be modified by blending it with corresponding scientific technologies to make it more effective and suitable to their farming situations. To handle the data conveniently, it was decided before hand that ITKs which scored above 15 (> 50%) in any of the two categories will be the recommended mode for generalisation of ITKs. The results revealed that altogether 22 ITKs at Sl.No 1, 2, 3, 4, 5, 7, 9, 10, 11, 12, 13, 18, 20, 21, 23, 24, 26, 27, 28, 29, 30, and 31 could be recommended by extension agencies directly to the farmers for their application, whereas nine ITKs at Sl.No 6, 8, 14, 15, 16, 17, 19, 22 and 25 need to be further modified for their popularisation through blending with corresponding scientific technologies in order to enhance their efficacy and effectiveness as well as their suitability, adaptability and compatibility with their farming situations and farming system components. The plant protection scientists were also of the opinion that to the maximum possible extent efforts should be made to prepare ready to use (RTU) products in order to avoid time consuming and cumbersome procedures. Such efforts will step up easy dissemination of the usable ITKs. The findings presented in the above table are summarised in the Table 4.4.7.2.

Table 4.4.7.2: Distribution of ITKs according to utilisation method suggested by the scientists

Utilisation method	Frequency
ITKs suitable for directly dissemination by the extension workers	22
ITKs need to be modified as per the farming situation and preference of mod of application	9
Total	31

Corresponding scientific technology (CST) for Blending with selected Indigenous technical Knowledge (ITKs)

As evident from Table 4.4.7.2, out of 31 ITKs altogether 22 ITKs were recommended for their direct dissemination among farmers by the extension agents and nine with corresponding scientific technologies. The scientists' respondents were further requested to suggest suitable CSTs for each such ITKs. The findings are presented in Table 4.4.7.3.

Table 4.4.7.3: Suggestions on suitable Corresponding Scientific Technology for blending with ITK

S.No	ITK recommended for blending	Corresponding scientific technology (CST)
1 (ITK 8)	Sinduwar leaves are boiled in water and then cooled and this solution is used sprayed to control paddy caseworm *(Nymphula depunctalis)*.	Application of Chlorpyriphos @ 1 lit/ha
2 (ITK 14)	Red colour insects and Bihar hairy caterpillar is controlled by applying mixture of wooden ash and kerosene oil when insects appear on leaves of cucumber and bottle gourd crops.	Application of Indoxacarb 15.80 SC (500 ml/ha)
3 (ITK 15)	Ash is dusted over Bihar hairy caterpillar to control it.	Application of Indoxacarb 15.80 SC (500 ml/ha)
4 (ITK 16)	Mixture of Sinduwar leaves, sand kerosene oil is used to control Bihar hairy caterpillar.	Application of monocrotophos @ 1.0 lit/ha
5 (ITK 17)	Wooden ash is dusted on the leaves at night to control potato blight.	a. Seed treatment by Matlaxyly 0.2% solution & b. Spraying twice of Ridomil MZ 0.15% solution at interval of 10 days
6 (ITK 19)	Dried neem leaves are mixed with dried wheat seeds to control it from weevil during storage.	Use of Aluminium phosphide tablet @ 4 tab/quintal grain
7 (ITK 22)	Blackgram is protected from insects by storing it with fingermillet.	Use of Methyl parathion dust @ 250 g/quintal grain
8 (ITK 25)	Leaves and seeds of custard apple *(Annona squamosa)* are broadcasted to control insects/pests of paddy crop.	Application of Cartop hydrochloride 4G granules @ 25kg/ha after three weeks of transplanting

Figures in parentheses indicate serial no of ITK in the list

Results and Discussion ....

A perusal of Table 4.4.7.3 indicates that for blending ITKs with their corresponding scientific technologies in order to enhance their effectiveness in management of pests and diseases, the scientists' respondents have varied opinions and suggestions. However those CSTs were taken into accounts which were recommended by majority of them (50-70%). The respondents further opined that the ITKs can be practiced along with the respective CSTs in intermediated doses and with perfect frequencies. For this there is need for conducting on-farm trials (OFTs) in different combinations of ITKs and CSTs.

The findings are in conformity with those of **Haverkort et al. (1991)** and **Lakra et al. (2010)**, who blended several ITKs with the CSTs for increasing effectiveness of ITKs in management of various pests and diseases. Blending of ITK with CST will help in generation of low cost, need-based, location-specific and eco-friendly appropriate technology to make them more readily acceptable by resource poor farmers **(Kumar and Ansari 2015)**. While encouraging the use of ITKs, some modifications may be made to make them scientifically rational by blending with corresponding scientific technologies to increase their acceptability **(Shadap and Dkhar, 2019)**.

The target users of ITKs are the tribal farming community so it becomes imperative to take their opinion too for generalisation of ITKs. Studies have shown that relatively old age people do not share their valuable knowledge to others mainly for three reasons; first is to maintain the monopoly in the community, secondly they worry due to a superstition that the effectiveness of ITKs would disappear when shared with others and thirdly the younger generation do not value the age old knowledge and their disinterest in such knowledge. Thus relatively younger people complained that they are unaware of the existence of such kind of knowledge. Therefore for generalisation it was felt necessary that the opinion of tribal farmers should be obtained for knowing about wider generalisation of ITKs. The findings are presented in Table 4.4.7.4.

Table 4.4.7.4 Opinion of tribal farmers on mode of dissemination of ITKs for generalisation

S.No	Mode of dissemination	Frequency	Rank preference
1.	Farmer to famer extension	45 (100)	I
2.	Farmer-scientist interaction	12 (26.66)	X
3.	Para professional workers	7 (15.55)	XII
4.	Key informants	38 (84.44)	III
5.	Panchayat meetings	22 (48.88)	IX
6.	ITK register maintained at village level	41 (91.11)	II
7.	Magazines/Pamphlets in vernacular languages	34 (75.55)	V
8.	Social media	29 (64.44)	VII
9.	Village Knowledge Centres	26 (57.77)	VIII
10.	Farmer field schools	35 (77.77)	IV
11.	Portals/Websites/Apps	9 (20)	XI
12.	Role model announcement during kisan mela /farmers meeting	33 (73.33)	VI
13.	Awareness through Public address system	41 (91.11)	II

Multiple responses entertained and Figures in parentheses indicate percentages

Table 4.4.7.4 indicates that tribal farmers preferred to get information pertaining to ITKs from their fellow farmers. Farmer to farmer extension was ranked first (100%) as the fellow farmers are well acquainted with the farming situations of each other.

Tribal farmers were found to be excited about the record maintained in ITK register (91.11%) to seek information related to different aspects of generalisation of ITKs. As the African proverb states that "*if an old man dies, whole library disappears*", Up keeping and maintenance of such register will serve as repository of such knowledge at local level. Simultaneously awareness through public address system was also ranked second (91.11%) by the tribal key informants in scaling up of the ITKs.

Obtaining information through key informants or opinion leaders ranked third (84.44%) as the preferred mode of dissemination of ITKs for its generalisation. The reason might be due to their experience, social prestige and trustworthiness. Due to these characteristics generally people used to visit them for valuable information from them.

Farmers field schools were ranked fourth (77.77%) as the preferred means of dissemination for generalisation of ITKs. Farmers field schools are a good platform to bring farmers and facilitators at one place and display the effectiveness of technologies where a follow up can help in building the confidence of farmers in practicing ITKs in farming.

Magazines and pamphlets in vernacular languages were ranked fifth (75.55%) as the tribal farmers know only their regional languages so for better outreach publications in vernacular language was preferred.

Award of role model farmer during kisan melas/farmer meetings ranked sixth (73.33%). A successful farmer practicing ITKs can be awarded as a role model in his/her community. This will not only bring sense of pride among the farmers to do better with ITKs but also empower and motivate other farmers to take up and utilise ITKs on a larger scale.

Social media like whatsapp, facebook, twitter, instagram etc are excellent platforms to share information at global level. This will facilitate better handling of information with different sections of the society and also helpful in documentation. So it was ranked as seventh (75.55%) most preferred means of dissemination.

Village knowledge centres were ranked eighth (57.77%). These centres have become hub for information sharing and getting any information with print outs which is cost-effective and helpful in providing advices in any problem.

Panchayat meetings ranked ninth (48.88%) which is convenient for the farmers to share all kind of information at a single place.

Farmers are reluctant to have a healthy discussion with scientists as they think outsiders are not empathetic with their conditions and outsiders always have blanket recommendations. That's why they least preferred scientist-farmer interaction as it ranked tenth (26.66%).

Portals/Websites/Apps ranked eleventh preferred means for generalisation of ITKs as the tribal farmers are not well versed with these digital applications.

Para-professional workers are also a source of information to the villagers in the study area. But the tribal farmers are least bothered about the information shared by them due to their least experience and expertise in ITKs so it was ranked twelfth (15.55%) and last by the tribal farmers.

Ponnusamy *et al.* (2009), Singh (2013), Pandey *et al.* (2017) and Rathore *et al.* (2021) suggested similar promotional strategies like farmer-farmer extension, promoting local innovators as role models and and incentives were more preferred by farmers. **Talukdar *et al.* (2012)** suggested popularising ITKs through awareness campaigns and trainings, and other traditional methods to scale up the use of ITKs in agriculture. Scholars in all these studies emphasized institutionalisation of ITK as it has immense utilitarian value in development process for wider applicability of ITKs.

4.5. Constraints encountered in utilisation of ITKs by tribal farmers

A participatory agricultural extension approach needs continuous reflection on the potentials and constraints of the target group i.e. farmers. Focus group discussion with tribal farmers yielded a number of constraints encountered by the tribal farmers in utilisation of ITKs in the study area. In order to prioritize the constraints, a schedule was administered to the tribal farmers to rate their opinion on a 3- point continuum. Based on the responses received, the various constraints were categorized under five major sections namely, i) Socio-psychological constraints ii) Technological constraints iii) Financial constraints iv) Extension-related constraints v) Policy-related constraints. The data obtained are presented in the Table 4.5.

A cursory look on Table 4.5 indicates that under socio-psychological constraints, 'lack of interest among youths' and 'lack of awareness among farmers' were ranked first (WMS=2.63). This might be due to the reason that the young generation is attracted towards modern lifestyle and migrate to cities for seeking better livelihood options leaving the traditional farming legacy behind. Similarly the reason for lack of awareness among farmers was due to the fact that tribal farmers remain isolated from the society and have rigid social structure and they are not aware of the scientific interventions and alternative knowledge systems prevalent in the society. They keep following the beliefs they have been practicing and are aloof of new learning opportunities. Second rank (WMS=2.60) was assigned to 'lack of motivation from peers'. Fellow progressive farmers do not support them in practicing ITKs as it is being regarded by them as outdated and irrelevant to modern day farming. 'Lack of conviction about returns' ranked third (WMS=2.31). ITKs are time consuming and desired results are obtained slowly. On contrary results of corresponding scientific technology (CST) are immediately visible so they prefer the quickest possible way to solve the problems.

Table 4.5: Distribution of tribal farmers according to their opinion on constraints encountered in utilisation of ITKs

(n=45)

S.No	Constraint	Most Important (3)	Important (2)	Least Important (1)	Total score	WMS	Rank
I.	**Socio-psychological constraints**						
1.	Inclination towards modern technologies	8	18	19	79	1.75	VI
2.	Lack of conviction about returns	14	31	-	104	2.31	III
3.	Lack of motivation from peers	36	-	9	117	2.60	II
4.	Negative attitude towards ITK	8	6	31	67	1.48	VII
5.	Difficulty in identifying indigenous materials	22	14	9	103	2.28	IV
6.	ITK changes from area to area	8	37	-	98	2.17	V
7.	Lack of interest among youths	38	-	7	121	2.63	I
8.	Lack of awareness among farmers	38	-	7	121	2.63	I
II.	**Technological constraints**						
1.	ITK is labour intensive	10	24	11	89	1.97	VI
2.	Inconvenient and time consuming nature of ITK	22	14	9	103	2.28	IV
3.	Over reliability of farmers on external inputs	22	14	7	101	2.24	V
4.	Inconvenience in preparation	24	21	-	114	2.53	III

Results and Discussion ....

5.	Mode of application is not well defined	34	11	-	124	2.75	II
6.	More reliance on Ready to Use (RTU) products	43	2	-	133	2.95	I
III.	**Financial constraints**						
1.	Lack of financial support	43	2	-	133	2.95	I
2.	Low economic returns	29	4	12	107	2.37	II
3.	Preference to costly external inputs in comparison to cost effective ITK	16	8	21	85	1.88	III
IV.	**Extension-related constraints**						
1.	Lack of expert guidance	29	16	-	119	2.64	I
2.	Lack of exposure among extension personnel towards ITK	25	18	2	113	2.51	II
3.	Lack of training	19	10	16	95	2.11	VI
4.	Lack of awareness campaigns	25	18	2	113	2.51	II
5.	Lack of research-based evidences in economic terms	3	42	-	93	2.06	VII
6.	Lack of information sources	23	4	8	85	1.88	X
7.	Lack of participatory technological validation	17	25	3	104	2.31	IV
8.	Lack of linkages and coordination among various stakeholders	23	20	2	111	2.46	III

Results and Discussion ....

9.	Limited scope for dissemination	20	15	10	100	2.22	V
10.	Lack of publications in vernacular languages	21	11	3	88	1.95	IX
11.	Lack of scientific evaluation and modification.	9	26	10	89	1.97	VIII
V	**Policy-related constraints**						
1.	No platform for sharing indigenous knowledge	42	3	-	132	2.93	II
2.	No provision for monetary assistance to disclosures of indigenous knowledge	44	1	-	138	3.06	I
3.	Extinction of many indigenous plants	18	13	14	94	2.08	VII
4.	Least effort made by the government agencies in popularising ITK	28	11	8	114	2.53	VI
5.	Less recognition of ITK work	41	-	4	127	2.82	III
6.	No provision of Prior Informed Consent (PIC) for commercialisation	30	15	-	120	2.66	V
7.	Industrialisation and urbanisation	38	1	6	122	2.71	IV
8.	Migration of tribal people from remote areas	34	1	10	114	2.53	VI
9.	Lack of database creation facility	24	1	-	114	2.53	VI

I. Socio-psychological constraints

'Difficulty in identifying indigenous materials' ranked fourth (WMS=2.28) among socio-psychological constraints as only elder persons have sufficient knowledge about the importance of indigenous plant materials and their insecticidal properties and it is very difficult for them to roam around the surroundings to collect the materials due to their age and health issues. Other important constraints reported were 'changing nature of ITKs, changes from area to area' (WMS=2.17) due to its location-specificity, inclination towards modern technologies (WMS=1.75) as there is no provision of ITK-based recommended package of practices and attractive returns and associated perks with CST force them to undo practicing ITK. 'Negative attitude towards ITK' (WMS=1.48) emerged at last rank as farmers are quite skeptical regarding the profitability and quickness in problem-solving through ITK.

II. Technological constraints

Under technological constraints, 'more reliance on Ready to Use (RTU) products' (WMS=2.95) was ranked first. It might be due to the fact that now-a-days people prefer quick method, and direct as well as immediate solutions rather than lengthy procedure of identifying, collecting and preparing products for solving the problem. Secondly, 'not well defined mode of application of ITKs' was identified as the next major constraint (WMS=2.75) as there is no standardised information are readily available on mode and dose of application of ITK. 'Inconvenience in preparation' was deliberated as the third (WMS=2.53) important constraint. The procedure of preparing the solution is cumbersome and time consuming. Fourth (WMS=2.28) rank was assigned to the statement 'ITK is inconvenient and time consuming', as it takes long time to control insect-pests. The results are slowly visible. 'Over reliability of farmers on external inputs' (WMS=2.24) was ranked fifth among all as the CST is easy to handle which may be applied directly and effects are seen immediately as well as problem is solved quickly. 'ITK is labour intensive' was assigned sixth (WMS=1.97) rank as more labour is required for preparing ITK due to its bulkiness.

III. Financial constraints

Under financial constraints, lack of financial support from government agencies got first ranked (WMS=2.95). It might be due to the reason that there is no special package and perks available for farmers practicing traditional faming which discourage them to practice it and on contrary many perks of credits, farm mechanizations etc are being given to farmers who adopt new scientific interventions. Low economic returns was assigned second rank (WMS=2.37) as it is low yielding in nature. Preference to costly external inputs in comparison to cost effective ITK was scored third rank (WMS=1.88) as standard package of practices are easily available

IV. Extension-related constraints

Under extension-related constraints, first (WMS=2.64) major constraint identified was 'lack of expert guidance' as there are very few ITK experts available in the country. Second rank (WMS=2.51) was given to 'lack of exposure to extension personnel towards ITK' and 'lack of awareness campaigns' as ITKs are available with tribal communities and they don't have interaction with the outer world, so extension personnel rarely encounter ITKs during their service period and have less orientation towards its existence and use. Furthermore, awareness campaigns are not organised to limelight the existence of ITK in the society, so they remain hidden from the development practitioners and other stakeholders. 'Lack of linkages and coordination among various stakeholders' was deliberated third rank (WMS=2.46) as no national body to regulate and scale up the use of ITK is in existence, so there are linkage issues in streamlining its usage. 'Lack of participatory technological validation' was identified as fourth major constraint (WMS=2.31) because rarely any validation work is done at research stations to know about the effectiveness of ITKs. Fifth constraint (WMS=2.22) was 'limited scope for dissemination'. There is also inadequate availability of audio-visual materials to showcase the relevance of ITKs prevalent in the area. 'Lack of training to extension professionals' was assigned sixth rank (WMS=2.11) as there was no training facility available on ITK-based package of practices. 'Lack of research-based evidences in economic terms' was deliberated seventh rank (WMS=2.06) by the tribal farmers as rarely any profitability based research findings are available with the scientific community. Eighth rank (WMS=1.97) was given to 'lack of scientific evaluation and modification' as meagerly any efforts are made to evaluate the ITK on different attributes and its refinement for scaling up its use for sustainable agricultural development. Last and ninth rank (WMS=1.95) was assigned to 'lack of publications in vernacular languages'. It might be due to the fact that nobody has ever been concerned about publishing relevant ITK literatures to broad base its utilisation.

V. Policy-related constraints

Under policy related constraints lack of provisions for monetary assistance to disclosures of indigenous knowledge was assigned as the first policy-related constraint (WMS=3.06). Since there is no policy regarding ITK and its practitioners so several development personnel exploit their knowledge without giving them any recognition and monetary rewards so they are skeptical to share their knowledge with the outsiders as they have intuition that people outside their community might misutilise their knowledge for personal gains. Second rank (WMS=2.93) was deliberated to 'no platform for sharing indigenous knowledge' as there is no common platform where all the knowledge bearers and originators can come up, discuss and share about relevant ITKs.

Less recognition of ITK work was assigned third rank (WMS=2.82) as it is considered as outdated, illogical, unscientific, marginalized and backward so less recognition is given by the scientific community and development workers and are ignored in many development projects. Fourth major identified constraint (WMS=2.71) was industrialization and urbanization as young generations do not want to follow the traditional lifestyle as they are attracted to the charm of modern cities and modern livelihood options rather than farming. So they migrate to cities for jobs and educational opportunities. No provision of Prior Informed Consent (PIC) for commercialisation was identified as fifth major constraint (WMS=2.66) and it is of more relevance in the context of Intellectual Property Rights. Many development projects exploit farmers and their knowledge without obtaining PIC and give no monetary rewards and recognition after commercialization of that ITK. So tribal farmers are at loss in sharing this important indigenous knowledge. Three constraints namely 'least efforts made by the government agencies in popularizing ITK', 'migration of tribal people from remote areas' and 'lack of database creation facility' were ranked seventh (WMS=2.53). It might be because no programmes and campaigns are organised to popularize ITKs so they are not accessible to other farmers. People are not continuing the legacy of traditional farming and move to cities to find employment for their socio-economic upliftment. Modern digital tools like ICT interventions are not promoted in ITK documentation and database are still not created. Many indigenous plants are on the verge of extinction ranked eighth (WMS=2.08) among all these constraints as the important indigenous materials are not maintained properly by the government agencies.

Similar constraints were determined under the studies conducted by **Sahu (2002), Noorjehan *et al.* (2005), Jayawardana (2007), Hosseni *et al.* (2011), Hathila (2013), Husain and Sunadaramari (2013), Malhari (2015), Naharki and Jaisi (2020), Sujeetha and Asokhan (2020)** and **Khatri *et al.* (2021)**. Inability in identifying indigenous materials, more time requirement, lack of skill, less yield and income, less recognition by scientific community, undefined dose of application, documentation, inclination towards modern technologies, older people being skeptical to share this knowledge with others and consideration being outdated were the major constraints that hinder the utilisation of ITKs in all the studies. The constraints identified by these studies also revealed that lack of interest of young generation is the sole reason for unpopularity and vanishing of ITKs.

4.6 Development of a framework for systematic documentation and scientisation of Indigenous Technical Knowledge

A framework is a real or conceptual structure intended to serve as a support or guide for the building of something that expands the structure into something useful. The framework assists in the identification of the linkages and relationships between indigenous technical knowledge and sustainable agricultural development. **Dekens**

(2007) stated the important steps in order to provide further policy recommendations is identifying how indigenous technical knowledge can be combined with other knowledge system such as scientific knowledge. Development of the framework emerges from participatory work between researchers, scientists, extension workers, tribal farmers and the non-government organizations.

In order to engage indigenous technical knowledge productively in development, **Agrawal (1995)** argues that there is a need to move beyond the dichotomy of indigenous versus scientific and work towards building bridges across the indigenous and scientific divide. This requires parity and integration between indigenous and scientific knowledge systems, demanding a mutual understanding of the cultural, material and epistemological basis of each. Hence, there is need for a participatory process in which indigenous knowledge is shown to have value and is kept within the community. It is essential that indigenous communities themselves have easy access to relevant research and information that may assist them in reducing the cost of cultivation. In an attempt to meet the requirements for sustainable agricultural development the framework discussed below has focused on the use of participatory techniques within a given community to integrate both indigenous and scientific knowledge. This will be a useful tool for identifying how the two sets of knowledge may be successfully integrated within the National Agricultural Research System.

The process framework focuses on the process as key to achieving outcomes on a step-by-step basis in a linear fashion. However it is a cyclic process with the framework designed to be flexible to suit any community, and with no specific guidelines as to how much time should be taken upon each step, thereby enabling the community to control the process. Importantly, this process is not static, because once an integrated strategy has been identified, the framework again allows for flexibility and revision of the process.

Framework development

Before developing such a process framework and consulting as well as working with tribal communities, it is essential to ensure that research is conducted in a dignified manner, following the communities' cultural values, norms and traditions and ensuring that the research contributes to their needs **(Louis, 2007)**. The researcher and the community together were able to determine the problems to be worked on and the possibilities for change. The researcher and the community were able to adapt and develop methods that worked best for a given community or locality **(Ivanitz, 1999)**. This approach attempts to acknowledge that researchers are not always right and that it is the community that knows its own situation best, thus avoiding the traditional power relations between a researcher and his or her subjects **(Ivanitz, 1999)**. The researcher is there as a facilitator to guide, assist and learn, but not to teach. The framework involves a partnership between the community, the researcher and associated stakeholders (for example, NGOs, government bodies) to identify a viable strategy for appropriate technology development. It has long been recognised that the top-down, science-centered approach to development has failed to deliver its promises **(Halani, 2004 and Fraser *et al.*, 2006)**. The bottom-up participatory approach, advocated a couple of decades ago, has also not yielded the desired results **(Halani, 2004)**. The proposed framework offers a potential solution to this dilemma, utilising and building upon the benefits of both indigenous and scientific knowledge bases.

The potential contribution of indigenous knowledge to uplift livelihood of the local people notwithstanding some people still believe that it is backward, conservative, inefficient, inferior and based largely on myths **(Titilola, 1990)**. There is need to develop frameworks capable of tapping and revisiting the existing knowledge and incorporating the same in development of sustainable production system. It is high time that scientific community to stop finding limitations and see the strengths in ITK so that it can complement the CST for better adoption and adaptation. Every knowledge system has its own strengths and weaknesses. We should look for better opportunities. Despite the fact that efforts have been made towards the changing agricultural scenario from a scientific perspective, research and policies directed towards the incorporation of ITK within agricultural systems are desperately needed. The below mentioned figure depicts the dimensions of the framework development.

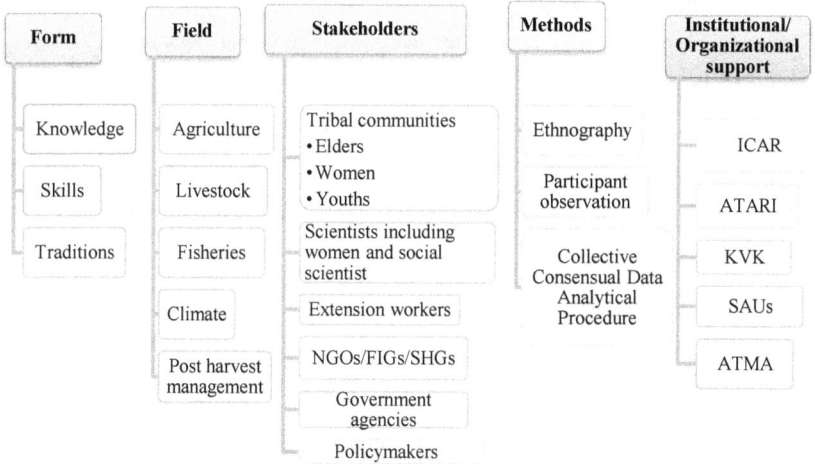

Figure 15: Dimensions of framework development

Major Planks of Framework

1. Prior Informed Consent (PIC)

It becomes imperative for research community to obtain PIC either from the tribal clan leader for the entire community or from the tribal farmers individually for equitable benefit sharing. It was observed that many researchers exploit the knowledge of tribal framers without giving them due recognition and any monetary assistance. Thus, to avoid such unavoidable exploitation PIC should be made mandatory before documenting knowledge of voluntary disclosers.

2. Community engagement

For appropriate technology development, it is imperative to involve communities at each and every level of planning, implementing, monitoring and promoting of ITKs. To initiate the whole appropriate technological development process, rapport building with the villagers is necessary. Establishing trust and rapport with a community is an essential first step prior to moving on to further steps in the framework. So it can be done with the help of tribal key informants. The first step is to initiate community engagement and to determine what are the major problems of the area and also define the problems from farmers' perspectives and its effect on agricultural productivity. Rapport building with the tribal community should be initiated through identification of key informants. The purpose of the visit should be explained properly and with the consent of tribal key informants a suitable place to hold meetings and focused group discussions can be fixed. Prior to meeting suitable arrangements for sitting and discussion should be made. Involvement of elders and women must be ensured.

3. Pilot study of the area

After exhaustive literature review identify an area where one will be studying ITKs. Try to categorize different aspects where ITKs are being applied having the problem. Visit the place personally or in a team and contact key informants. Discuss about the motive of coming and ask them to schedule a meeting with the villagers for the same.

4. Initial preparations for documentation

A multi-disciplinary team should be involved to identify the needs and priorities of the farmers of the study area. It must include a woman scientist as tribal community may have restriction for women to interact with the outsiders, a social scientist to understand the socio-psychological and economic condition of the farmers and a leader identified through key informant techniques or sociometric and informant rating. A para professional would complement the team as he/she will be from the community and well acquainted with the agro-ecological system. Participatory techniques like venn diagram, social mapping, resource mapping, transect walk etc would complement the documentation. Library professional is required for archiving and cataloguing. Arrangements for photography/ videography will be required.

5. Documentation of ITKs

Documentation can either be made from primary sources or secondary sources. A thorough review of literature revealed that many researches have been done in the past to identify and document ITKs in different aspects of agriculture but due to unavailability of a proper format of documentation, the work is scattered and not accessible for compilation for the directory or database creation. Thus a format has been suggested so that other researchers may follow in future researches so that relevant information could be documented properly of a particular ITK. Name, problem, mode of application, frequency, community, disclosure's name, contact number, address and photograph etc needs to be recorded in the format so that a directory of ITKs can be created for different fields.

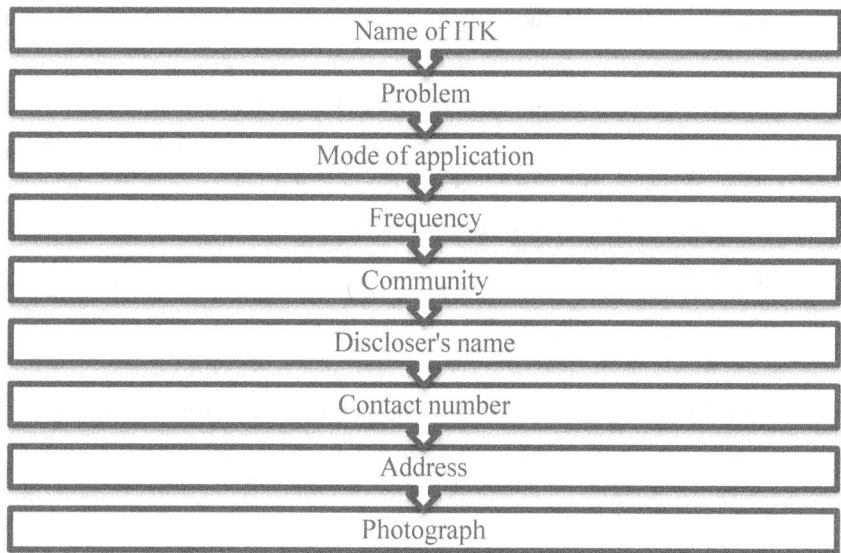

Figure 16: Items in the format for documentation of ITKs

The present framework has been developed involving the end of three main stakeholders i.e. users, extension personnel and researchers. During documentation of the ITKs the three stakeholders should be involved as given here under:

User end

After identification of tribal key informants, proposal should be taken to the community and a subsequent meeting should be called with community members at a common meeting place. The meeting is an opportunity for villagers to discuss important issues with the researcher and other stakeholders, including the government and NGOs. Then ITK and related information should be elicited from the community members on different aspects as suggested above.

Extension end

The researcher or facilitator is there to guide and to listen but not to direct. The role of extension personnel should be not to teach and train the community but to facilitate community and knowledge mobilization. Extension personnel must be competent enough to identify right ITK materials and document the relevant information. Inventory creation with the help of library information professionals for cataloguing and archiving is also an important role of extension personnel. Training and capacity building should be required for extension personnel for understanding the social, agro-ecological condition and cultural setting of tribal communities. Trainings to conduct participant observation and ethnography studies, data gathering and assessment tools should be organised for them.

Research end

The task of finalizing a proper ethical protocol through Prior Informed Consent format lies in the hand of research community through discussion with policy makers, development practitioners and other stakeholders. A common data gathering tool with standardized format consisting of name of ITK, problem, mode of application, frequency, discloser's name, community, contact number and photographs with proper guideline to documentation and scientisation of ITKs should be prepared.

6. Scientisation of ITKs

i. Particularisation of ITKs

ITKs are practices and traditions of indigenous communities for solving their day to day problems to adapt to the changing environmental condition. Every knowledge is not of utilitarian value, some knowledge is just myths and beliefs that have been followed since time immemorial without knowing the logic behind using it. So to sort out appropriate ITKs is an important step in the process of development of sustainable agricultural practices. Thus particularisation is an important step of screening out ITKs that can be utilised for developmental purposes.

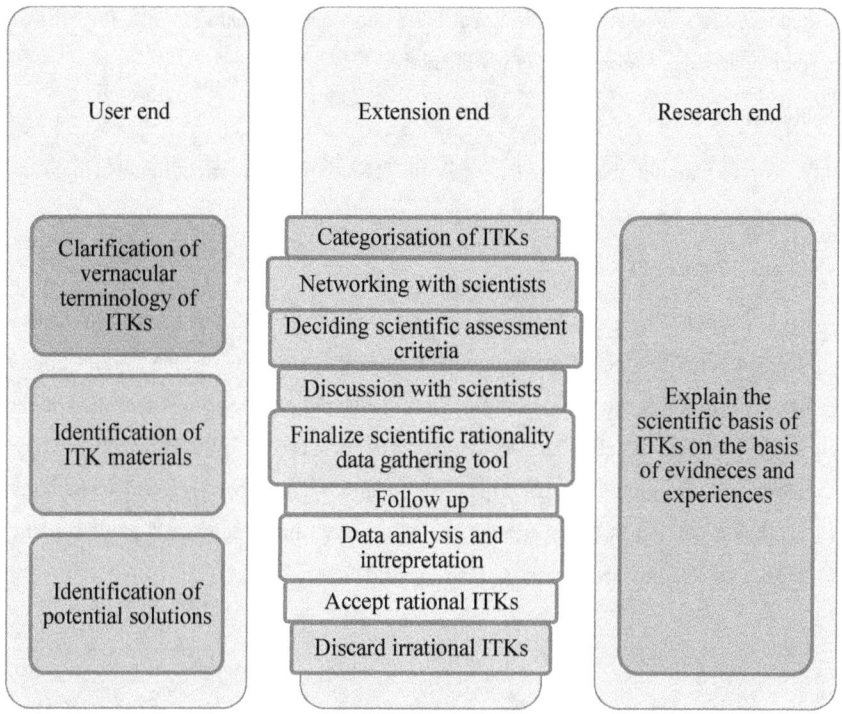

Figure 17: Particularisation of ITKs involving the three main stakeholders

User end

The role of user is to assist extension personnel in clarifying vernacular terminologies related to ITKs and other information needed, identification of ITK materials and potential solutions within the community and area to solve the prioritized problems.

Extension end

Categorization of ITKs according to different problems as well as linkages and networking with the scientists of different disciplines to establish scientific rationality of ITKs should be done followed by deciding relevant scientific rationality assessment tools in discussion with the scientists and finalizing scientific rationality data gathering tool, follow up, skills for data analysis and interpretation, acceptance of rational ITKs by discarding irrational ITKs and finally preparation of a final list of particularised or rational ITKs for validation.

Research end

Explaining the scientific basis of ITKs based on scientific evidences or experience in respective fields by the research scientists.

ii. Validation of ITKs

Validation means assessing the effectiveness of ITKs on certain parameters decided either by scientific community or farming community or both. Since farmers are well aware of their socio-physical field situations, it is assumed that they better understand their situation and decide the practices accordingly so we can also go for scientific and community participatory validation. The most preferred community validation method is Quantification of Indigenous Knowledge (QuIK) followed by Mean Perceived Effectiveness Methodology (MPEM).

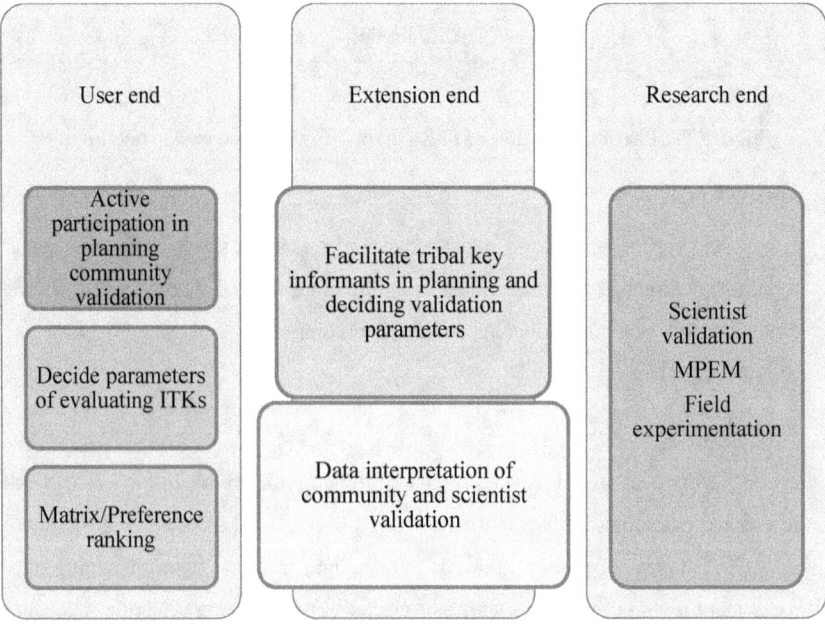

Figure 18: Validation of ITKs involving the three main stakeholders

User end

Evaluating ITKs on decided parameters through use of preference or matrix ranking tool.

Extension end

Facilitating tribal key informants in planning and deciding parameters and data interpretation.

Research end

Deciding scientific parameters to establish the effectiveness of ITKs through field experimentation (On Farm Trials/Frontline Demonstrations).

iii. Generalisation of ITKs

Several works have been done so far but due to unavailability of a proper strategy to scale up the use of ITKs, it is not fully utilised in farming. So a proper standard strategy to scale up the use of ITKs is required according to the scientists' and farmers' preferences.

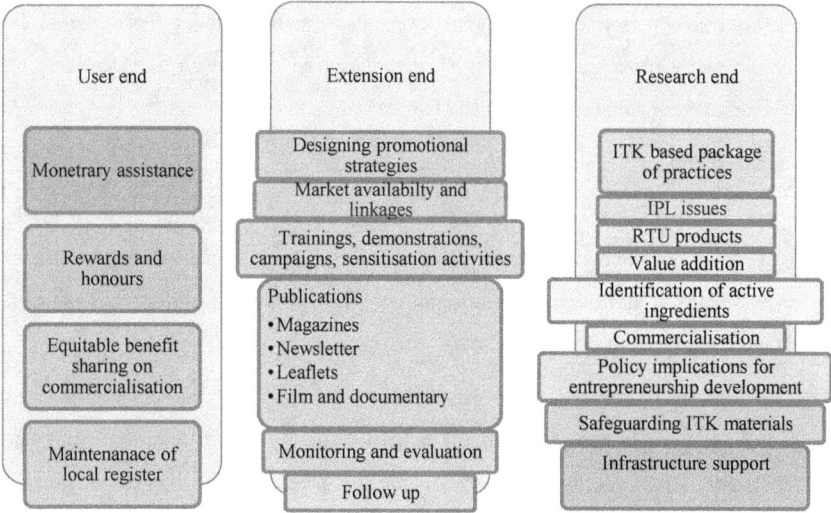

Figure 19: Generalisation of ITKs involving the three main stakeholders

User end

Monetary assistance to disclose ITKs will motivate them to disclose and the rewards and honors will bring sense of pride and increase respect among them in the community. Equitable benefit sharing on commercialization of ITKs will help the community to actively involve in value addition and commercialization of ITKs. Simultaneously local register can be maintained by community at local level to assist other fellow farmers.

Extension end

Designing promotional strategies for generalisation of ITKs should be followed through establishing market linkages. Besides, trainings, demonstrations, campaigns and sensitization activities should be carried out including publications, monitoring and evaluation and follow up. Traditional media should be preferred as mode of communication. Apart from this, ITKs magazines, newsletters, leaflets, films and documentaries should be prepared and published. For archiving and indexing, role of both the extension workers and library professionals is of utmost importance. Both should complement each other's role. Field survey and data should be gathered by extension personnel whereas in close discussion archiving task should be completed by library professionals so that it can be utilised on a wider scale by development workers, researchers and farmers.

Research end

ITK based package of practices, Intellectual Property Right issues, ready to use product development, value addition, commercialization, policy implications for entrepreneurship development, safeguarding ITK materials and infrastructure support should be provided and strengthened.

It is very important to concretize ITK into a system. By linking the indigenous knowledge systems with research and extension, the outputs of the research can be made more fertile and usable (**Pandey *et al.* 2017**). So identification, documentation and incorporation of ITK in agricultural extension organization are essential for appropriate technology development **Lenka and Satpathy, (2020).** Strengthening the capacity of regional research and extension organisations and bringing research-extension-farmers together in validation and dissemination of ITKs would help in sustainable agricultural development **Mushtaq et al. (2020)**. Roles and responsibilities of extension system, policy makers and administrators for ITK documentation and preservation were also defined in the study of **Kanagasabapathi and Sakthivel (2016)**. A standard framework including detail of each activity to be followed at various stages of incorporating ITK into agricultural system for sustainable agricultural development has been recommended by **Rajasekharan (1993)**.

4.7 Success story

In order to demonstrate the value of ITKs, an attempt was made to document a success story which is presented as follows:

Socio-economic Upliftment of Tribal Farming Community of Jharkhand through Upscaling Indigenous Rice Varieties

Divyayan Krishi Vigyan Kendra (KVK) run by R K Mission, Ranchi, is a well-recognized institution for its exemplary work in the tribal belt of Jharkhand. An awareness programme was organised under the ageis of Protection of Plant Varieties and Farmers' Rights Authority (PPV&RA) through Indian Council of Agricultural Research (ICAR) in order to identify and document farmers' varieties of different crops across the country through Scientist-Farmer Interaction. Divyayan KVK took an initiative to register indigenous rice varieties cultivated in the area of its operation. Altogether 187 rice varieties cultivated by tribal farming communities were identified and analysed for their distinctiveness, uniformity and stability (DUS) test. Out of 187 rice varieties, 35 were registered under PPV&FRA. A remarkable feature of this process was that the varieties developed by tribal farming communities were registered in their names which provided them identity and recognition.

In order to bring improvements and expedite the process, a Project was submitted by Divyayan KVK on '"Commercialisation of Selected Indigenous Rice Varieties of Tribal Farmers" to NABARD for providing support to marginalised tribal farmers'. Market survey was carried out to know the consumer preferences with regard to selected rice varieties. It was found that non-basmati but scented rice variety was commonly preferred by the local people of Ranchi. After market survey two varieties, namely, *Bhutku* and *Tulsi Mukul*, non-*basmati*, but scented varieties were selected for their multi-location trials for analysis of various attributes including aroma, taste and yield. The two rice varieties, however, were relatively low yielders in comparison to other improved varieties prevalent in the area. Keeping this in view the KVK developed organic package of practices to add value to the produce. A system of seed production was also evolved by the KVK. Every possible measure for purification of the seed was taken care. Organic manures and pesticides (*Sanjivani*, *Panchagavya*, Azolla and Bioagents) were the important aspects of the package including green manuring. The KVK devised a mechanism to buy back the seed from farmers @ Rs. 40/kg and after processing sale back to the growers @ Rs. 50/kg. Dehusked rice is marketed by the KVK @ Rs. 150/kg. On the basis of cost and benefit sharing with the growers. On the basis of average yield @25q/ha and sale of dehusked rice @ Rs. 15000/q i.e. Rs. 240000/ ha a farmer was earning as gross income. The net income is computed to be on an average Rs 200000 per ha with B: C ratio of 5.0.

This brought a spectacular change in economic condition of the tribal farm families owing to various socio-economic transformations.

This is a case of KVK showing the way to the tribal farmers about taking and adopting innovative methodologies to develop plant varieties. The efforts of the KVK motivated farmers in developing and popularising indigenous plant varieties. They have the potential to develop and cultivate rice varieties. It brought sense of pride among the tribal farmers. The empowerment of tribal farmers was done by PPV&FRA which was facilitated by Divyayan KVK.

Chapter 5 SUMMARY AND CONCLUSIONS

The basic component of any country's knowledge system is its Indigenous Technical Knowledge. It encompasses the skills, experiences and insights of people, applied to maintain or improve their livelihoods. This rich resource and indigenous knowledge base has tremendous potential to address the current concerns of conventional agriculture like depletion and degradation of the natural resource base, poor productivity and the problems related to pests and diseases. ITK is a cumulative body of knowledge and techniques handed down through generations by cultural transmission of the relationship of living beings including humans with one another and their environment. ITK practices are farmer friendly, socially accepted, economic, environmentally sound, and suited to the specific local and environmental conditions.

Sustainability is something that is talked about considerably these days. In our acute need to save environment, we are making strides towards more secured alternatives. At this juncture, it becomes imperative to take a step back and think about the genesis of agriculture. If the fundamental practices and resources in agriculture are utilized more sustainably, the successive strata would be improved significantly. Over time, ITK has proved itself to be a valuable resource for the researchers and scientists to work on and develop suitable technologies. In this way, it has also facilitated the participation of local communities in the development of better innovations. This has not only paved way for eco-friendly techniques but has also promoted self-sufficiency. Hence, there is an urgent need to document and preserve the indigenous knowledge for its proper utilisation in the Indian agricultural context. ITK holds immense potential for development, especially at the grassroots level.

Assessment of this precious knowledge resource for its scientific rationality could be a step towards their integration in the formal research system. The integration of indigenous knowledge with scientific agricultural practices could lead to easy adoption of technologies by the farming community resulting in achieving sustainability in agriculture. ITK integration with improved scientific agricultural practices could make agriculture more sustainable. Understanding the perception of researchers on the indigenous pool could be the first stage of incorporation of this precious knowledge base in the formal research system and generation of technologies that are appropriate and sustainable with ensuring faster rate of adoption among the farming community.

Not many efforts have been made so far to collate this vast pool of knowledge in the context of managing and preserving ITK. Inadequate frameworks for proper documentation and scientisation of ITKs have limited the easy accessibility to farmers, researchers, academicians, policy makers and development practitioners.

Therefore, an effort has been made to identify the process of evolving scientific practices from experts and comparing this with what is being practiced at the field level. The study also aimed at identifying the constraints in the process of generalisation. Based on this, a process framework has been recommended for collating and preserving ITKs for sustainable agricultural development. Therefore, a research study entitled, "Scientisation of Indigenous Technical Knowledge of Tribal Farmers in Ranchi district of Jharkhand" was undertaken with the following specific objectives:

5.1 Objectives

1. To identify the process of systematic documentation and scientisation of Indigenous Technical Knowledge.
2. To study the process of scientisation of Indigenous Technical Knowledge about pest and disease management among tribal farmers.
3. To delineate the constraints encountered in utilisation of Indigenous Technical Knowledge by tribal farmers.
4. To develop a framework for systematic documentation and scientisation of Indigenous Technical Knowledge.

5.2 Research methodology

Descriptive research design was used for this study. There were three categories of respondents consisting of ITK Experts, plant protection scientists and the tribal farmers. A total number of 55 ITK experts spread across the country and 30 plant protection scientists were selected randomly from the list prepared. The selection of tribal farmers was done by adopting the multistage sampling procedure. Tribal farmers were also utilised as the key informants in this study. Jharkhand was identified as the universe and Ranchi district was selected as the locale of the study. Two tribal dominated blocks of the district i.e. Angara and Tamar were selected purposively. Two villages each namely Uludih and Jaspur from Angara and Amhesa and Dhurleta from Tamar being tribal dominated were selected randomly for the study. Selection of tribal farmers was made through snowball sampling. A total of 45 tribal farmers were selected as the respondents for the study. Delphi technique was used to reach at consensus by the ITK experts for identifying the process of systematic documentation and scientisation. Rationality analysis of selected ITKs was done by sending the list of ITKs to the plant protection scientists, as the first step of scientisation i.e. particularisation. Three types of rating scales i.e. 3-point rating scale of Dhaliwal and Singh (2010), 4-point rating scale of Venkatesan and Sundaramarai (2014) and 5-point rating scale of Hiranand (1979) were used. Validation was done both through community validation and scientist validation. Community validation was done by QuIK method with tribal farmers and scientist validation through Mean Perceived Effectiveness Methodology by the scientists. For generalisation, scientists were asked to indicate their opinion on whether an ITK can be directly disseminated to the farmers or it needed blending, so blending suggestions were also requested. Preference on mode of dissemination was also obtained from the tribal farmers for better utilisation of the ITKs. The constraints encountered in the utilisation of ITKs were investigated using a 3-point continuum i.e. score 3 for most important, 2 for important and 1 for least important constraints. Thereafter analysing the outcomes of objectives 1, 2 and 3, a process framework was prepared and recommended for systematic documentation and scientisation of ITK. Mailed questionnaires and interview schedules were used as quantitative tools for data collection. The focus group discussion, participant observation and transect and matrix ranking were used as qualitative tools for data collection. The data so collected was analysed, tabulated, and interpreted by using statistical procedures like frequency, percentage, arithmetic mean, standard deviation, standard error, weighted mean score and Duncan Multiple Range Test.

5.3 RESULTS AND DISCUSSION

The demographic profile of tribal farmers and ITK experts were documented and presented below:

5.3.1 Demographic profile of tribal farmers

- Altogether 60 per cent of the tribal farmers were females and 40 per cent were males. The findings highlighted the importance of women's representation and contributions in tribal farming systems.
- Out of total tribal farmers, the highest proportion of the respondents i.e. 71.11 per cent belonged to old age group followed by middle-aged (24.44%) and young (4.45%). This indicated that old age people were the knowledge bearers holding vast knowledge about ITKs which might be lost if they do not share this knowledge with the youngsters.
- Altogether 46.66 per cent of the tribal farmers belonged to Oraon community followed by Munda (24.46%), Ho (15.55%) and Kharia (13.33%).
- Majority of the tribal farmers had education up to primary level (31.12%) followed by middle school (20.00%) and high school (11.12%). A very less number of respondents belonged to the category of graduate and above (8.88%). The remaining respondents were either illiterate (6.66%) or can read and/or write only (28.88%). This indicated that the respondents in the study area had low level of education.
- Out of total tribal farmers, highest proportion had marginal size of land holdings (57.78%) followed by small (20.00%), medium (13.33%) and large (8.89%). Findings revealed that more than 75 per cent of tribal key informants had small and marginal size of land holdings.
- The highest proportion of the respondents i.e. 57.78 per cent was having high farming experience followed by medium (31.11%) and low (11.11%) experience. This indicated that they had been practicing this oral tradition for a long time and thus contributing to environmental protection.

> Altogether 57.77 per cent of the tribal farmers had low level of risk orientation followed by 24.45 per cent and 17.78 per cent who had medium and high levels of risk orientation respectively. The reason behind this might be that they remained isolated from the mainstream of society having minimum interaction with the outside world and belonged to rigid social structure with lower educational background.

> The organizations prevalent in the study area were village panchayats, co-operative credit society, milk co-operative society, rural youth club, Self Help Groups (SHGs) etc of which some tribal farmers were either members or office bearers. It was found that 42.22 per cent of the respondents were not associated with any of the formal organizations. Altogether 33.34 per cent had membership of only one organization and 8.88 per cent had membership of more than one organization and 15.56 per cent were found to be the office bearers.

> Majority of the tribal farmers (60%) showed low innovativeness, while 35.55 percent exhibited medium innovativeness and remaining 4.45 percent exhibited high innovativeness.

5.3.2 Demographic profile of ITK experts

In the final (3rd) round of Delphi, gender-wise distribution shows that cent percent of the experts were males and majority belonged to the age group of 51-65 years (64.70%), holding designation of Director/ Dean of SAUs or Director/Assistant Director General of ICAR (64.70%) with experience between 10-15 years (88.23%) involved in extension (52.94%) followed by research (35.29%) and teaching (11.77%) and involved in ITK related work to a greater extent (82.35%).

5.4 Identification of the process of systematic documentation and scientisation of Indigenous Technical Knowledge

> The results of three Delphi rounds enabled in identification of expanded list of total 120 statements from the experts and it was categorized into five main domains namely, methods and activities, competencies required, institutional mechanism, criteria and barriers.

- In order to know the degree of their agreement regarding need and relevance of the study, experts opined that there is a strong need for developing a policy framework for effective utilisation of ITKs, need to formally recognize the rights of farmers in order to equitably share the benefits and scientific validation of ITKs will generate unique knowledge which can be integrated with modern approaches for developing sound technologies. However, all other statements were also rated strongly for their consideration in identification of a systematic process of documentation and scientisation of ITKs.

- An attempt was also made to seek opinion of Delphi experts about their awareness of specific methods of documentation and under headings/sub-headings, different scales for measuring rationality, methods of validation, and preferences for generalisation. The experts felt that a combination of suitable methods should be used for documentation of ITKs as opined by cent percent of the ITK experts. The methods most preferred by the experts were interaction with community leaders including elders, rapid rural appraisal, participatory rural appraisal, case study, key informant method, historical timeline, interview method, participant observation, brain storming methods would give better documentation results and would help in proper collection and identification of ITKs from the study area.

- Among headings and sub-headings to be covered in documentation of ITKs, 'name of ITK', 'purpose of ITK', 'community practicing that ITK' and 'availability of ITK material' were most preferred sub-headings to be followed in documentation of ITK followed by extent of adoption of ITK. Percentage of family using ITK was found to be of no relevance for documentation purpose by the experts as only six per cent experts showed their preference to this section.

- The most preferred scale to assess the scientific rationality of ITKs was Dhaliwal and Singh (2010) scale which has 3-point scoring procedure followed by 5- point rating scale of Hiranand (1979) and 4-point rating scale of Venkatesan and Sundaramarai (2014).

- For validation of ITKs, Quantifying Indigenous Knowledge (QuIK) method was most preferred method of validation followed by Mean Perceived Effectiveness Methodology (MPEM). Field experimentation was least preferred as it is time consuming and costly.

- Generalisation of ITKs should be scaled up so it is important to know whether ITK is as effective as or at par with the corresponding scientific technology. After ascertaining this it should be recommended for large scale dissemination followed by utilising ITKs through ready to use (RTU) products. When ITK is not effective at par with Corresponding Scientific Technology then further experimentation of ITKs for enhancing its effectiveness was most preferred followed by conducting multilocational trials.

- After obtaining the results of the PIC format and the opinion on need and relevance of the study, awareness and preference of the different methods of documentation and scientisation of ITKs, different statements were framed on different aspects of documentation and scientisation of ITKs to get dichotomous response of the experts in round 2 and round 3 to achieve the consensus. The statements were categorised under five domains by the experts and they were: methods and activities to be followed for documentation and scientisation of ITKs, competencies required for personnel involved, institutional mechanism required, criteria and barriers in ITK related studies.

- Under the domain of documentation, 13 statements were framed from the opinions received from the experts. Almost all the statements reached at consensus. Out of those 13, experts expressed their cent-per-cent agreement on 9 statements i.e. Statement. No. 1, 3, 4, 5, 10, 11, 12 and 13 followed by 88.23 per cent agreement on 2nd statement (i.e. studies on ITKs be conducted on anthropological lines) and 8th statement (i.e. document the experiences of focus group discussion) and 76.47 per cent agreement on 7th statement (i.e. decide a convenient time and place for focus group discussion with farmers). Only for the statement at Sl.No. 6 i.e. 'transect walk with elders', experts

Summary and Conclusions

showed varied level of opinion i.e. 47.05 per cent agreement and 52.94 per cent disagreement.

- The process of scientisation was followed after documentation of ITKs. The scientisation process was conceptualized as a three sequential steps of particularisation, validation and generalisation.

- In particularisation section of 'methods and activities' domain, there were three statements out of which two i.e. 'identification of needs and problems of farmers' and 'identification of location-specific ITKs available to solve the problem prioritized' reached at cent- per-cent consensus of the experts followed by statement at Sl.No. 2 i.e. 'rank analysis for prioritizing the major problems to be solved' with 94.11 per cent of agreement.

- In validation section of methods and activities domain, a total number of 14 statements were listed out. Of the 14 statements, seven statements (Sl.No. 3, 5, 6, 7, 10, 12 and 14) received cent-per-cent agreement of the experts. In respect of statement at Sl.No. 11 i.e. 'validation through field/ laboratory experimentation', 94.11 per cent of agreement was reached followed by statements at Sl.No. 1, i.e. 'identification of needs and problems of farmers' and Sl.No.9 i.e. 'validation through Quantification of Indigenous Knowledge (QuIK)' (88.23%) and statement at Sl.No. 2 (conducting trials at different locations or multilocational trials) got 82.35 percent of agreement. This is the only section where maximum number of statements attained consensus with varied level of disagreement. For statements at Sl.No. 4 'observing the performance' and Sl. No.13 'mass validation to know the side effects', the level of disagreement was 94.11 per cent followed by statement at Sl.No. 4 i.e. 'validation through surveys' with 88.23 per cent of disagreement.

- Altogether 14 statements were listed under generalisation section of methods and activities. Statements at Sl. No. 1, 4, 5, 6, 7, 9, 10, 11, 13 and 14 received cent-per-cent agreement of the experts. However, statement at Sl.No.8 (provision of regular appointment of experts representing agriculture, health, engineering, resource conservation and innovators) received 94.11 per cent followed by statement at Sl.No.3 (very common ITKs may be identified and comments of researchers can be taken) and Sl.No.12 (incorporation of validated ITKs in the package of recommendations relevant to each discipline/sectors), 88.23 per cent of agreement of the experts. There was only one statement i.e. 'wide publicity to be given through ICTs (Sl.No.2) in this section which received consensus on disagreement received 94.11 per cent of disagreement of the experts.

> Under the competencies required domain, nine statements were identified by the experts. The experts expressed their cent-per-cent agreement with the statement i.e. 'attitude to respect ITK and farmers' wisdom', 'orientation/ training/ exposure/ capacity building to incorporate ITK in National Agricultural Research System' and 'sensitization of scientists and extension workers regarding myths attached to ITKs' followed by 'adequate knowledge about ITKs' (94.11%) and 'mechanism formulation for different activities related to ITK studies and their upscaling' (76.47%). Varied opinions were emerged in this domain as there were no major demarcations between the level of agreement and disagreement for the statements like 'designing strategies and linkages to promote ITKs through student researches (52.94 % for agreement) and (47.05% for disagreement) and 'establishment of a proper body to conduct academic activities and their monitoring for scaling up the use of ITKs' achieved 58.82 per cent for agreement and 41.17 per cent for disagreement respectively.

> Under "institutional mechanism" domain of ITK documentation and scientisation (particularisation, validation and generalisation), a total number of 20 statements were identified by the experts. Almost all statements reached at consensus in the third round. The experts expressed their cent-per-cent agreement on the statements related to 'formation of FPOs/ FIGs/ SHGs/ Forums of ITK wisdom bearers', 'Gram Panchayats should take a lead in popularising ITKs", "scouts should be utilised', 'a national level institute should be established for coordinating ITK researches', 'village schools should be involved in ITK-related activities', 'package of practices should be

formulated taking ITKs into consideration', 'Zonal Research Stations should include ITKs in their experiments', 'a common networking platform should be established', 'linkages of national and international bodies should be initiated and strengthened', 'village clusters should be formed to practice ITKs', 'a national authority should be established', 'computerized and updated database' and 'methodological procedures should be clearly defined' and 'OFT/FLDs should be properly designed'. As it was felt that it would pave the ways for integration of ITKs in developmental work. It was followed by 'farmer-scientist interaction' and 'role of KVKs in validation and ATMA in dissemination of ITKs' (94.11%) and 'ITK cell in every R&D organisations (88.23%)' and "specific portals should be designed (76.47%)'. Since the recognition of ITK has just started scratching the surface so recent advancements with mobile apps and websites would take time to come into force, majority of experts expressed their disagreement (88.23%) on designing and developing mobile apps for ITK work. Similarly the experts expressed their disagreement (88.23%) with the statement that farmer radio clubs should be organised as the ITK work has to start first from grassroots' level with full participation of the community.

> Altogether 16 particulars were considered under the broad domain of "criteria" to be used for systematic documentation, particularisation, validation and generalisation of ITKs. Almost all particulars were reached at consensus at *Round 3*. The experts showed their cent-per-cent agreement with items at Sl.No. 1, 2, 3, 4, 5, 6, 7, 9, 12, 13, 14 and 16. 'Ability of ITK for large scale demonstrations' (94.11 %) followed by 'marketability of ITK' (88.23%), 'problem solving ability of ITK' and suitability of ITK for validation (76.47%) of agreement was expressed by the experts.

> A total number of 25 particulars were identified under the domain of "barriers" that might obstruct the work of systematic documentation, particularisation, validation and generalisation of ITKs. Out of 25 particulars listed in this section, the experts expressed cent-per-cent agreement on 19 particulars (Sl.No. 1, 3, 4, 6, 7, 8, 11, 12, 13, 14, 15, 16, 17, 18, 19, 20, 21, 23

and 25). Poor accessibility of ITKs is due to low interest among the users as they are attracted to modern lifestyle and did not want to follow the legacy of traditional farming, ITK wisdom bearers don't want to disclose ITKs to other members (100% agreement) to maintain monopoly in the community. Low profits and returns (100% agreement) are also a major reason behind the restricted use of ITKs. People are not aware of the utility of ITKs (100% agreement) and how sustainable it is. Low efficacy in comparison to CSTs, no blending and restricted use due to geographical limitations, IPR issues (94.11%) followed by farmers' reluctance to share and lack of role model (88.23%), negative attitude of stakeholders towards ITK (76.47 %) attained agreement.

5.5. Scientisation of indigenous technical knowledge about pest and disease management among tribal farmers

5.5.1 Particularisation of ITKs

It was decided to find out the extent of scientific rationality of selected ITKs mailing the listed ITKs to 30 plant protection scientists to judge their rationality on three types of selected scales developed by different social scientists as well as to see the consistency in the opinion of scientists on different scales.

5.5.1.1 Rationality analysis on a 3-point rating scale of Dhaliwal and Singh (2010)

The ITKs which scored total rationality score more than 60 was deliberated as rational and less than 60 as irrational by the plant protection scientists. Thus it can be concluded that scientists exhibited varied levels of rationality on different ITKs about pest and disease management. Altogether 31 ITKs (70.45%) scored above 60, which indicated that these were scientifically rational and rest 13 (29.55%) were rated to be irrational and discarded by the scientists for the next step i.e. validation.

5.5.1.2 Rationality analysis on a 4-point rating scale of Venkatesan and Sundaramarai (2014)

ITKs listed at Sl.No. 1, 2, 3, 8, 11, 12, 14, 15, 16, 18, 19, 21, 22, 23, 24, 25, 26, 27, 28, 29, 30, 32, 34, 35, 36, 39, 40, 42 and 43 were adjudged rational whereas

ITKs at Sl.No. 4, 5, 6, 7, 9, 10, 13, 17, 20, 31, 33, 37, 38, 41 and 44 were deliberated as irrational by the scientists either on the basis of their scientific evidence and their experience of working in the respective fields. It can be concluded that 65.90 percent ITKs were reported to be rational which were accepted for validation and 14 ITKs (25.10%) were reported to be irrational and discarded for the next step.

5.5.1.3 Rationality analysis on a 5-point rating scale of Hiranand (1979)

Altogether 32 documented ITKs (ITK at Sl.No. 1, 2, 3, 7, 8, 10, 11, 13, 14, 15, 16, 18, 19, 20, 21, 22, 23, 24, 25, 26, 27, 28, 29, 30, 32, 34, 35, 36, 39, 40, 42 and 43) were adjudged highly rational as they received rationality scores above 3.5 and four ITK practices (Sl.No. 31, 33, 37 and 38) were found to be moderately rational which received rationality scores between 2.5 and 3.5. The remaining eight ITKs (ITKs at Sl.No. 4, 5, 6, 9, 12, 17, 41 and 44) were reported to be irrational which received rationality score less than 2.5. Thus altogether 81.81 percent ITKs were found to be rational and 18.19 percent ITKs were found to be irrational, so discarded for the next step of scientisation i.e. validation

5.5.1.4 Comparative Rationality Analysis of 3 Types of Rating Scales

This was done to understand the differences as well as the consistency between the results obtained by three types of rating scales. Most of the ITKs were found rational in all the three scoring procedures. On the 3-point scale of Dhaliwal and Singh (2010), a total of 31 ITKs were found to be rational, on 4-point scale of Venkatesan and Sundaramarai (2014), 28 ITKs were found to be rational and on 5-point scale of Hiranand (1979) altogether 36 ITKs were rated to be rational. Thus it can be inferred that altogether 30 ITKs at Sl.No. 1, 2, 3, 8, 11, 12, 14, 15, 16, 18, 19, 20, 21, 22, 23, 24, 25, 26, 27, 28, 29, 30, 32, 34, 35, 36, 39, 40, 42 and 43 were rated to be rational by the scientists based on their expertise, experience and scientific evidences. So far consistency of the scales is concerned majority of the ITKs (30) were rated to be rational on all the three types of scales followed by seven ITKs rated to be irrational at Sl.No 4, 5, 6, 9, 17, 41 and 44.

5.5.2 VALIDATION OF ITKs

Validation of ITKs was done by two methods i.e. Quantification of Indigenous Knowledge method and Mean Perceived Effectiveness Methodology.

5.5.2.1 Validation by Quantification of Indigenous Knowledge (QuIK) method

A total of 31 scientifically rational ITKs were to be validated but it was a difficult task to gather all the 45 tribal farmers at one place and involve them in QuIK method, further time constraints was a limiting factor. So it was decided by the researcher, tribal farmers and the scientists to take up five commonly used ITKs for the QuIK method.

The results analysis of Duncan Multiple Range Test (DMRT) shows that in all the five cases (i.e. Rice hispa, Rice caseworm, Bihar hairy caterpillar, Rice gall fly and Banki disease were found to be superior to Corresponding Scientific Technology (CST) in terms of cost-effectiveness, environment friendliness and farming system compatibility whereas CST was preferred more in terms of effectiveness in controlling pests/diseases, quickness in problem solving and ease in preparation. Experiences from the discussion with tribal farmers revealed that ITK-1, ITK-2 could be viable alternatives to control Rice hispa, Rice caseworm, Bihar hairy caterpillar, Rice gall fly and Banki disease are adaptable to the agro-ecological situation of the tribal farming community.

5.5.2.2 Validation of ITKS by Mean Perceived Effectiveness Methodology (MPEM)

Out of 44 listed ITKs about pest and disease management, 31 ITKs were found to be rational by the experts and accepted for validation in the particularisation step of scientisation. Six parameters namely, efficacy, accessibility, cost-effectiveness, observability, adaptability and simplicity were identified to assess the mean perceived effectiveness of the particularised ITKs. The results showed that out of 31 ITKs listed, 29 were found highly effective, whereas ITK 4 and ITK 15 were marked as moderately effective. Not a single ITK was reported under less effective category.

5.5.3 GENERALISATION OF ITKs

The results revealed that altogether 22 ITKs at Sl.No 1, 2, 3, 4, 5, 7, 9, 10, 11, 12, 13, 18, 20, 21, 23, 24, 26, 27, 28, 29, 30, and 31 could be recommended by extension agencies directly to the farmers for their application whereas nine ITKs at Sl.No 6, 8, 14, 15, 16, 17, 19, 22 and 25 need to be further modified for their popularisation through blending with corresponding scientific technologies in order to enhance their efficacy and effectiveness as well as their suitability, adaptability and compatibility with their farming situations and farming system components. The scientists respondents were further requested to suggest suitable CSTs for each such ITKs.

The target users of ITKs are the tribal farming community so it becomes imperative to seek their opinion for generalisation of ITKs. The results indicated that tribal farmers preferred to get information pertaining to ITKs from their fellow farmers. Farmer to farmer extension was ranked first (100%) as the fellow farmers are well acquainted with the farming situations of each other. Tribal farmers were found to be excited about the record maintained in ITK register (91.11%) to seek information related to different aspects of generalisation of ITKs. Simultaneously awareness through public address system was also ranked second (91.11%) by the tribal key informants in scaling up of the ITKs. Obtaining information through key informants or opinion leaders ranked third (84.44%) as the preferred mode of dissemination of ITKs for its generalisation. Farmers field schools were ranked fourth (77.77%) as the preferred means of dissemination for generalisation of ITKs. Magazines and pamphlets in vernacular languages were ranked fifth (75.55%) as the tribal farmers know only their regional languages so for better outreach publications in vernacular language was preferred. Award of role model farmer during kisan melas/farmer meetings ranked sixth (73.33%). Social media like whatsapp, facebook, twitter, instagram etc are excellent platforms to share information at global level. This will facilitate better handling of information with different sections of the society and also helpful in documentation. So it was ranked as seventh (75.55%) preferred means of dissemination. Village knowledge centres were ranked eighth (57.77%). Panchayat meetings ranked ninth (48.88%) which is convenient for farmers to share all kind of

Summary and Conclusions ....

information at a single place. Farmers were reluctant to have a healthy discussion with scientists as they think outsiders are not empathetic with their conditions and outsiders always have blanket recommendations. That's why they least preferred scientist-farmer interaction as it ranked tenth (26.66%). Portals/Websites/Apps ranked eleventh preferred means for generalisation of ITKs as the tribal farmers are not well versed with these digital applications. Para-professional workers are also a source of information to the villagers in the study area. But the tribal farmers are least bothered about the information shared by them due to their least experience and expertise in ITKs so it was ranked twelfth (15.55%) and last by the tribal farmers.

5.6 Constraints encountered in utilisation of ITKs by tribal farmers

Based on the responses received, the various constraints were categorized under five major sections namely, i) Socio-psychological, constraints ii) Technological constraints iii) Financial constraints iv) Extension-related constraints v) Policy-related constraints.

- Under socio-psychological constraints, 'lack of interest among youths' and 'lack of awareness among farmers' were ranked first (WMS=2.63). Second rank (WMS=2.60) was assigned to 'lack of motivation from peers'. 'Lack of conviction about returns' ranked third (WMS=2.31) followed by 'difficulty in identifying indigenous materials' (WMS=2.28), 'changing nature of ITKs changes from area to area' (WMS=2.17), 'inclination towards modern technologies (WMS=1.75)', 'negative attitude towards ITK (WMS=1.48) respectively.

- Under technological constraints, 'more reliance on Ready to Use (RTU) products' (WMS=2.95) was ranked first. Secondly, 'not well defined mode of application of ITKs' was identified as the next major constraint (WMS=2.75). Inconvenience in preparation was deliberated as the third (WMS=2.53) important constraint. Fourth (WMS=2.28) rank was assigned to the statement "ITK is inconvenient and time consuming". Over reliability of farmers on external inputs (WMS=2.24) was ranked fifth. 'ITK is labour intensive' was assigned sixth rank (WMS=1.97).

- Under financial constraints, 'lack of financial support from government agencies' got first ranked (WMS=2.95) followed by 'low economic returns' (WMS=2.37) and 'preference to costly external inputs in comparison to cost effective ITK' (WMS=1.88) respectively.

- Under extension-related constraints, first (WMS=2.64) major constraints identified were lack of expert guidance followed by 'lack of exposure to extension personnel towards ITK' (WMS=2.51) and lack of awareness campaigns, 'lack of linkages and coordination among various stakeholders'(WMS=2.46), 'lack of participatory technological validation' (WMS=2.31), 'limited scope for dissemination' (WMS=2.22), 'lack of training to extension professionals' (WMS=2.11), 'lack of research-based evidences in economic terms' (WMS=2.06), 'lack of scientific evaluation and modification' (WMS=1.97), 'lack of publications in vernacular languages (WMS=1.95) respectively.

- Under policy related constraints lack of provisions for monetary assistance to disclosures of indigenous knowledge was assigned as the first policy-related constraint (WMS=3.06). Second rank (WMS=2.93) was deliberated to "no platform for sharing indigenous knowledge" followed by 'less recognition of ITK work', 'industrialization and urbanization' (WMS=2.71), 'no provision of Prior Informed Consent (PIC) for commercialization' respectively. Three constraints namely 'least efforts made by the government agencies in popularizing ITK', 'migration of tribal people from remote areas' and 'lack of database creation facility' were ranked seventh (WMS=2.53) together. Many indigenous plants are on the verge of extinction ranked eighth (WMS=2.08) among all these constraints.

5.7 Development of a framework for systematic documentation and scientisation of Indigenous Technical Knowledge

The process framework for documentation and scientisation of ITK involved user, extension and research systems as the major stakeholders. Seeking prior informed consent from the tribal farmer respondents, community engagement, pilot study and initial preparations were suggested to be the starting points. Meeting with villagers, proper capacity building of extension personnel and standardization of proper data gathering tools were recommended as the important measures for documentation from the ends of user, extension and research systems. For particlarisation, identification of ITK materials from user's end, networking with scientists from extension's end and explanation of scientific rationality from researcher's end were suggested to be major planks of the framework. For validation, evaluation of ITKs by users through preference ranking, facilitation of tribal key informants by the extension personnel and field experimentation by research scientists were the key aspects and for generalisation, monetary assistance to users for disclosure, designing of promotional strategies by extension system and development of ITK-based package of practices by research system were suggested to be the major plank of the framework.

5.8 CONCLUSIONS

- The findings led to conclude that majority of tribal farmers were female (60%) of old age (71.11%) belonging to Oraon community (46.66%) having education up to primary (31.12%) and middle level (20%) and marginal size of holding (57.78%) with high farming experience (57.78%) having lower level of risk orientation (57.77%) and lower participation (42.22%) with low innovativeness (60%).

- In the final (3rd) round of Delphi, gender-wise distribution shows that cent percent of the experts were males and majority belonged to the age group of 51-65 years (64.70%), holding designation of Director/ Dean of SAUs or Director/Assistant Director General of ICAR (64.70%) with experience between 10-15 years (88.23%) involved in extension (52.94%) followed by research (35.29%) and teaching (11.77%) and involved in ITK related work to a greater extent (82.35%).

- The ITK experts opined that a combination of suitable methods should be used for documentation of ITKs.

- Among headings and sub-headings to be covered in documentation of ITKs, 'name of ITK', 'purpose of ITK', 'community practicing that ITK' and

- 'availability of ITK material' were most preferred sub-headings to be followed in documentation of ITK followed by extent of adoption of ITK.
- The most preferred scale to assess the scientific rationality of ITKs was Dhaliwal and Singh (2010) scale which has 3-point scoring procedure followed by 5- point rating scale of Hiranand (1979) and 4-point rating scale of Venkatesan and Sundaramarai (2014).
- For validation of ITKs, Quantifying Indigenous Knowledge (QuIK) method was most preferred method of validation followed by Mean Perceived Effectiveness Methodology (MPEM).
- In generalisation, if ITKs are found effective at par with corresponding scientific technology should be recommended for their large scale dissemination followed by utilising ITKs for Ready to use products and if found not effective at par with corresponding scientific technology then further experimentation is required.
- Under documentation domain, altogether eight statements were agreed upon by the majority of the experts, out of which ITKs studies conducted on anthropological lines and experiences gained from focused group discussion were found to be most appropriate.
- In particularisation section of methods and activities domain two statements i.e. identification of needs and problems of farmers and identification of location-specific ITKs available to solve the problem prioritized reached at cent-percent consensus of the experts.
- Under validation section, QuIK method was preferred followed by conducting trials at different locations.
- Under generalisation section, ten statements received cent-percent agreement of the experts followed by the statements i.e. very common ITKs may be identified and comments of researchers may be taken and incorporation of validated ITK in the package of recommendations relevant to each discipline/sector.

- Under competencies required domain, attitude to respect ITKs and farmers wisdom and incorporation of ITK in National Agricultural Research System got cent-percent agreement by the ITK experts.

- Under institutional mechanism domain, almost all the statements reached at consensus, among which Gram Panchayats should take a lead in popularising ITKs, scouts should be utilised and a national level institute should be established were prominent.

- Similarly under the criteria domain, almost all statements were reached at consensus followed by marketability of ITK and problem solving ability as well as suitability of ITK for validation.

- Under barriers domain, poor accessibility of ITKs was due to low interest among the users, negative attitude of ITK wisdom bearers, do not disclose ITKs to other persons and low profits and returns as well as low efficacy of ITKs in comparison with corresponding scientific technologies.

- On 3-point rating scale altogether 70.45 percent ITKs were found to be scientifically rational and rest 29.55 percent were rated to be irrational and discarded for validation.

- On 4-point rating scale, 65.90 percent ITKs were found to be rational and 34.10 percent ITKs were reported to be irrational and discarded for next step of scientisation.

- Similarly on 5-point rating scale, altogether 81.81 percent ITKs were found to be rational and 18.19 percent irrational.

- So far consistency of the three types of scales is concerned 68.18 percent ITKs were rated to be rational and 15.90 percent were rated to be irrational. However on the rest 15.92 per cent of the ITKs varied opinions were received.

- Five ITKs which were considered for QuIK analysis namely Rice hispa, Rice caseworm, Bihar hairy caterpillar, Rice gall fly and Banki disease were found to be superior to Corresponding Scientific Technology in terms of cost-effectiveness, environment friendliness and farming system compatibility whereas CST was preferred more in terms of effectiveness in controlling pests/diseases, quickness in problem solving and ease in preparation.

- The results of validation of ITKs through Mean Perceived Effectiveness Methodology exhibited that 29 out of 31 ITKs were found to be highly effective whereas only two ITK 4 and ITK 15 reported to be moderately effective and not a single ITK was reported to be less effective.

- For generalisation of selected ITKs i.e. large scale dissemination, it was found that 22 ITKs were opined to be recommended by extension agencies directly whereas nine ITKs opined to be further modified for their generalisation through blending with CSTs in order to enhance their efficacy and effectiveness adaptability.

- Farmer to farmer extension was recommended by the key informants (tribal farmers) for generalisation of the ITKs followed by maintaining ITK register and creating awareness through different extension methods including publication of extension literature and use of information communication technology.

- Framework for documentation and scientisation of ITK was developed involving user, extension and research systems respectively.

5.9 Implications of the study

Holistically the entire research had started its journey in identifying a systematic process for documentation and scientisation of indigenous technical knowledge through experts opinion and ended with a strategic process framework for systematic documentation and scientisation of indigenous technological knowledge in the context of research and extension.

- It may be recommended that those indigenous technical knowledge bases or techniques may be nurtured and manifested in the present ecosystem as well as in the similar type of ecosystem in case of preventing the people's health hazard, climate change, agrarian development and livelihood sustenance.

- The scientifically validated indigenous technical knowledge could be generalised and disseminated to different ecosystems for its future manifestation and application.

- The study has recommended that a compendium of the indigenous technical knowledge in the area will be helpful. So for feeding the indigenous technical knowledge base in the ICT system, the developed content will prove its worth to acquaint the local people of other areas regarding the indigenous technological knowledge practices. The future study can be conducted to explore the gender based indigenous technological knowledge utilisation. Similar studies can be conducted to analyse the efficacy of the proposed research extension framework based on indigenous technological knowledge and scientific knowledge. The future studies can be conducted in case of exploring the indigenous technological knowledge associated with climate change adaptation and mitigation. The future studies can be conducted in case of utilising the indigenous technological knowledge for media management and Information Communication Technology (ICT).

- Sustainable agricultural practices through use of ITKs that have evolved over the years could provide answers to the current crisis in the agriculture sector in respect of crop production. It is therefore, imperative that the knowledge of ITKs in crop production is widely disseminated among the farming community, researchers, academicians, administrators, policy makers. The State Government needs to create an enabling environment, through appropriate policy interventions, for inclusion of this knowledge into mainstream agriculture.

- Indigenous Technical Knowledge (ITK) encompasses mechanisms to stabilize production in a risk-prone environment without external subsidies and to limit environmental degradation. Such stabilizing qualities of (ITK) must be supported and complemented by agro-ecological practices that enhance the production factors and natural resources potential of ITK. That also provides diversification guidelines on how to assemble functional biodiversity.

- The knowledge related to indigenous technology is depleting day by day. Sharing ITK within and across communities can help enhance cross-cultural understanding and promote the cultural dimension of development. ITK is important for both the local communities and the global community.
- An inventory for better accessibility of ITKs in agriculture and allied field would be made.
- Development of appropriate technologies through blending with CST considering farmer's socio-cultural background.
- Empowerment of farmers as considered as key actors in planning and execution of projects.
- A ready to use (RTU) product prepared from well validated ITK would enhance the adoption, profitability and sustainability.
- A standard framework to collect and compile ITK-related data for successful generalisation and amalgamation with modern technologies.
- The development partners need to recognize the role of Indigenous Knowledge, understand its working in the context of the local communities, and integrate systematically the most effective and promising of such practices into the development programs they support.
- The potential disappearance of many indigenous practices could have a negative effect primarily on those who have developed them and who make a living through them. A greater awareness of the importance of ITK can play in the development process is likely to help preserve valuable skills, technologies and problem solving strategies among the local communities. Therefore, preserving the ITK capital can enrich the global community and contribute to promoting the cultural dimension of development.
- The findings will also help to serve as a caution to us to conserve plants with insecticidal and pesticidal properties before they become extinct.
- Commercial exploitation and patenting will be possible only after conducting a thorough scientific study on these plants.

- It was revealed from the major findings of this investigation that majority of the ITKs were found valid and effective as per the observations made by the tribal farmers. These need to be validated scientifically and experimentally along with the identification and isolation of active ingredients present in the materials used under ITKs. Such studies will provide scientific rationality for use of ITKs in future.

- Since, the ITKs seem to be cheaper, locally and easily available in remote areas and have lesser side effects; the use of these ITKs may be encouraged. Proper blending of ITK with the CST could be placed best in today's demand for eco-friendliness in particular and sustainability in general. Refresher training courses on ITK should be organised based on field problems.

- Involvement of tribal farmers and non-government organisations at each stage of the project formulation, implementation, review and monitoring process is an effective method of sharing knowledge and skills.

- Documentation and subsequent validation (by QuIK method) of all the available ITKs in any region could be helpful for further scientifically oriented similar works.

- Emphasis should be given on documentation and validation of relevant indigenous practices that perceived as most successful during their experimental trials.

- Regional work stations should be set up for the people who are interested in ITKs. It is also necessary to establish sub centers in interior places and in remote areas of the country to impart to say above objective.

- Emphasis should be given for changes in the curriculum for agriculture and allied graduates. The curriculum should be revised with inclusion of indigenous eco-friendly practices.

- The documented indigenous practices can be taken up by different institutions to test the validity in the laboratory.

- The success story documented under the study showed that the ITKs have tremendous wealth to be studied and utilised further.

5.10 Suggested areas for future research

- Documentation and scientisation of ITKs in agriculture and allied fields needs to be further explored in different tribal areas of Jharkhand as well as in different regions of the country.
- Assessment of awareness and knowledge of extension personnel and scientific community about the relevance and application of ITK-based practices in agriculture and allied fields.
- Development of appropriate extension mix for dissemination of locally relevant ITKs through vernacular languages targeting the resource poor farm families.
- Designing appropriate ICT interventions for further exploring and popularising ITKs.
- Developing a framework for monitoring ITKs and its impact on the communities.
- Developing a social marketing strategy to change the attitude of extension personnel, scientists, policy makers regarding ITK as primitive, underdeveloped, irrational etc.
- Standardising different formulations of ITKs for different problems and thereby developing Ready to use (RTU) products.
- Developing strategies for bringing about positive changes in the attitude of extension personnel, scientists, policy makers and planners regarding ITKs so that ITKs may not be considered as primitive and underdeveloped.

Summary and Conclusions ....

www.ingramcontent.com/pod-product-compliance
Lightning Source LLC
LaVergne TN
LVHW010202070526
838199LV00062B/4471